THE ANALYTICS REVOLUTION
IN HIGHER EDUCATION

THE ANALYTICS REVOLUTION IN HIGHER EDUCATION

Big Data, Organizational Learning,
and Student Success

Edited by

Jonathan S. Gagliardi, Amelia Parnell,

and Julia Carpenter-Hubin

Foreword by *Randy L. Swing*

Published in association with AIR and ACE

STERLING, VIRGINIA

Library of Congress Cataloging-in-Publication Data
Names: Gagliardi, Jonathan S., editor. | Parnell, Amelia R., editor. |
Carpenter-Hubin, Julia, editor.
Title: The analytics revolution in higher education : big data,
organizational learning, and student success / edited by Jonathan S.
Gagliardi, Amelia Parnell, and Julia Carpenter-Hubin ; foreword by
Randy L. Swing.
Description: First edition. |
Sterling, Virginia : Stylus Publishing, LLC., 2018. |
Includes bibliographical references and index. |
Identifiers: LCCN 2017055080 (print) |
LCCN 2018008161 (ebook) |
ISBN 9781620365786 (uPDF) |
ISBN 9781620365793 (ePub, mobi) |
ISBN 9781620365762 (cloth : alk. paper) |
ISBN 9781620365779 (pbk. : alk. paper) |
ISBN 9781620365786 (library networkable e-edition) |
ISBN 9781620365793 (consumer e-edition)
Subjects: LCSH: Education, Higher--Research--United States--Data
processing. |
Education, Higher--Research--United States--Statistical methods. |
Educational statistics--United States. |
Universities and colleges--United States--Administration--Data
processing.
Classification: LCC LB2395.7 (ebook) |
LCC LB2395.7 .A63 2018 (print) |
DDC 378.007--dc23
LC record available at https://lccn.loc.gov/2017055080

13-digit ISBN: 978-1-62036-576-2 (cloth)
13-digit ISBN: 978-1-62036-577-9 (paperback)
13-digit ISBN: 978-1-62036-578-6 (library networkable e-edition)
13-digit ISBN: 978-1-62036-579-3 (consumer e-edition)

Printed in the United States of America

All first editions printed on acid-free paper
that meets the American National Standards Institute
Z39-48 Standard.

Bulk Purchases
Quantity discounts are available for use in workshops and for
staff development.
Call 1-800-232-0223

First Edition, 2018

CONTENTS

A paradigm shift is taking hold in American higher education. In its briefest form,
the paradigm that has governed our colleges is this: A college is an institution that
exists to provide instruction. Subtly but profoundly we are shifting to a new paradigm:
A college is an institution that exists to produce learning. (Barr & Tagg, 1995)

*T*he *Analytics Revolution in Higher Education: Big Data, Organizational Learning, and Student Success* presents a clear and consistent message that a paradigm shift is taking place around data and analytics in higher education. Of course, declaring that a paradigm shift is upon us does not make it so. For example, the promise (or threat) of instructional videos and massive open online courses (MOOCs) have not proven to be as transformational as once predicted. In comparison, the shift from teaching-centered to learner-centered higher education is a paradigm shift that has largely come true with significant impact on higher education structures, functions, and outcomes. There are parallels to be drawn with the forecasted paradigm shift in institutional research (IR) presented in this book.

Three key conditions of higher education data and analytics support the view that a paradigm shift is underway; this is not just another soon-to-pass, jargon-filled fad-du-jour. Each proved true the observations of Robert Barr and John Tagg (1995) and can be tested against the ideas put forth in the chapters that follow.

First, paradigm shifts are often well underway before anyone thinks to write that they are happening. Evolution rather than revolution is a hallmark of paradigm shifts. Barr and Tagg (1995) were reporting the ongoing shift in teaching versus learning that was apparent, especially in community colleges. By naming and clarifying the changes in teaching and learning practices, they greatly accelerated the pace of change. In describing the paradigm shift in IR, the *Aspirational Statement for Institutional Research* (Swing & Ross, 2016) likewise notes that it is "not a prediction of a distant future; rather, it reflects changes that are already observable" (p. 7). Nobody disputes that new practices are already in place. Data and analytic tools are widely distributed across postsecondary institutions as never before. Democratization of data and decentralization of analytic tools have already significantly changed the data ecosystem in higher education.

Second, paradigm shifts occur because of foundational changes in the supporting environment. Bower and Christenson (1995) dubbed these *disruptive innovations* and observed that, over time, new customers and new business models arise from them. The case can easily be made for a paradigm shift in data and analytics based on the influx of new technologies and new services provided in data-related higher education decision-making. Likewise, it is readily observable that disruptive innovations have created new consumers of data and established new business models for the production of data analytics, providing energy to fuel a paradigm shift.

Third, paradigm shifts gain permanency when external pressures are applied to existing, established professional practices. Paradigm changes are a combination of "push" and "pull"—both inside the impacted field and outside. It is wise to question whether a paradigm shift is actually underway if the primary beneficiaries are only established practitioners themselves. In response to Barr and Tagg's proposal, sides were drawn over teaching philosophies and practices, with "sage-on-the stage" traditional lecturers expressing the most concern about moving away from teaching-as-doing to learning outcomes. Similarly, the changes in IR have been embraced by many professionals in the field and deemed threatening by others—a sign that this is a movement created by both "push" and "pull" dynamics. There is a natural cycle of adoption in paradigm shifts and that appears to be the case across the field of IR today.

Borrowing from Barr and Tagg (1995), the analytics paradigm shift can be stated as the following:

> In its briefest form, the paradigm that has founded IR is this: IR exists to *provide accurate data and analytics*. Subtly but profoundly we are shifting to a new paradigm: the IR function exists to support decision makers—students, faculty, staff, administrators, and other stakeholders. (para. 1)

The difference is in accountability for IR being used by and useful to those making decisions.

The *Aspirational Statement for Institutional Research* focused on (a) decision support for a broad array of decision makers and stakeholders and (b) assuring that decision makers have the capacity to use data independently to inform decisions on their own timeline. An additional aspect was mentioned only briefly and will serve as the closing point of this foreword. Decision support in the new paradigm includes leadership in questioning and predicting decisions that are arising or should be advancing on agendas. Supporting decision makers at the point when decisions are on the table is essential IR work, but not sufficient to meet the future demands of higher education stakeholders. Leadership roles in IR include identifying issues and opportunities that should have priority in decision-making cycles. Readers are encouraged to review *Scholarship Reconsidered* (Boyer, 1990) to consider how his ideas about the Scholarship of Integration, Scholarship of Application, and Scholarship of Teaching fit the changing role of IR in higher education.

The markers of a true paradigm shift are present in the field of IR. This book serves to further document a rapidly changing professional field. More importantly, the evidence shows that a reimagined IR function will be essential to meeting the challenges facing higher education in a rapidly changing landscape.

Randy L. Swing
Executive Director
Association for Institutional Research (2007–2016)

References

Barr, R. B., & Tagg, J. (1995, November/December). From teaching to learning—A new paradigm for undergraduate education. *Change: The Magazine of Higher Learning*, 12–26.

Bower, J. L., & Christensen, C. M. (1995). Disruptive technologies: Catching the wave. *Harvard Business Review*. Retrieved from https://hbr.org/1995/01/disruptive-technologies-catching-the-wave

Boyer, E. L. (1990). *Scholarship reconsidered: Priorities of the professoriate*. Princeton, N.J: Carnegie Foundation for the Advancement of Teaching.

Swing, R. L., & Ross, L. E. (2016, March/April). A new vision for institutional research. *Change: The Magazine of Higher Learning*, 6–13.

W hen asked to choose growing areas of future importance to their successors, only 12% of college and university presidents identified using institutional research (IR) and/or evidence to inform decision-making (Gagliardi, Espinosa, Turk, & Taylor, 2017). This finding was unexpected and startling given how consistently members of the higher education community, government, and the media have championed the importance of data analytics in realizing higher education innovations big and small. It was also revelatory; after all, if the exponential growth and democratization of data and analytics tools are to be used to their fullest extent, college and university leaders must first harness the untapped potential of IR and the growing number of analytics offshoots.

The Analytics Revolution in Higher Education: Big Data, Organizational Learning, and Student Success seeks to help leaders of public colleges, universities, and systems do just that. Helping institutional leaders optimally leverage data analytics functions to improve decision-making is an important first step in facilitating higher education reform. It's also messy work.

In the wake of an environment fraught with change, decision makers are faced with a host of pressures. Students need better insights to navigate complicated pathways to earn an affordable credential of quality. Faculty and advisers are trying to use data analytics to help facilitate improved student outcomes. Chief academic officers and provosts, deans, and department chairs are tasked with optimizing their academic enterprises. Presidents are using data to create new and sustainable higher education business models while preserving the unique mission and value of their institution.

Recent innovations in data and technology have created an information tsunami that not only holds great promise but also presents myriad challenges. While there is more data—big and small, structured and unstructured—than ever before, sifting through it to create insight that facilitates action has grown more difficult as accountability and cost pressures have magnified demands for analysis. Many leaders are struggling to juggle this growing sea of demands, which may seem counterintuitive given how accessible data and analytics tools now are. Some are throwing up their hands because there can be too much data to know where to start, and the barriers to entry are seemingly too high, costly, and risky. Even so, the tide cannot be stemmed; the analytics revolution is here to stay.

Realizing the value of the analytics revolution while mitigating the associated risks (e.g., cost, infrastructure, privacy and security, and perverse consequences) requires a unique blend of skills and competencies that are seldom found within one organizational or administrative unit. These include expertise in data governance, stewardship, and analytics; the ability to effectively communicate, teach, and facilitate; and the technical know-how to build and administer dynamic data repositories. Making sense of it all requires a commitment of resources into the development of a data-enabled campus. IR functions have a lead role to play in that.

We created this book to aid college and university leaders in leveraging their analytics functions to harness data in all forms to facilitate organizational learning and student success, with focus on the IR functions of public colleges and universities, and systems.[1] Our personal and professional experiences have made apparent the importance of IR and related analytics functions to the future of higher education. These functions—including IR, information technology (IT), in addition to the numerous other data-savvy shops—have yet to be fully utilized in creating much needed change in higher education.

Together, these functions are being tasked with facilitating organizational transformation through the use of data analytics. They must reframe existing relationships and develop new partnerships, which is hard given that such efforts can have implications for the future nature of analytics units. As the need for contextualized insight increases, IR and other analytics functions have sought to develop and maintain sound principles of data governance and stewardship at a time when creating a consistent version of the truth is tougher than ever. Without a campus-wide commitment to data-informed decision-making, and absent the kinds of resources needed for a data-informed culture to take root, such efforts can, and most likely will, fall short. Only through a collaborative model can analytics functions be made cohesive enough to deliver on the needs of colleges and universities, and students. As such, this volume is directed at all audiences—institutional researchers, information technology officers, and decision makers at all levels—who recognize that the analytics revolution can be used to great effect.[2]

To begin, the environmental factors influencing IR and analytics functions are detailed. Then the authors provide an overview of the development of IR and analytics functions and the changes that are currently underway. This includes an overview of the impact that other institutional functions (e.g., IT, business intelligence, and student affairs) are having on the creation of campus-wide data cultures. Following this, specific college, university, and system efforts at reinventing IR and analytics structures are described, highlighting how the analytics revolution manifests itself in context-dependent ways. The volume concludes by unpacking key challenges and opportunities facing campus leaders in their efforts to effectively use IR and analytics functions by exploring key themes that can help college leaders make the most of the analytics revolution.

We believe in the power of IR and the role it plays in facilitating higher education reform that benefits students, first and foremost. We hope the content in this volume aides you in doing so.

Jonathan S. Gagliardi
Amelia Parnell
Julia Carpenter-Hubin

Notes

1. It is worth pointing out that, while this volume focuses on public IR and analytics functions, we believe that many of the lessons are broadly applicable to colleges and universities regardless of sector.

2. With a title like *The Analytics Revolution in Higher Education*, you might expect to be inundated with page after page of dazzling visualizations and methods. This volume offers little of that. Instead, it focuses on the organizational changes necessary to harness data analytics effectively.

Reference

Gagliardi, J. S., Espinosa, Lorelle L., Turk, J. M., & Taylor, M. (2017). *The American college president study 2017*. Washington, DC: American Council on Education.

.

ACKNOWLEDGMENTS

First, thank you to JoAnn and Anthony Gagliardi, Robert and Amanda Hunter, and Don Hubin for their love and support as we worked to make *The Analytics Revolution in Higher Education* a reality.

The Analytics Revolution in Higher Education is really a reflection of the collective wisdom of the field. Each of us has benefited from the guidance of our mentors. Their support has been instrumental in making this work a reality, with special thanks to Jason Lane and Randy Swing.

We would also like to express our appreciation to those contributors who wrote chapters, adding their expertise and experience to the creation of *The Analytics Revolution in Higher Education*. Additionally, we would like to thank David Brightman of Stylus Publishing for guiding us through the process of creating *The Analytics Revolution in Higher Education*, and the American Council on Education and the Association of Institutional Research for supporting this work. We are grateful to Chris Brewer, Jamey Rorison, and Bobby Sharp for their careful review of the volume.

Finally, we would like to acknowledge the countless analytics professionals whose efforts have made a difference in the lives of students. We cannot imagine where higher education would be without their energy and commitment.

THE ANALYTICS REVOLUTION IN HIGHER EDUCATION

Jonathan S. Gagliardi

We are living through an analytics revolution. More data was created over the last two years than in the entire previous history of humankind[1] (IBM, 2016; Marr, 2016). Those numbers will be dwarfed in the coming years as the digital universe grows to include over 50 billion devices and over 180 billion zettabytes of data by the year 2025 (IDC, 2014; Marr, 2016). For example, transmitting all that data through a broadband Internet connection would take over 450 million years, according to a recent article in the *Economist* ("Data Is Giving Rise," 2017). By the turn of the decade, approximately 1.7 megabytes of new information will be created every second for each person on Earth (Evans, 2011; Gantz & Reinsel, 2012; Marr, 2016).

Still, raw data is of limited utility. To extract value, it needs to be mined, refined, integrated, and analyzed for insight. When responsibly and effectively used, the insight drawn from data propels progress and innovation. The potential benefits are too many to ignore for people, firms, and governments, many of which have taken measures to accelerate their analytics maturity. Successfully doing so has become big business in recent years. In 2015, revenues from analytics software reached $122 billion, and that number is expected to rise to $187 billion in 2019. The market for predictive and prescriptive analyses is skyrocketing (Columbus, 2016). More firms are recognizing the value of putting data to work to promote organizational transformation. So powerful is this analytics revolution that in 2013 the term *big data* was added to the Oxford English Dictionary. A fad this is not; the analytics revolution is here to stay.

While this analytics revolution has been unfolding, American colleges and universities have been facing choppy waters. The U.S. system of higher education, highly regarded by many, has shown signs of dysfunction in recent years. In fact, America is no longer the most highly educated nation in the world (OECD, 2016). This can be attributed, in part, to the convergence of stagnant graduation rates, persistent equity gaps, ballooning tuition, mounting student debt, and other countries getting serious about postsecondary education. These factors, coupled with social, political, and economic changes, have weakened the public trust in higher education, eroded state and federal financial support for the pursuit of a college credential, and created an affordability problem. Sensing a crisis, stakeholders from government, the private sector, and civic society have renewed their calls for higher education reform by demanding transparency and accountability and creating lofty educational attainment goals known collectively as the *completion agenda*. Still, improvement has been a slow and difficult process.

Colleges and universities have tried to reassess and reconfigure their business models in hopes of better serving students, communities, and economies in response to this growing crisis (Soares, Steele, & Wayt, 2016). These efforts to improve student outcomes while driving down costs have primarily focused on the large-scale adoption of programs, practices, and services designed to optimize remediation, shorten time to degree, reduce excess credits, and streamline credit transfer, all while enhancing teaching, learning, and advising in a cost-effective manner (Complete College America, 2017). Doing so can be hard because institutions are trying to standardize output with fewer resources and increasingly varied input, but it is not impossible. Data analytics are at the heart of gathering the evidence and insights needed to accomplish the transformational changes demanded by the current climate. In recent years, robust data analytics have been shown to be a key ingredient to strategic innovation.

Even though the higher education community has turned the corner and embraced the analytics revolution, a multitude of barriers stand in the way of any given campus doing so. While data and analytics tools are plentiful, the reality is that most institutions are not yet able to use them optimally, for a host of reasons. These can include: insufficient or misaligned resources, endless information demands, disjointed or rigid infrastructure, mismatches in skills and expertise, and the absence of data-enabled executives (Gagliardi & Turk, 2017). The presence of any of these challenges can be formidable enough to undermine the development of an analytics culture, and a large share of campuses experience a handful of them. So, how can colleges and universities overcome these barriers to harness the power of data analytics?

This volume seeks to help college and university leaders[2] harness the analytics revolution in ways that promote student success, organizational vitality, and innovation. The rest of this chapter will provide the reader with an overview of some of the challenges and opportunities facing colleges and universities in their quest to harness the analytics revolution. It will then home in on how institutional research (IR) is being reshaped by this fundamental shift in how data are being used in higher education. It is important to note that this volume does not focus on methods, analyses, or visualizations; rather, it focuses on identifying the keys to developing a dynamic, campus-wide analytics culture and function centered around IR.

Harnessing the Analytics Revolution

If effectively harnessed, the massive amount of information born out of the analytics revolution can allow institutions to better understand student needs; enhance the quality of teaching, learning, and advising; drive down costs; and predict and avoid risks (Cai & Zhu, 2015; Denley, 2014). Despite this, the sheer volume of data and the multitude of tools for analysis are inconsequential to colleges and universities unless the conditions exist for their effective use. In fact, while artificial intelligence and machine learning grab headlines, most colleges lack that level of analytics sophistication, and they do not need it. Many institutions would benefit from a solid foundation of data that is based on *accuracy, timeliness, relevancy, integration,* and *security.*

Accuracy

As the sheer volume of available data increases so do pressures to use it, making it important to develop procedures to ensure that it is of quality and usable in contextualized ways. There are multiple steps in acquiring, processing, and analyzing data. These include data discovery, extraction, reformatting, uploading, normalizing, enriching, comparing, presenting, and integrating workflow (Wheeler, 2017). These procedures help to ensure that new insights gleaned from data analytics are trustworthy ones.

Timeliness

Data and insight need to be delivered in timely and accessible ways, otherwise their usefulness may be lost regardless of their accuracy. This is especially true for colleges and universities that are seeking out real-time solutions to the challenges facing students. The longer it takes to acquire, process, and analyze data related to each element of the student lifecycle, the less likely it is that insights can be used for predicting risks and prescribing solutions for students.

Relevancy

Translating accurate and timely data into programs or services that support students and decision makers is often aspired to but seldom achieved. In some ways there is so much data it becomes difficult to sort the good from the bad. With so much data to sift through, the matter of identifying the right analytics tools and infrastructure becomes more important. As the need for accurate real-time insight increases, analytics leaders must be prepared to deliver insights, products, and services that matter to the end user.

Integration

Decision makers want access to insight in near-real time, which means that the steps of acquiring, processing, and analyzing data need to happen quickly. A major barrier to delivering accurate, timely, and relevant insight has been a lack of integration. The difficulties in sewing together data from disparate sources originate from a host of challenges, including differences in storage, definition, structure (or lack thereof), and intended use (Gagliardi & Wellman, 2015). At a time when unstructured data, which can be incredibly rich, account for 90% of enterprise data, determining ways to extract value often hinges on connecting it with other data sources (Vijayan, 2015). This makes effective integration an even more important step toward creating dynamic data and insight.

Security

Indeed, it can be difficult to create data that are simultaneously accurate, timely, and integrated while also making them accessible to decision makers in realtime. On top of that, data need to be protected and to be used ethically. Policies and best practices surrounding data privacy and security, intellectual property, and ethical practices all warrant careful attention (Ekowo & Palmer, 2017). According to Sun (2014), analytics functions should work to adopt practice standards, adhere to best practices to maintain privacy and security, and create ethics review boards to mitigate the many risks associated with the analytics revolution, big data, and predictive analytics. Once data are accurate, timely, relevant, integrated, and secure, institutions can focus on building out the infrastructure and culture necessary to become more data-informed.

Infrastructure

The right infrastructure is needed to acquire, process, and analyze data from diverse sources in relevant ways that are secure. In the Higher Education

Data Warehousing Forum's[3] most recent survey of top issues facing its members,[4] over half (57%) of respondents chose data governance as their top issue. Six of the top 12 categories were related to technology. These included data quality (45%), metadata and data definitions (42%), predictive analytics (35%), data visualization (34%), integration (33%), and self-service (30%) (Childers, 2017).

Culture

Investing in quality data, insight, and the underlying infrastructure requires that campuses reorient their cultures toward a collaborative model of data-informed decision-making. Without a culture of analytics, efforts to embed analytics can generate concerns around diluting quality, eliminating choice, tracking students, cutting programs and jobs, and the loss of institutional identity. Leadership must champion the use of data and be intentional about tying data analytics into a future vision focused on student success and institutional sustainability. The rewards are many for campuses willing to invest in infrastructure and culture, which are preconditions for safely and effectively harnessing the analytics revolution.

Improving Student Success

The major reward of better leveraging the analytics revolution is student success. For example, Austin Peay State University used a grade-prediction model to place students in courses that offered them the highest likelihood of success. The program, called Degree Compass, proved effective. Over 90% of students who took the recommended courses earned an A or a B. Moreover, the grades of students after Degree Compass was introduced were five standard deviations higher than those of students prior to its implementation. It was eventually scaled across the Tennessee Board of Regents. Since its initial deployment in 2011, similar models have been adopted at institutions across the country (Denley, 2014; Gagliardi, 2015).

In another instance, Georgia State University (GSU) increased its graduation rates from 32% in 2003 to 54% in 2015; graduation rate gaps for low-income, underrepresented, and first-generation students were also closed (Georgia State University, 2016). Between 2009–2010 and 2015–2016, the credit hours at completion for bachelor students decreased from 140 to 133. One contributing factor to GSU's success was the analysis of 10 years of student financial data and approximately 140,000 GSU student records, which eventually became the baseline for the development of their predictive analytics platform (Georgia State University, 2016).

Each of these universities methodically built out their analytics capacity. Eventually they were able to use predictive analytics and principles of behavioral economics and choice architecture to better guide students along their education pathway with great success (Denley, 2014; Thaler & Sunstein, 2008; Wildavsky, 2014). The potential exists for all institutions to do so, as long as they know where to start, and IR is the ideal partner for figuring it out.

Opportunities for Institutional Research

IR has a leadership role to play in ensuring that campuses realize the full potential of the analytics revolution while mitigating the associated risks. This includes satisfying the growing sea of demands for insights that improve student outcomes and institutional productivity. The function is well positioned to guide the creation of knowledge, advise in policy and strategy, and drive innovation through a data-informed lens. This is because IR functions possess a unique combination of institutional memory and domain expertise, in addition to a rich understanding of the opportunities and challenges facing students and institutions (Cheslock, Hughes, & Umbricht, 2014). These characteristics make IR unique in its capacity to create relevant organizational intelligence that informs action.

In that vein, leaders of IR are exploring how to acquire, process, and analyze data in ways that lead to better decisions. They are also using the analytics revolution to create new kinds of visualization products, real-time business intelligence, and self-service platforms that appeal to leaders and power users alike. They are opening the door to more sophisticated analyses, better insight, and a more collaborative and nimble model of analytics led by IR.

In recognition of this emerging model, the Association for Institutional Research published a statement of aspirational practices for IR leaders and practitioners. It emphasizes a hybrid model of analytics (Swing & Ross, 2016). In this model, IR is charged with

- nurturing the profusion of IR across the institution,
- teaching data analytics best practices,
- facilitating campus-wide data-informed decision-making,
- providing professional development in data analytics, and
- focusing on student-centered responses.

By embracing these roles, IR leaders can modernize and enhance their capacity to guide institutions through an intentional process of transformational change (Swing & Ross, 2016). To do that, there are several challenges that must be overcome.

Growing Pains

The demands for insight and analysis stemming from the analytics revolution have grown in complexity and rapidity, resulting in the exertion of great pressures on colleges and universities to demonstrate accountability and performance. These pressures are reshaping how analytics are practiced in higher education, with substantial implications for the nature of IR. They also are bending the traditional analytics structures of campuses. In many cases, this has contributed to the profusion of analytics across institutions, albeit in a disconnected and loosely structured way. This is good in some ways, as being too rigid can counteract adaptability, but it also has its drawbacks. For example, data exist within student and academic affairs, budget and finance, facilities and capital planning, and personnel, but too often they remain disconnected.

The stresses caused by the ongoing democratization of data analytics can be threatening to IR. As more members of the campus community practice data analytics, they also adopt some functions and roles that have traditionally belonged to IR. This can create issues of ownership on matters such as data and can increase competition for scarce analytics resources. It can also create apprehensions about the accuracy of data and analysis, as those who are conducting it may lack the formal training and experience to use data safely, wisely, and effectively. As analytics use becomes a more widespread activity, IR has a role to play in identifying, nurturing, and empowering new analytics users and creators, which will have the effect of scaling data analytics across campuses. The cultural and structural challenges in doing so are immense, and this will be a difficult process for most institutions.

Data analytics of varied quality is another consequence of the profusion of IR and the democratization of data. As analytics shops continue to sprout up, they often collect their own data and conduct their own analyses in isolation of other campus units. The data collected by these small shops can range in quality because resources, expertise, and methods for data governance and stewardship and analysis can vary greatly from place to place. A lack of uniformity in data definitions and parameters, collection procedures, infrastructure, and record-keeping can drastically impact the quality and meaning of data analytics. These barriers can further limit cross-functional comparability, which is already diluted in its effectiveness due to being topically stove-piped. As a result, effectively assessing program and service productivity based on cost and outcomes has remained elusive for many colleges and universities.

Pop-up analytics shops, disconnected data of varied quality, and the emergence of analytics roles outside IR frequently lead to different answers to the same questions. The difficulty in pinning down a single version of the truth presents external reporting and accountability challenges, which can impact the bottom line. Internal challenges related to progress monitoring and continuous improvement also exist. Together, these challenges can place a high degree of stress on traditional IR functions that are accustomed to being the gatekeepers of the data. This point is significant because IR functions have operated in a world focused on compliance and accountability reporting for decades. This world carries with it specific rules and roles that shape the behavior of IR functions. As those rules and roles change, conflicts between IR and other functions can reach a boiling point. These changes make it more difficult for IR to centrally exert a high level of quality assurance.

Requests for analysis and insight continue to grow in volume and become more diverse in nature. Particularly, they are being asked to strike a balance between reflective analyses and compliance reporting (e.g., Integrated Postsecondary Education Data System [IPEDS]), and predictive and prescriptive analyses that often entail forecasting and that generate insight that adds value to decision-making beyond historical counts. Such a balance is difficult to achieve, given that a large portion of reflective analyses are often required by the federal or state governments and have big dollars tied to them even though they are becoming increasingly misaligned with data analytics needs. Some IR shops must forgo analyses that might be more aligned with serving the needs of contemporary and future students due to capacity constraints. Although the talent exists within IR to fulfill compliance reports, maintain quality, and conduct predictive and prescriptive analyses, the question is whether the capacity exists within IR to do it all at once.

Regardless, that is what IR is being asked to do. Leaders now want forward-looking analyses on top of the kinds of work that have shaped the function over time. Being plucked out of a very narrow set of rules and activities has been a jarring experience for some IR leaders and professionals. So, even though IR and analytics functions have begun to evolve to better meet contemporary demands for insight, it should be no surprise that there have been, and will continue to be, growing pains. The analytics revolution necessitates some degree of change, and change is hard. Even with all of their inherent challenges, these developments also offer a rare chance for campuses, and by extension, IR, to overcome the scarcity of analytics resources and capacity that are too often present.

Guiding Principles

Real structural shifts are occurring in the way that institutions function, and they require a reconsideration of how data analytics are used in order to facilitate organizational learning and student success. Institutions must reassess the users of data analytics, the composition and purpose of analytics functions, and the products created to drive improved performance. The following separate but interconnected strands are meant to guide the reader throughout this volume.

Data-Enabled Executives

Strong leaders with a future vision that includes the continuous use of data analytics provide the starting point for using data to make better decisions. These leaders must be willing to follow the data where they lead them to confront the many challenges facing students and institutions today. This top-level commitment to data and evidence helps to set the expectation of continuous organizational learning and improvement, and it helps to drive the organization toward an aspirational vision for the future. Aspirational goals and a commitment to data-informed practices help to create the environmental conditions necessary for the use of analytics across all corners of the campus.

Strategic Senior Executives

Aspirational college and university leaders who are data informed can be isolated. To avoid this, there is a growing need for a strong core of senior leaders who are committed to using insight to assess and direct talent and resources. This is particularly true during times of resource contraction and growing accountability and performance pressures. Leaders and their senior executives need evidence to have difficult conversations about where to strategically invest in academic programs, student services, and other administrative functions. Without an evidence base, these conversations can foment campus unrest. Aspirational goals require strategies that are accompanied by targets and progress monitoring that can only be achieved through a deep commitment to the use of data at the most senior level.

Investment of Talent and Resources

Many colleges and universities are data rich and insight poor. This is because data are often of varied quality and disconnected, creating scenarios where decisions are made with incomplete information. As the saying goes, "garbage in, garbage out." Additionally, even the most robust analytics structures often fall short of providing decision makers with forward-looking insight and instead are largely reflective in nature. To overcome these barriers, time, money, and talented people must be given the support and infrastructure needed to meet demands for insight. Still, at a time when analytics are needed the most, many campuses are unable to invest the necessary resources into the data infrastructure and skills needed to use data analytics differently.

Campus Cultures Empowered to Use Data

Leaders must use their ingenuity to combat the resource constraints that can make it difficult to make needed infrastructure and talent investments in data analytics capacity. In recent years, the expansion of access to data and analytics tools has been used as an opportunity to counteract resource scarcity. The desire to use data analytics is permeating campuses widely and deeply. Leaders can use this to create diffused capacity models that buck what are often rigid and understaffed analytics structures. Giving deans, department chairs, faculty, advisers, students, and other members of the campus community the access to data needed to create insight is one creative way that can nurture a campus-wide culture of data-informed decision-making.

IR as a Translator, an Adviser, and a Coach

The effective diffusion of data analytics is best done with guidance from IR, which has a rich understanding of institutional history and context. These functions are well versed in data governance and stewardship. The unique blend of skills and competencies offered by IR leaders and professionals allows for nuanced analysis, interpretation, and storytelling, all of which are key design elements of effective analytics solutions. Even if IR functions lack the capacity to create every product or conduct each analysis, they have the talent and legitimacy to partner with the entire campus community to use data analytics better and routinely. By placing IR in the role of teacher, facilitator, and communicator, senior leaders are more likely to see and realize the value of the analytics revolution. As such, IR leaders and professionals should be the hub of dynamic and collaborative data analytics teams due to their blend of skills and competencies. They are ideally positioned to coordinate campus-wide efforts at scaling data analytics.

Dynamic and Collaborative Teams Led by IR and IT

The changing nature of analytics users and consumers has implications for the kinds of analyses, reports, and visualizations that are needed by any given audience. Fact books, data dashboards, accountability reports, artisanal surveys and analyses, and business intelligence are all distinct products. Successfully creating these products and projects is best done collaboratively with information technology (IT). Together, IR and IT must nimbly manage teams that could include database architects, software engineers, quantitative and qualitative experts, communicators, quality assurance experts, project managers, experts, and students. These distinct skills and competencies are rarely found in any single administrative or academic unit. As such, the composition of teams must be carefully constructed and orchestrated so that they are coherent and stable, yet sufficiently flexible. Analytics leaders and professionals need the legitimacy and latitude to marshal these assets effectively, and IR can offer it. In many ways, IT is the tool by which good research and analysis can be scaled out across campuses under the guidance of IR functions.

Summary

IR offices can lead the charge. They are uniquely situated to ensure that the emergence of the analytics revolution is promising, not perilous. IR is confronting a new reality that is full of opportunities and challenges. The growing interest in higher education has been serving and will continue to serve the sector well, pushing institutions and systems to transform their business models by making changes that promote student success and benefit the public as a whole. Internally, the desire has increased among senior leaders, administrators, faculty, advisers, and staff to use decision analytics to benefit students and ensure that the institution continues to grow. These stakeholders see the potential for transformational change. Externally, benefactors that include state legislators, the federal government, and philanthropies are demanding more evidence and forecasting than ever before. All are hungry, not for more data, but for more insight, effective storytelling, and predictive analyses. Strong IR is a precondition for meeting these diverse and competing demands.

Doing so will be tough. New demands aren't replacing old ones; they are being added to them. In the near term, this will place significant strain on IR functions, which are being asked to do more with less. As data and analysis become more widespread, some stakeholders are deciding to pass on engaging with IR, choosing instead to mine, analyze, and communicate their own insight. This transition has been facilitated by growing volumes of data and data warehouses with sophisticated business intelligence that allow for users to explore more data in real time without assistance. The resulting differences in the unit of analysis, technical definitions, the rise of new reporting formats, metrics and ratings, and differences in methods, analysis, and interpretation represent major changes to the ways that institutions operate, and this will naturally impact IR.

As such, deep-seated cultures must be confronted as the analytical map gets redrawn before our eyes. Structures must be reorganized and long-standing arrangements, rules, and routines will change due to a more diffuse culture of data and changes in demand for insight. The role of IR is expanding from data governance, stewardship, and compliance to include translator and storyteller. The most prominent change is that IR is no longer the sole broker of data and analysis. Now, IR must shift to the role of teacher, ensuring that data and analyses are accurate, timely, relevant, integrated, and secure. IR must also become a catalyst for using data analytics to drive actions that benefit students. This likely means getting more comfortable with consequential validity for the purposes of decision-making, which is quite different from statistical validity.

Ultimately, it is easy to construct reconfigurations of IR that are hypothetically elegant, particularly when cultures, politics, and resources are left out of the equation. However, in the real world these are among the most important considerations one can make when conceptualizing any kind of change. To facilitate the successful transition of IR, stakeholders across institutions must work together and confront the messy, contentious spaces that reflect competing demands, diverse agendas, and rarely the capacity to do it all. Without the necessary resources, professional development, and investment, IR will continue to struggle to balance some of its traditional roles and responsibilities with the desire for real-time data and forecasting that will drive the academy in the future. At its heart, a culture of data must be diffused to and embraced by everyone involved in facilitating student success and organizational learning. That is not easy, as such efforts are challenging, fluid, and as prone to regress as they are to progress without constant attention and support.

Still, these pressures suggest that creating a diffused model of IR would seem to be a reasonable solution, if not for the tensions that arise from changing arrangements and the culture clash that comes along with redrawing the map, whether it be in IR or elsewhere. Despite the bumpy road, it will be worth it, as the profusion of analytics carries with it unexpected resources, staffing, and capacity. It can be done. IR has proven incredibly resilient and dynamic in the past. As evidenced by the following chapters, it is proving to be so in the present, and hopefully, well into the future. IR is too integral a part of the success of American higher education for that not to be the case.

Conclusion

We are living through an analytics revolution. It could not have come at a better time for colleges and universities, many of which have been tasked with an ambitious reform agenda centered on student success. Simply put, colleges and universities must figure out how to make the necessary structural changes to harness the analytics revolution. To do so successfully requires visionary leadership, strategies, resources and talent, a culture of data-informed decision-making, and a more dynamic and collaborative analytics culture with IR at its core.

Notes

1. According to IBM, 2.5 quintillion bytes of data were created between 2014 and 2016.

2. These include senior executive roles such as presidents, provosts, chief institutional researchers, chief information officers, and other senior executives.

3. The Higher Education Data Warehousing Forum (HEDW) is a network of higher education colleagues dedicated to promoting the sharing of knowledge and best practices regarding knowledge management in colleges and universities, including building data warehouses, developing institutional reporting strategies, and providing decision support.

4. The HEDW's members include technical developers and administrators of data access and reporting systems, data custodians, institutional researchers, and consumers of data representing a variety of internal university audiences.

References

Cai, L., & Zhu, Y. (2015). The challenges of data quality and data quality assessment in the big data era. *Data Science Journal, 14,* 2. DOI: http://doi.org/10.5334/dsj-2015-002

Cheslock, J., Hughes, R. P., & Umbricht, M. (2014). The opportunities, challenges, and strategies associated with the use of operations-oriented (big) data to support decision making within universities. In J. E. Lane (Ed.), *Building a smarter university: Big data, innovation, and analytics* (pp. 211–238). Albany, NY: SUNY Press.

Childers, H. (2017, November 30). 2017 HEDW Survey of top 10 issues [Web log post]. Retrieved from https://hedw.org/2017-hedw-survey-of-top-10-issues/

Columbus, L. (2016, August 20). Roundup of analytics, big data & BI forecasts and market estimates, 2016. *Forbes.* Retrieved from https://www.forbes.com/sites/louiscolumbus/2016/08/20/roundup-of-analytics-big-data-bi-forecasts-and-market-estimates-2016/#79e616d26f21

Complete College America. (2017). *The game changers.* Retrieved from http://completecollege.org/the-game-changers/

Data is giving rise to a new economy (2017, May 6). *Economist.* Retrieved from https://www.economist.com/news/briefing/21721634-how-it-shaping-up-data-giving-rise-new-economy

Denley, T. (2014). How predictive analytics and choice architecture can improve student success. *Research & Practice in Assessment, 9*(2), 61–69.

Ekowo, M., & Palmer, I. (2017, March 6). Predictive analytics in higher education. *New America.* Retrieved from https://www.newamerica.org/education-policy/policy-papers/predictive-analytics-higher-education/#introduction

Evans, D. (2011). *The Internet of things: How the next evolution of the Internet is changing everything* [White paper]. Retrieved from http://www.cisco.com/c/dam/en_us/about/ac79/docs/innov/IoT_IBSG_0411FINAL.pdf

Gagliardi, J. S. (2015). From perpetuation to innovation: Breaking through barriers to change in higher education. In J. E. Lane (Ed.), *Higher education reconsidered: Executing change to drive collective impact* (pp. 61–96). Albany, NY: SUNY Press.

Gagliardi, J. S., & Turk, J. M. (2017). *The data enabled executive.* Washington DC: American Council on Education.

Gagliardi, J. S., & Wellman, J. (2015). *Meeting demand for improvements in public system institutional research: Progress report on the NASH project in IR.* Washington DC: National Association of System Heads.

Gantz, J., & Reinsel, D. (2012, December). *The digital universe in 2020: Big data, bigger digital shadows, and biggest growth in the far east* [Video file]. Retrieved from https://www.emc.com/leadership/digital-universe/2012iview/analyst-perspective-john-gantz-david-reinsel.htm

Georgia State University. (2016). *2016 status report.* Retrieved from http://success.gsu.edu/files/2017/01/Georgia-State-University-2016-Complete-College-Report-with-Appendix-10-26-16.pdf

IBM. (2016). *Big data.* Retrieved from https://www.ibm.com/analytics/us/en/technology/big-data/

IDC. (2014). *The digital universe of opportunities.* Retrieved from https://www.emc.com/collateral/analyst-reports/idc-digital-universe-2014.pdf

Marr, B. (2016, November 1). 20 mind-boggling facts every business leader must reflect on now. *Forbes.* Retrieved from https://www.forbes.com/sites/bernardmarr/2016/11/01/20-mind-boggling-facts-every-business-leader-must-reflect-on-now/#35486aa20dcd

OECD. (2016). *Education at a glance 2016: OECD indicators.* Paris, France: OECD Publishing. http://dx.doi.org/10.1787/eag-2016-en

Soares, L., Steele, P., & Wayt, L. (2016). *Evolving higher education business models: Leading with data to deliver results.* Washington DC: American Council on Education.

Sun, J. C. (2014). Legal issues associated with big data in higher education: Ethical considerations and cautionary tales. In J. E. Lane (Ed.), *Building a smarter university: Big data, innovation, and analytics* (pp. 27–56). Albany, NY: SUNY Press.

Swing, R. L., & Ross, L. E. (2016). *Statement of aspirational practice for institutional research.* Association for Institutional Research. Retrieved from http://www.air-web.org/aspirationalstatement.

Thaler, R. H., & Sunstein, C. R. (2008). *Nudge: Improving decisions about health, wealth, and happiness.* New Haven, CT: Yale University Press.

Vijayan, J. (2015, June 25). Solving the unstructured data challenge. *CIO.* Retrieved from http://www.cio.com/article/2941015/big-data/solving-the-unstructured-data-challenge.html

Wheeler, B. (2017, March 13). Who is doing our data laundry? *EDUCAUSE Review.* Retrieved from http://er.educause.edu/articles/2017/3/who-is-doing-our-data-laundry

Wildavsky, B. (2014). Nudge nation: A new way to use data to prod students into and through college. In J. E. Lane (Ed.), *Building a smarter university: Big data, innovation, and analytics* (pp. 143–158). Albany, NY: SUNY Press.

2

HIGHER EDUCATION DECISION SUPPORT

Building Capacity, Adding Value

Daniel R. Cohen-Vogel

Over the last five years, the University of North Carolina–General Administration (the UNC system office) has undertaken a series of transformations aimed at growing and reshaping the university system's data and analytics capacity. More than simply updating a set of outdated technologies and processes, the driving principle behind these efforts was, and still is, getting a diverse set of stakeholders the information they need when they need it. To be candid, UNC has tackled an ambitious agenda, and some of its efforts are still works in progress; however, UNC has also had some big successes. The process UNC went through to identify the problem and to plan and implement solutions is driven by the same factors that are driving change in the institutional research (IR) profession generally.

This chapter describes the UNC system's transformative data and analytics endeavors within a broader discussion of the evolving higher education decision support role. This chapter is framed around the components of a vision for the future of UNC system decision support. Of course, much of this vision and the context that shaped it are relevant for individual institutions, public or private. And it is obvious from some of the contributions to this volume that many other institutions and systems are responding to the same conditions.

As UNC began to plan and execute various changes—and note that *UNC* is used interchangeably in this chapter to refer to the system office (UNC–General Administration) and the multicampus University of North Carolina overall—UNC–General Administration conducted some casual research and used the findings to frame the problem as follows. The IR function at the system office and across UNC's constituent institutions developed largely as a compliance reporting and information summary function.

The bulk of time was spent producing state and federal required reports, static fact books, statistical abstracts, and submissions to various regional and national organizations, so that those organizations may produce similar kinds of products.

Figures 2.1a and 2.1b summarize information gathered through conversations with the UNC IR offices in 2012 as the system office was developing a business case for an overhaul of its roughly 20-year-old process for collecting and reporting data. Figure 2.1a describes the current state, an estimate based on historic data of effort spent on various activities. Figure 2.1b describes the preferred state, where the system's IR leaders thought their offices should be aiming. Two points come through in these charts. First, there was a general sense that too few value-added activities were occurring and that more such activities were needed. Second, there were a lot of balls that still had to be kept in the air and a lot of activities (surveys, accreditation activities, compliance reporting, etc.) that must be sustained, at least in the short run, regardless of any new directions to be pursued.

This self-assessment is consistent with what some have observed about the national development of the IR function. In a book about the first 50 years of the Association for Institutional Research, William Lasher (2011) writes about the emergence of IR functions, describing the "survey era" of the first few decades of the twentieth century, followed by significant growth in the number of IR administrative units at universities in the 1950s and 1960s. This period is notable for dissemination of the business case for IR and for specific IR practices and training. The period saw the creation of interstate higher education organizations (e.g., SREB, WICHE, SHEEO) and growing federal and private foundation interest in IR. The first half of the twentieth century is also a period that saw great growth in accreditation of higher education institutions. For example, most of the institutions that would later make up the UNC system were accredited by SACS from the 1920s through the 1950s. Early IR activities were largely focused on surveys and descriptive analyses of various aspects of the institutions (e.g., faculty, facilities, and finances) as well as support for accreditation processes (Lasher, 2011).

Lasher (2011) also cites work suggesting that "the spread of statewide coordination had a material effect on the birth and growth of institutional research" (p. 15), pointing to John Dale Russell's early "pioneer" efforts in New Mexico as one of the first examples of system-level activities. And although the policy issues and primary audiences of the system office differ somewhat from those of individual institutions, IR activities at the system level seem to have mirrored those of institutions, with most effort put toward

Figure 2.1a. Where we have been: Disproportionate effort on reporting and compliance.

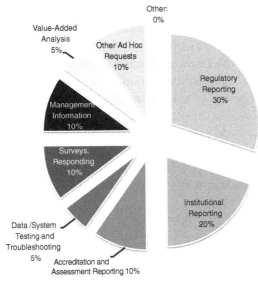

Figure 2.1b. Where we are headed: A shift toward value-added information.

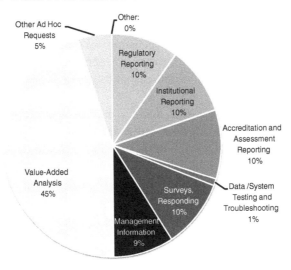

Note: The percentages in Figure 2.1a and Figure 2.1b are based on observation and conversations with the UNC IR offices specifically regarding data-specific IR functions. Excluded from the categories are managerial or administrative time and time spent on campus workgroups or committees. Those activities consume significant time but were not expected to be affected by UNC data system advances and so are not included in the assessment of IR offices' time allocation.

developing fact books and other descriptive analyses of centrally collected data, conducting system-wide surveys, and supporting system-level compliance reporting.

UNC as a multicampus university—its beginning as a public higher education system—started with consolidation of a few institutions in 1931, and the creation of the 16-campus system occurred in 1971.[1] The proceedings of early North Carolina Association of Institutional Research (NCAIR) meetings—the organization was founded largely by UNC staff at an inaugural meeting at UNC-General Administration in 1973—suggest that focus on fact books, surveys, and self-studies continued to be the bread and butter of IR.[2] Moreover, as a historical account in *NCAIR—Its Story* notes, the 1971 creation of a statewide university governing board itself shaped the emphasis of IR offices, concentrating their efforts on data gathering and reporting (Ussery & Ballou, 1985).

For the UNC system office as well as higher education institutions nationally, the late-twentieth-century focus of IR offices on compliance reporting was most significantly affected by the rise of the U.S. Department of Education's higher education surveys, HEGIS (1971–1972 to 1986–1987) and then Integrated Postsecondary Education Data System (IPEDS) (1985–1986 to the present). The number and breadth of these surveys has increased over time, and the reporting standards contained in them as well as a statutory mandate (Higher Education Amendments of 1992; see 20 U.S.C. 1094(a)(17)) and financial penalties for noncompliance have elevated their importance and the role that federal reporting has played in determining data standards, workloads, and overall focus of campus and system IR units.

A challenge for UNC—one that has faced the profession generally for decades—has been to develop sufficient capacity to provide actionable management information to decision makers. In addition, often there has been a tension among institutional researchers, some of whom gravitate toward a reporting role in which the IR office provides data alone and some of whom see their role as providing interpretation, context, and analysis to support decisions. Lasher wrote about this when describing debates within the profession in the 1970s and 1980s (Lasher, 2011). Those debates express some of the same concerns that UNC leadership have expressed in recent years. They want better access to information that helps them understand problems and develop solutions. They want analytical capacity.

The UNC system office's historical focus on reporting and compliance-related activities rather than analytics might not in itself have engendered major changes and certainly would not necessarily have led to the disruptive changes the office pursued. However, the broader context has bumped up against a traditional focus and limited capacity and provoked the university to change. The rest of this chapter will touch on some of those contextual factors and then discuss several ways in which the traditional IR function can, and arguably must, evolve to meet the demands of a changing higher education landscape, to become much more of a true decision support function.

Context: Pressure to Change

To some degree, there have always been pressures urging the profession toward more value-added, decision support activities. Lasher (2011) points to debates on that subject going back more than 60 years, and efforts to provide evaluative, actionable information certainly predate those debates. Whether at an institution or system level, there have always been multiple stakeholders with divergent interests, evolving demands of the labor market, and changing social and political streams. Yet, basic compliance monitoring and regulatory reporting has dominated. However, recent trends have presented a unique combination of pressures and opportunities to refocus and change the traditional business model.

Shrinking Public Budgets

A sluggish economy combined with a changing political landscape have driven real state appropriations per students down, and public institutions have substituted tuition dollars and made cuts to offset those declines. For example, the Center for Budget and Policy Priorities calculated an 18% (or nearly $1,600) decline in inflation-adjusted, per-student state support for higher education from 2008 to 2016 (Mitchell, Leachman, & Matterson, 2016). Fiscal pressures are incentives to become more efficient and effective in activities such as enrollment management and student success, and it is necessary to improve data and analytical contributions to support such efficiencies.

Changing Politics and Attitudes Toward Higher Education

Growth in the U.S. college-educated population has come on the heels of expanding higher education options and state and national pushes for increased educational attainment. Yet, the twenty-first century started with a decade of zero overall job growth and a housing bubble that drove up household debt (Irwin, 2010). It is no wonder that there has been growing public focus on tuition and other higher education cost increases and on student debt, as Americans (and their elected officials) question the higher education value proposition generally. Discussions of disruptive changes and new business models in higher education have emerged against this economic and political backdrop.

Changing Technology

Computing power, networking and communications developments, and accompanying software improvements have put great tools at people's fingertips. The capacity to send, receive, and store data and to conduct analyses and create data visualizations has dramatically expanded. These innovations present opportunities as well as challenges, not the least of which are expectations put on higher education analytical units to keep up with leading-edge capabilities.

Twenty-First Century Expectations

"Better data faster" was a catch phrase UNC-General Administration first heard from colleagues at East Carolina University, and the system office borrowed the phrase often in describing the expectations of its leadership and other stakeholders. These audiences do not always know specifically what they want, but they generally express that what they have been getting is not approachable enough, flexible enough, "clean" enough, or timely enough. And technological advances heighten their sense of urgency not to fall behind. Decision makers have gotten used to Google, Amazon, and smart TVs, and they are looking for their information technology and IR units to catch up.

Within this context, UNC is looking for ways to meet a diverse set of stakeholders' current and future demands, when the bulk of IR offices' activities—and their data systems, organizational structures, and skill sets—were built primarily with historical demands in mind. As the world changes, so must investments in capacity, so that technological, organizational, and human infrastructures will support current and future needs. The imperative is to add value to the academic enterprise by informing decision-making at all levels to improve student outcomes and operational efficiency. And these endeavors occur against the backdrop of a world of increasing technological sophistication and real-time feedback. So, higher education analytical units are driven to provide many audiences with timely and sophisticated windows into the academic enterprise. The UNC story over the last five years was authored with this future in mind. UNC has reenvisioned and begun to transform its historical IR function to build system *decision support* capacity.

Developing a UNC Data System as an Analytics Foundation

Through various iterations and to various audiences, UNC has presented its efforts most often in terms of a pyramid on which value-added (decision support, analytics, etc.) activities are supported by a large foundation that is the data system (see Figure 2.2). The data system must provide the flexibility to conduct required reporting with relatively low effort, but it must not be built as a reporting tool. Its primary purpose is to support decision-making—to support student success and operational efficiency—and to do so at multiple levels.

The development of UNC's Student Data Mart—the UNC system data warehouse—began with an explicit understanding of these requirements. It would be the "better data faster" foundation to support analytics and data visualization, tie into state initiatives (e.g., reverse transfer program, statewide longitudinal data systems), maintain required state and federal reporting, and serve as a shared warehouse and single source of data truth for the system. It is flexible enough to respond to changing needs, and the data collected are captured at a scale and frequency that reflect underlying business practices. Moreover, the new data system includes more than the data elements that the system office needs, as was the case with the legacy system. Rather, the data model reflects campus-specific as well as standard system needs.

Figure 2.2. Data foundation: The big lift, necessary to support analytics.

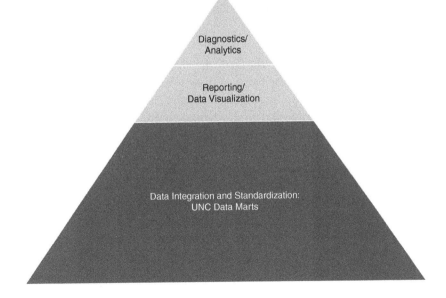

This feat would have been impossible to accomplish without highly competent and high-performing staff, which is the system's greatest asset. (And they were also the biggest risk, as turnover in certain positions would have temporarily hobbled the project and delayed pursuit of the vision.) It is a reminder that an effective data system is not simply a set of hardware and code but is built on sound business practices and communication and requires skills to maintain and extract meaning from it.

Moreover, the UNC Student Data Mart project's success was due in part to the clarity of vision and scope articulated from the start and to extensive planning and communication throughout. It also benefitted from strong and sustained leadership support. An additional factor in the project's success as well as a spillover benefit of the new data system has been the changing nature of both system-campus relationships and, at the institution level, the changing roles of the business units and the intracampus interactions required for implementation and maintenance of the new reporting environment. Campus IR units no longer extract data from various sources to massage and compile into submissions to the system office. Instead, the data are pulled by the system office directly from the institutional enterprise resource planning (ERP) systems, and the campus research office's role on each campus is to be the arbiter of data quality and coordinator of data management by campus business units (registrar, admissions, financial aid), which are now directly responsible for fixing erroneous data in the ERP system and modifying business practices, where appropriate. A few universities performed this function well already, but for many it took a significant culture change to develop a shared responsibility for accurate data.

An Analytics Ecosystem

With the data foundation established, the challenge is how best to get the data and information into the hands of those who can use it to affect changes on the campus. Seeking to build a shared analytical platform for the system on top of the Data Mart foundation, when the UNC system office put out a request for proposals in 2016 for an analytics platform, the description of the platform that the system office envisioned included the following parameters: portable, flexible, modular, nonproprietary, sustainable, and scalable. The rationale was to invest in future analytics capacity with a mind-set that considers that capacity as deriving from a data and analytics ecosystem, largely indifferent to the tools and ERP systems that different units or campuses are using. Although such an open, flexible ecosystem is an appropriate aim in general, given the speed of technological change in the industry overall, this is especially important in the context of a university system with a system office and 17 diverse constituent institutions managing 17 ERP systems and a wide range of data tools and skill sets.

More Effective, Shared Human Capacity

Human capital is the biggest challenge in building and maintaining analytical capacity and effective decision support. Successful investment in human capital requires answers to fundamental questions such as the following: What skills are needed? Which skills should be hired, and to what extent should existing staff be trained to achieve those skills? Which skills should be farmed out?

It is clear that the skills and orientation necessary for compliance reporting and fact books are different and less specialized than those needed for customer needs assessment, data visualization, diagnostic analysis, and predictive analytics. Many institutions and system offices have difficulty hiring and retaining employees with more advanced skills, and doing so is expensive, particularly in the context of tight budgets. This problem is more acute in lower resourced institutions and those away from urban centers, and there is certainly such a contrast in North Carolina between the Research Triangle and Charlotte job markets and employment opportunities in the eastern and western edges of the state.

Moreover, public institutions sometimes struggle against the constraints that state personnel rules and system human resources offices present. As part of the broader labor market context in which institutions and systems develop human capacity in a rapidly changing data and analytics field, human resource offices must also reenvision themselves as talent acquisition and retention functions in addition to, and ultimately more prominently than, their traditional roles as guardians of state rules and agents of risk avoidance.

Shared human resources

Just as recent UNC efforts have been to develop a shared data warehouse and analytics platform in addition to other central technology resources (e.g., banner hosting for a subset of UNC institutions), UNC is also investing in and exploring further shared human capacity opportunities. For years, the UNC system office has populated nearly all the IPEDS surveys for the 16 constituent universities, the only exceptions currently being the institutional characteristics surveys and academic libraries survey. Recently, as a by-product of the Student Data Mart implementation and the system office resources that came out of strong IR–IT collaboration on that project and others, UNC established an ERP support team. This group developed the baseline code that was customized to meet the needs of each institution during the

Student Data Mart implementation, and the group was also able to distribute banner modifications and guidance to help campuses respond to policy changes and data quality problems more efficiently and inexpensively than by hiring consultants or maintaining such skill sets at each institution. The continuity and strength of these support team members encourages campuses to trust that the system office has their interests in mind, shares their priorities, and is invested in their success. And it is worth emphasizing that for this shared function to be successful in supporting a collective pursuit of data integrity, trust is a necessary condition for institutional teams to speak openly and honestly about data "dirty laundry."

In part as a recognition of the value of the ERP support team and in part in response to the limited skill sets and lack of programmer depth among UNC constituent institutions, the UNC system office and some institutional counterparts also have begun discussing opportunities to develop shared programmer/analyst support in the system office as well as building into the system analytics platform contract some shared data science services to support system needs.

Distributed analytical capacity

Within the system office and at many constituent institutions, future efforts should include an exploration of new models of analytical support. This may mean developing a more distributed approach, one that discards the notion of a single IR unit and allows for the analytics function to be managed or coordinated from a central point but situated within different business units. A more effective approach may include a matrix organizational structure rather than a traditional organizational chart. And at the scale of a higher education system, such a distributed model may involve creative ways to leverage the strengths on campuses. For example, UNC has many strong universities and a collective wealth of bright and innovative employees. The system needs to look more to approaches that facilitate the sharing of expertise across universities in the areas of data visualizations, analytical studies, predictive models, and more.

Reducing the Burden of Compliance Reporting

System offices have an opportunity to free up analytical capacity significantly by reducing regulatory barriers imposed by state and federal reporting requirements.

State Reporting

UNC has begun to tackle state reporting requirements that were initiated administratively as well as those that have accumulated over the years from legislative and governing board actions. Each reporting requirement should be considered in basic cost-benefit terms: Does it add sufficient value to justify the cost of maintaining the data and production process?

- *Uncluttering self-imposed reporting burdens.* Without too much reflection, it becomes apparent that many of the routine, annual reports that were historically compiled from institutional data submissions and published as (sometimes voluminous) documents each year are often not required by the governing board or legislature but rather are historical artifacts. They were created at a time when system needs and technological options were different. They are largely informational works that do not support any specific action and often get little or no immediate attention. Not all reports are outdated or unnecessary, and some reports can be useful as sources of consistent response to information requests throughout the year. However, interactive dashboards, downloadable data sets, and targeted information briefs often allow for more efficiency in meeting the needs of different stakeholders, including internal data queries. Furthermore, the process of assessing the value of age-old reports provides an opportunity to engage with stakeholders and demonstrate interest in their needs—that is, to provide system office leadership and governing board members with what they want to know rather than what analysts think they should want to know.

- *Engaging governing board and legislature to streamline system policies and state statutes.* Legislative bodies and governing boards often create reporting requirements to express the importance of an issue or to confirm that enacted policies have been implemented. And sometimes reporting requirements are a next-best measure when there is not sufficient political support to pass a statute or policy. Over the years, required reports multiply due to a "flypaper effect." Recently, the UNC Board of Governors charged system office staff with combing through the UNC policy manual to identify no-longer-necessary and nonactionable reporting requirements. With legislative requirements, a similar review is worthwhile as well, and the process also creates an opportunity to reach out to legislative stakeholders to check in about what kinds of information they need as opposed to sending current legislators reports that may represent past members' concerns or focus on outdated policies or programs.

Federal Reporting

The system's engagement with national organizations, federal relations, and bureaucratic processes should be used as avenues to reduce the significant burden of the IPEDS, which has ballooned over the years and arguably imposes costs far in excess of its value. Significant attention has been given in recent years to the costs of regulation in higher education, including the cost of IPEDS. The Task Force on Federal Regulation in Higher Education—which included among its members the UNC System president and a chancellor of one of the system's constituent institutions—recognized generally the burden of IPEDS and also pointed to specific burdensome IPEDS reporting issues (e.g., HR survey and SOC codes not well suited to higher education, military/veterans benefits reporting that could come from other federal agencies) (Task Force on Federal Regulation of Higher Education, 2015). A subsequent Vanderbilt University study attempted to estimate the cost of federal regulatory compliance (Vanderbilt University, 2015). That report also touched on the cost of IPEDS compliance, and UNC system staff had the opportunity to provide input to the consultants commissioned to produce the study.

With a renewed push from some in Congress to develop a federal unit-record data system for higher education, an intensified focus on the burdensome and inefficient aspects of IPEDS surveys and related bureaucratic processes is even more pressing. Without addressing the deficiencies of the current system, attempting to navigate the complexities of data standardization and meaningful derivations of metrics from a unit-record data system that would span the huge and evolving array of higher education institutions nationally will almost certainly result in a proverbial "garbage in, garbage out" data system.

The system office can mitigate the impact of federal reporting in multiple ways. There are positive economies of scale that a higher education system can gain from centralizing IPEDS reporting, as has been the case within UNC. However, the frequency of changes to the IPEDS surveys, the often-insufficient lead time to respond to changes, and the occasional disconnection of the reporting requirements from the realities of the higher education enterprise are ongoing challenges. In addition to serving as an aggregator in sending data up to Washington, system offices may also serve their constituent institutions by leveraging their collective voices to mitigate the demands coming down.[3]

Communicating

Although communication skills have always been relevant, their value is growing in importance as part of the response to the changing contexts discussed earlier. Higher education, particularly public higher education, is increasingly having to make a case for itself. Politicians and the media are responding to and sometimes fueling the intensity of questions regarding the higher education "value proposition." Why should families pay for this service? Why should policymakers allocate scarce resources to the enterprise? What is the return on their investments? Whether directly to governing boards, legislatures, or media outlets, or indirectly through institutional and system office leadership, effective decision support necessitates effective communication.

It is a significant challenge to reach these key stakeholders with priority messages that are the results and interpretations of analyses. Amidst the swirl of information and demands competing for the policymakers' attention, sometimes the challenge is to move an analytical finding from the edge of their consciousness to an impactful component of a particular policy or programmatic decision, a task further compounded by the audience's diversity of perspectives and experiences. Addressing this challenge effectively means addressing external perceptions of research and analytics offices, the tools used to convey information, and staff communications skill sets.

Rebranding

It may seem relatively insignificant, but in the UNC system office the recent name change—from "institutional research" to "data and analytics"—was an acknowledgement of where the unit is headed as well as a part of helping external audiences to understand what the unit does. *Institutional research* is not widely understood among noninstitutional stakeholders. *Data and analytics* and *decision support* are more widely familiar concepts. Making ourselves approachable is a part of navigating through the swirl.

Transparency and Accountability

These buzzwords express expectations placed on higher education institutions and systems. They are particularly relevant to the public higher education system, for which the legislature, governing board, and media are key audiences. The system office is also accountable to the institutions it regulates and for which it advocates. UNC's efforts to create user-friendly data tools—the UNC Data Dashboards, for example—are an important component of providing transparency and accountability. Paying some attention to areas that are not part of the traditional IR skill set—in particular, the aesthetics and user-friendliness of data tools—is part of a more outward focus. Although UNC had created some interactive data tools more than a decade earlier, they were largely geared toward an internal audience, such as other institutional researchers. Orienting the next generation of those products toward external audiences and a broader set of internal audiences can go a long way toward ameliorating misconceptions and mistrust that emerge in the current climate.

Communication Skill Sets

Often, the impact of analytical work is dependent on how effectively it is communicated in written and verbal presentation. Analysts, programmers, and researchers often tend to be introverts and are unlikely to have received training in how to write for and speak to policymakers, institutional leaders, the business community, and the media. Addressing those important audiences in a manner that effectively conveys key information is a skill set to be developed, just like writing SAS code.

Next Steps

A key premise of UNC's recent investments in building analytical capacity is that the traditional IR function must evolve to meet the demands of a changing higher education landscape, to become much more of a true decision support function. And the UNC system's investments have succeeded in providing the foundational technologies and business processes necessary to support that analytical capacity. This chapter also touches on other efforts to develop the human capital and greater orientation toward stakeholder needs that help to sustain UNC's investments and more fully realize its vision.

Yet, there are aspects of system analytical capacity that the chapter has not addressed that are also crucial building blocks to realizing the benefits from UNC's investments: governance and culture. And these are still works in progress.

Effective governance and a culture of data-informed decision-making to reap the fruits of data and analytics have long been understood as needs, and they are rightfully talked about as significant barriers. An EDUCAUSE Center for Applied Research study over a decade ago presented a framework for understanding the environment for higher education analytics in which organizational factors (decision-making style, governance, and accountability; culture of evidence; staff analytical skill) were presented as overarching factors in that environment (Goldstein & Katz, 2005).

The development of UNC's new Student Data Mart substantially moved the system forward with standardization of definitions and underlying business practices as well as communication around data quality. However, challenges remain in derivation of information from the data and interpretation thereof. UNC has yet to develop rules governing data sharing and the vetting and dissemination of information to various stakeholders. Some system policies affecting data definitions and reporting still require clarification and alignment.

Development of a data-informed culture at all levels in the system is vital. Aligning leadership expectations and practices with what is both feasible and valuable in the data and analytics space is a challenge at both the institutional and system levels, perhaps made more challenging in systems with high degrees of politicization and leadership turnover. A data-informed culture requires a commitment shared by leadership and analytical support units to creating the time, space, products, and receptivity to drawing actionable meaning from the data. Moreover, in a resource-constrained environment— is there any other?—the propensity of decision makers to pursue new "shiny objects" can crowd out more immediately valuable investments. Often, basic diagnostic analyses are low-hanging fruit and can be more actionable and sustainable tools than sophisticated predictive models.

With a clear vision and the resources, organization, and cultural framework to sustain it, IR can and should become the decision support function that our systems and institutions need. UNC has taken some big steps toward its decision support vision. How the system further develops a broad analytical ecosystem, human resources, and the governance and culture described previously will determine how that vision continues to unfold.

Notes

1. The University of North Carolina became a 17-campus university in 2007 with the addition of the North Carolina School of Science and Math, a statewide public high school for juniors and seniors.

2. Perhaps more accurately stated, the ad hoc committee that initiated the NCAIR inaugural meeting at UNC-General Administration was composed almost entirely of UNC representatives, except for the inclusion of the president of the National Laboratory for Higher Education. However, the inaugural meeting included other higher education institutions, as did the first slate of association officers.

3. This is not to suggest that these demands are solely the result of Department of Education actions. Congress creates reporting requirements, of course. And so do other executive branch agencies. Recent indications that the Office of Management and Budget may require the breaking out of various subgroups of "Asian/Pacific Islander" and to create a subgroup of "White" that is for "Middle Eastern" people are examples of poor data practice (i.e., combining language, skin color, geographic origin, national or regional identity, and cultural identity into one "race" field) that creates added cost, reduces data quality, and adds potential conflict with FERPA vis-à-vis other reporting requirements, such as graduation rates reported by increasingly disaggregated racial subgroups.

References

Goldstein, P. J., & Katz, R. N. (2005). *Academic analytics: The use of management information and technology in higher education* (Vol. 8, pp. 1–197). Boulder, CO: EDUCAUSE Center for Applied Research.

Irwin, N. (2010, January 2). Aughts were a lost decade for U.S. economy, workers. *Washington Post*. Retrieved from http://www.washingtonpost.com/wp-dyn/content/article/2010/01/01/AR2010010101196.html?hpid=topnews

Lasher, W. F. (2011). The history of institutional research and its role in American higher education over the past 50 years. In G. Rice, M. A., Coughlin, & R. Howard (Eds.), *The Association for Institutional Research: The first 50 years* (pp. 9–52). Tallahassee, FL: Association for Institutional Research.

Mitchell, M., Leachman, M., & Matterson, K. (2016, August 15). *Funding down, tuition up*. Washington DC: Center for Budget and Policy Priorities. Retrieved from http://www.cbpp.org/sites/default/files/atoms/files/5-19-16sfp.pdf

Task Force on Federal Regulation of Higher Education. (2015). *Recalibrating regulation of colleges and universities*. Retrieved from http://www.acenet.edu/news-room/Pages/Task-Force-on-Government-Regulation-of-Higher-Education-Main.aspx

Ussery, R. M., & Ballou, L. R. (1985). *NCAIR—Its story: A history of the North Carolina Association for Institutional Research*. Chapel Hill, NC: North Carolina Association for Institutional Research.

Vanderbilt University. (2015). *Federal regulatory cost burden: A multi-institutional study overview and findings*. Retrieved from https://news.vanderbilt.edu/files/Regulatory-Compliance-Report-Final.pdf

3

CULTURAL AND ORGANIZATIONAL STRUCTURES AND FUNCTIONS OF INSTITUTIONAL RESEARCH

Julia Carpenter-Hubin and Jason Sullivan

Two recent studies from the Association for Institutional Research (AIR) have endeavored to describe the current nature of institutional research (IR). The first study attempts to define the field of IR as the set of things IR professionals do (Lillibridge, Swing, Jones, & Ross, 2016), and the second study attempts to describe the types of environments in which IR professionals operate (Swing, Jones, & Ross, 2016). At the broadest level, the function of IR involves the collection, analysis, or reporting of any data used to inform decision-making within an institution or system of institutions of higher education. At the smallest and most isolated end of the spectrum, the organizational structure for IR professionals within an institution involves one individual reporting within a specific department, such as information technology (IT) or business and finance.

To accept that the structure of IR can appropriately be described as ranging between the full spectrum of these two configurations, one must assume that either some institutions are not using data in a widespread way to inform decision-making, at worst simply collecting the minimum necessary for operational purposes and federally mandated reporting, or that much of the function of IR is being done outside of IR offices, possibly by individuals who would not consider themselves IR professionals. Each of these, in many instances, is true.

As the amount of data available to inform decision-making increases, as our ability to transform that raw data into meaningful information increases, and as the utility of that information increases, we must expect that the resources devoted to tasks within the broad function of IR will increase. We must also expect, however, that these activities will be taking place everywhere on campus that decisions are being made. It is important to note that throughout this chapter, *IR function* refers to any analysis and research conducted about the institution, while the *Office of Institutional Research* (OIR) is intended to refer to a specific unit on campus. For example, an institution may have a centralized OIR that provides analysis and reporting primarily on topics related to students. In such a scenario, analysts focused on other topics would report to a relevant business function area. Much of the research and reporting work related to human resources (HR), for example, might be performed by a team reporting to the chief HR officer. Thus it would be an IR function, but one that is performed outside the OIR. When we realize that federally mandated reporting (along with responding to publisher surveys) are the only activities considered to be solely within the domain of IR professionals, whereas the largest and most central offices have double digit staffing levels with a vice-president-level director, it becomes obvious that the effects of an analytics revolution may be very different for some institutions. With this in mind, we should examine some of the most common arrangements of organizational structure and distribution of IR tasks within different types of institutions, determine the conditions required for analytics to be effective, and propose a new configuration for the function of IR.

IR Today

OIRs can be structured very differently in terms of size and degree of centralization. Reporting structures vary as well. Institutions will address the conditions for effective analytics differently, depending in large part on the structure of their OIR.

Current IR Structures

According to data from the AIR National Survey of Institutional Research Offices (Swing, Jones, & Ross, 2016), most two- and four-year not-for-profit (NFP) institutions are structured as highly centralized OIRs, while only about a third of the for-profits have structures that fit this description. The four-year NFP institutions tend to be larger, with 20% reporting that they have five or more FTE employees. The four-year NFP institutions have a greater focus on research as opposed to reporting and other IR functions, with professional, nonmanagerial staff spending significant time on data collection efforts such as surveys. Along with the increased size and scope of IR at four-year NFP institutions comes an increased likelihood that IR functions are being done outside of a traditional OIR, with more than a quarter indicating that most IR work is done outside of a central IR office.

For-profit (FP) institutions are much more likely than two- and four-year NFP institutions to report that they operate in a highly distributed model, without any central IR office. The difference (43% at FP institutions, compared to 8% for two-year and 12% for four-year NFP institutions respectively) is probably much larger in reality, as response rates, even among institutions with published contact information associated with IPEDS data reporting, were dramatically lower among FP institutions, and the likelihood of having such contact information was extremely low compared to NFP institutions. One can speculate that one reason for nonresponse might be the lack of individuals who identify as IR professionals, and evidence would suggest that this is more likely to be the case within a category reporting relatively few offices of IR.

In highly distributed IR structures, it is difficult to generalize about the depth of IR function being performed at the institution, as one office may have multiple individuals dedicated to doing sophisticated predictive modeling, while others are simply including basic counting tasks as ad hoc "other duties as assigned."

Even among institutions with large, centralized OIRs, there are almost certainly individuals doing basic analytics on department-specific data, and even among institutions that report having no office explicitly devoted to reporting and analytics, a majority of survey respondents indicated the presence of a full-time senior-level manager of IR. The prototypical models we've listed likely represent conceptual models of IR that exist in the minds of survey respondents from these institutions as much as, if not more so than, they represent actual organizational structures of employees performing IR functions. Most institutions, for example, do not include financial data under the purview of IR, so data on salaries, budgets, and financial aid are handled and analyzed by staff completely segregated from the OIR (if that office exists on campus). At these institutions, IR may still be seen as following a highly centralized and integrated model, as long as the person describing the model does not consider some analyses (e.g., budget modeling) to be IR. In reality, most institutions have some types of data that are handled at a high, central level, some types of data that are integrated across various silos, and some data that are kept segregated. When this is explicitly recognized and each accounts for a significant share of the IR work being done, the only way to give a single characterization to the conceptual model of IR being done is to label it a *hybrid model*.

Evolution of IR Structures

This variety in models for IR operations is not new. As John S. Chase noted in 1979, "The heterogeneity of our institutions and the varied external and internal pressures to which they are subjected will produce IR offices that differ in their organizational locations, roles, and responsibilities" (p. 15). In his 1990 monograph *The Nature and Purpose of Institutional Research*, Joe Saupe goes a step further, noting that IR may happen primarily outside of OIRs. Saupe writes that

> at some colleges and universities, a conscious decision had been made that each unit in central administration will be responsible for IR relating to the activities of that unit. There may be no formally identified OIRs in these institutions, but this does not mean that the activity is absent. . . . At other colleges and universities, OIRs have been established in recognition of the fact that the activity requires specialized expertise and full-time attention. (p. 3)

In that same year—and again more than 20 years later—Volkwein (2012) described a 4-part IR ecology as follows:

1. *Craft structures* are one- and two-person offices that focus primarily on mandatory reporting and do a modest amount of number-crunching.
2. *Small adhocracies* are two- and three-person offices that, in addition to mandatory reporting, engage in applied research projects and some policy analysis. They often carry out analytical activities collaboratively with other administrative offices.
3. *Professional bureaucracies* usually centralize analytical activities that support the entire institution in a single office of four or more staff. Along with responsibility for internal and external reporting, staff in these offices usually carry out more sophisticated research projects than those in other structures.
4. *Elaborate profusion* describes a decentralized arrangement with analysts in various academic or business units producing analysis and reporting relevant to their own organizations. While this work may be coordinated across the campus, more often it is the case that these analysts operate within their own silos.

Volkwein posited that, over time, craft structures may evolve into small adhocracies and small adhocracies into professional bureaucracies. Craft structures may multiply on a single campus, such that the structure develops into an elaborate profusion. While such evolutions may have taken place on some campuses, survey data show that over half of all OIRs have fewer than 3.0 FTE staff (Swing, Jones, & Ross, 2016).

IR Reporting Lines

The Association for Institutional Research's recent survey of IR leaders found that most OIRs report to either the office of the president or the provost, with IR at two-year NFP institutions more likely to report to the office of the president, IR at four-year institutions more likely to report to the office of the provost, and IR at FP institutions almost evenly split. About 20% of IR offices at FP and four-year NFP institutions report to other offices, including business affairs, student affairs/student services, or technology/IT, while closer to 30% of IR offices at two-year NFP institutions have those reporting lines.

OIRs with different reporting lines are likely to have different research foci.

> One generalization that is safe to make is that the practice of IR tends to be shaped by the part of the organization that it is located in. As a result, if IR is in student services it is more likely to be doing studies of student life and campus climate. If IR is lodged in academic affairs it is much more likely to be engaged in studies of faculty workload, salary equity, and faculty research and scholarship. If it is in business and finance, it is much more likely to be carrying out studies that support the resource allocation process and making revenue projections. (Volkwein, 2008, p. 10)

What is perhaps more interesting is the flip side of this generalization—if IR is in student services, it is much *less* likely to be doing studies of faculty workload or salary equity, or engaging in studies that support the resource allocation process. If IR is in academic affairs, it may be less likely to be engaged in studies of student life and campus climate. Leadership in the areas less likely to be the focus of IR studies are no less in need of data. The majority of OIRs report having no responsibility for such analyses as institutional budget/finance modeling, class scheduling/demand studies, or salary equity studies (Swing, Jones, & Ross, 2016). It is highly unlikely that such studies are not happening on the majority of campuses, but rather that they are taking place within the relevant functional offices.

As the need for data analysis to support decision makers grows on campuses, institutional researchers must expand their focus from providing the information that most accurately fits the definitions required in mandatory reporting to determining what data will best answer new, and sometimes vague, research questions. They will need to anticipate the needs of their constituents as well, often determining the questions that should be raised as well as developing the data-based responses to those questions. Understanding which of these questions can best be answered by OIRs and which by the relevant functional offices is a key issue to address as we consider the future of IR.

Effective Analytics Now and in the Future

For analytics to be effective, a number of conditions need to be met. This is true in the present, and these conditions will not change in the future. As IR professionals, we are well aware that analytics, including those we ourselves produce, do not always meet all of these conditions due to a host of challenges that can be difficult to overcome. While the conditions that need to be met will not change, the challenges that will need to be overcome as the nature of data collection and retrieval changes, and as our model of the IR function evolves or is revolutionized, will also change. Some of these conditions, the current challenges, and the foreseeable changes to these challenges include the topics discussed in the following sections.

Accuracy

Analytics are not effective when the data presented do not accurately reflect the world we're trying to understand. This includes data that are not replicable, data that are not representative, data that are improperly defined, data that are improperly cleaned, data that are improperly processed, and data that are improperly analyzed. When doing centralized reporting, the biggest threat to accuracy is simple human error at some stage of the process, committed by an individual who would recognize a mistake if it were pointed out.

Going forward, challenges to accuracy will involve data being analyzed by people who are distant from the data collection (e.g., deans pulling financial aid data), data being analyzed in a black box (coding errors in complicated analyses can be difficult to spot unless they are egregious; inappropriate or unexpected definitions or assumptions can go undetected), data from diverse sources being joined imperfectly (double counts, missing populations), and data being pulled from unreliable sources (social networks, biased samples). Good data governance policies and increased data literacy will be essential in meeting these challenges.

Clarity

Analytics are only effective when definitions are understood, strengths and limitations of information are recognized, and implications are unambiguous.

Going forward, challenges to clarity will be similar to contemporary challenges: The types of models we can examine will only continue to grow more sophisticated (many decision makers cannot be expected to interpret statistical models, and our current models already embody more complexity than can be easily reduced for wide consumption), the distance between data consumers and data collection will continue to expand, even when both populations are data literate (prospective students cannot be expected to be well versed in the conventions of labor economists), and efforts to comprehend complex data encourage thinking based on unreliable cognitive biases (humans are predisposed to see weak evidence as strong evidence and to interpret ambiguous evidence as though it supports a particular decision; Gilovich, Griffin, & Kahneman, 2002). We currently rely on experts to be gatekeepers of data analytic information and on experienced communicators to provide clear interpretations. As data consumption moves toward a self-serve model, continued development of software tools that can automate some of this expertise will be essential in meeting these challenges.

Informativeness

Effective analytics provide predictions and inferences that embody a relatively low amount of uncertainty, and complicated analytics only add to informativeness when they provide more knowledge than more easily obtained methodology. Essentially, analytics need to enable one to make a better decision than one was able to make without them.

Going forward, challenges to informativeness will come from the sheer number of analyses that will be available but provide little new information to the decision maker. Sometimes this will be because an analysis describes a small effect (e.g., the 8% of students who take Econ 212 are 1.2% more likely to graduate in 4 years—give or take 1%—than the 92% who do not), and at other times it will be due to redundancy (many researchers dislike some aspect of the "H-Index" of scholarly productivity, and as a result there are more than 10 variants that can be reported; it is extremely rare that reporting multiple versions of H provides significantly more actionable information than simply reporting the traditional version).

Relevance

Analytics are most effective when they provide the information we need, rather than simply the information we have available. If decision makers cannot explain what pattern of information would make a difference to their thinking prior to seeing the results, the analytics are not likely to be truly relevant.

Going forward, the biggest challenges to relevance will be the easy availability of irrelevant information. This will be a challenge both because the temptation will exist, as it always has, to use the data you have whether or not they are the data you need, and because finding the needle you've hypothesized to be relevant gets harder to find as the haystack grows. We will continue to have more and more data, and most of it will not be relevant for a particular decision. Ideally, our software would be intelligent enough to provide the data relevant to answering natural language questions, but for the foreseeable future, this is an area in which central OIRs can be highly effective through connecting decision makers to networks of experts.

Completeness

The most effective analytics should incorporate all available relevant sources of data, including interactions among data elements.

The biggest current challenge in providing holistic data in higher education is that data were and are collected for narrow purposes, which can make locating, standardizing, and integrating data a nearly insurmountable challenge, even when these data are freely shared among units. Advances in the private sector, in fields such as marketing, health care, and finance, have already gone a long way toward overcoming this challenge in other domains. The biggest challenge going forward will be to implement these methodologies at institutions of higher education.

Timeliness

Effective analytics ideally take place in real time and reflect the world as it exists at the time decisions are being made. Currently, the time lag between the world as it exists and the world as it existed when the data were demonstrably correct typically ranges from 18 hours (e.g., operational data from close-of-business yesterday), to 18 months (e.g., end of prior fiscal year).

Over the last several years we have begun to collect most of our data in real (or near-real) time, typically from sources such as transactional operational systems, learning management systems, and online surveys. We currently can transform much of that data into accurate, relevant, clear, informative, and holistic decision support material and deliver it to decision makers. Unfortunately, each of these processes may involve manual and semiautomated effort from a different human expert and need to be done on an ad hoc basis only after a request is received. As a result, analytics that can support decision-making are often not available when they can have the greatest impact. Technology will help overcome this challenge, but changes to the way we collect, locate, and manage both data and expertise will also be essential in ensuring timeliness.

Developing Structures That Better Support Effective Analytics

Across our campuses, the demands for data to support decision-making continue to increase. New tools make data ever easier to retrieve, report, and analyze. But access to data, even when combined with high levels of analytical skills, does not guarantee sufficient understanding of analyses. Budget modeling, class demand studies, and salary equity studies are but a few examples of IR that require a high level of specific subject matter expertise and are not currently the domain of most OIRs. None of the three—budgets, demand for classes, or salaries—are best considered alone, however. Budgets may determine the number of classes that can be offered, or the number of classes needed to fulfill demand in particular areas may impact how budgets are allocated. Dollars needed to achieve salary equity would have to be entered into a budget model. These are but a few examples that demonstrate the need for subject matter data specialists to be combined with an overarching understanding of the institution as a whole. Centralizing the subject matter data specialists would be highly problematic—removing them from their colleagues who do the day-to-day transactional work in finance, enrollment services, or human resources offices would diminish their intimate knowledge of their data domain and the people and practices those data represent. Abolishing any kind of centralized function would reduce the ability of an institution to ask the cross-cutting questions most meaningful to the institution as a whole.

Over the past several decades, we have tried more and less centralized models at our various institutions. We, and our colleagues in other offices across our campuses, have been more and less satisfied with the outcomes of changes to our models, with no model as the clear winner. We need to break with our current direction and develop a new model, one that may in fact be more revolutionary than evolutionary.

Fortunately, we have a model for this, and that model is right under our noses. Higher education research has always been divided into multiple disciplines, for years with little overlap between those disciplines. More and more, however, researchers are coming together to collaborate across different disciplines. The National Academies define (2004) *interdisciplinary research* as

> a mode of research by teams or individuals that integrates information, data, techniques, tools, perspectives, concepts, and/or theories from two or more disciplines or bodies of specialized knowledge to advance fundamental understanding or to solve problems whose solutions are beyond the scope of a single discipline or area of research practice. (p. 2)

We can compare the separate data reporting and analysis by topic at many institutions to disciplinary research. For example, just as we need disciplinary specialists in economics, engineering, agriculture, and environmental sciences in order to conduct research leading to a more sustainable and resilient economy, so too do we need specialists in budget and planning, human resources, and student enrollment patterns if we are to improve student success and higher education affordability. We don't expect the economist to become an engineer in order to contribute to the interdisciplinary team, and we don't expect the leader of the interdisciplinary group to become expert in all the participating disciplines. It is critical that the leadership of both the interdisciplinary research group and an OIR that draws on the knowledge and skills from across the campus understands which are the most critical research questions, what knowledge is possessed by whom, and how to bring those who possess that knowledge together with the right tools to answer those questions.

Institutions need to recognize that all the various staff across the campus who provide data and information to answer questions and support decision-making are conducting IR. We must figure out how to make sure they have the right data at the right time to answer their questions, and that they have the support they need to answer questions on their own or to go to other experts when the questions exceed their capacity to answer them. Thus a centralized OIR becomes the hub of a knowledge network that connects data users to other data experts, supports researchers with statistical and technical skills, and leads research teams that are interdisciplinary in the sense that they bring together data analysts from multiple units within the institution. Multiple chapters in this volume discuss research collaborations between the OIR and one or more other units, both within and beyond institutional boundaries. The degree to which these collaborations are formalized vary, and no single collaborations model has yet emerged as preeminent. What is clear, however, is that OIR leadership must assume the role of chief IR networker—the leader of and connection point for analyst/researchers throughout the institution, campus, or system.

References

Chase, J. (1979). Time present and time past. *New Directions for Institutional Research, 23,* 15.

Committee on Facilitating Interdisciplinary Research, Committee on Science, Engineering, and Public Policy. (2004). *Facilitating interdisciplinary research.* Washington DC: National Academies Press.

Gilovich, T., Griffin, D., & Kahneman, D. (2002). *Heuristics and biases: The psychology of intuitive judgment.* Cambridge, UK: Cambridge University Press.

Lillibridge, F., Swing, R., Jones, D., & Ross, L. (2016). *Defining institutional research: Findings from a national study of IR work tasks.* Retrieved from https://www.air-web.org/Resources/IRStudies/Pages/Defining-IR-Focus-on-Senior-Leaders.aspx

Saupe, J. (1990). *The functions of institutional research* (2nd ed.). Tallahassee, FL: Association for Institutional Research.

Swing, R., Jones, D., & Ross, L. (2016). *The AIR national survey of institutional research offices.* Retrieved from http://www.airweb.org/nationalsurvey

Volkwein, J. F. (1990). The diversity of institutional research structures and tasks. *New Directions for Institutional Research, 60,* 7–26.

Volkwein, J. F. (2008). The foundations and evolution of institutional research. *New Directions for Institutional Research, 141,* 5–20.

Volkwein, J. F., Liu, Y., & Woodell, J. (2012). The structure and functions of institutional research offices. In R. D. Howard, G. W. McLaughlin, W. E. Knight, and Associates (Eds.), *The Handbook of Institutional Research* (pp. 22–39). San Francisco, CA: Jossey-Bass.

4

DATA ANALYTICS FOR STUDENT SUCCESS

Elaborate Profusion of Institutional Research Into Student Affairs

Amelia Parnell

The foundation for this discussion is built on studies from the field that address the structure, reporting lines, and roles of institutional research (IR) offices, all of which influence the decentralization of the IR function. The exact functions of an IR office are sometimes ambiguous; Terenzini (1999) suggests that the history of the question, "What is IR?" spans decades and Parmley (2009) states that describing IR to those who are not familiar with the profession can be as challenging as trying to dispel prevailing myths such as the institutional researcher as a bean counter. Volkwein (2008) studied the ecology of campus IR offices and proposed that four types exist based on institutional size and degree of development: craft structure, adhocracy, professional bureaucracy, and elaborate profusion. He further suggests that elaborate profusion results from environments where research is conducted in silos that are spread across the campus and contends that such fragmentation and decentralization is the result of each dean and vice president asking their staff to carry out their own studies for purposes such as enrollment management, budget projections, or studies of student life. Over the past decade, analytical tools and technology have become useful and accessible to nearly all staff, and data is now more democratized. These conditions have led to the analytics revolution that we are currently experiencing, which is marked by divisions and departments exercising more ownership of their information and relying less on a central office of IR.

Pressures and Factors

As shown in Figure 4.1, the pressures faced in postsecondary institutions that are particularly relevant to institutional researchers are manifold and multidimensional in nature and are often in tension with one another. Internal demands may contrast with external demands, academic and administrative cultures differ, and institutional needs may vary from professional needs (Volkwein, 1999). Regarding the decentralization of IR, three additional factors appear to be woven within these pressures: varying information needs at the department and institution levels; vague distinctions between IR as a profession or practice; and changing roles and demographics of IR professionals.

These pressures and factors are not exclusively connected to IR; divisions of student affairs are also experiencing these shifts. Student affairs divisions, which are typically composed of multiple functional units including advising, health and wellness, student activities, conduct, recreation, and many others, often have multiple data collections and several types of data consumers, both internal and external. Though the functions of student affairs are mostly cocurricular, the programs and activities contribute to students' acquisition of skills and competencies, and as a result, professionals are increasing their capacity to assess the efficacy of those functions. This work often involves assessing learning outcomes, which connects student affairs to academic affairs. Perhaps this is why college and university presidents identified assessment of student learning outcomes as an area of growing importance in the future (Gagliardi, Espinosa, Turk, & Taylor, 2017). The changing demographics of IR professionals also relates to student affairs, as new hires are often expected to make data-informed decisions, both with their own data and in connection to larger institutional data.

Internal Versus External Demands

In addition to providing data and reports to internal consumers, IR offices are increasing their delivery of information to consumers outside of the

Figure 4.1. Pressures and factors influencing IR decentralization.

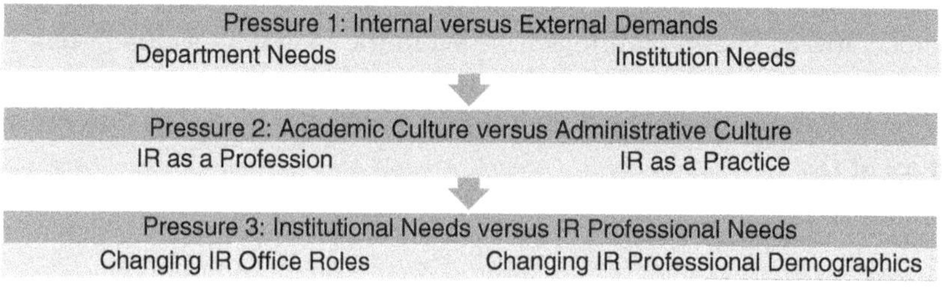

Pressure 1: Internal versus External Demands
Department Needs   Institution Needs

Pressure 2: Academic Culture versus Administrative Culture
IR as a Profession   IR as a Practice

Pressure 3: Institutional Needs versus IR Professional Needs
Changing IR Office Roles   Changing IR Professional Demographics

institution, such as the press, external agencies, foundations, and other non-governmental entities. Centralized IR offices are involved in department-level activities such as self-studies and accreditation, as well as studies related to students' progress, performance, engagement, and satisfaction. Swing and Ross (2016) suggest that new roles are emerging for institutional researchers, which include consulting with departments across the institution to find connections between their data and institutional data. This is particularly relevant to institutions that are conducting predictive analyses of behavioral data. For example, as more institutions gather information from students' identification cards to track their involvement in cocurricular activities, student affairs divisions are partnering with institutional researchers to broaden their understanding of the influence of such activities on academic outcomes. Institutions that use predictive models will inevitably have to address issues related to data governance, student privacy, and ethics as they find the balance between monitoring students' progress, informing students about how their information will be used, and appropriate decision-making. Therefore, as institutional researchers and other campus practitioners establish new partnerships, it is critical that such collaborations address how these issues will be resolved. In an ideal scenario, the central IR office would frequently collaborate with departments to conduct specialized research. Volkwein, Liu, and Woodell (2012) argue that teamwork with other departments is critical to many areas of campus research, considering that 7 of every 10 IR offices participate in such activities as administrative policy research, environmental scanning, and studies of faculty workload. However, low numbers of central IR office professionals may make teamwork with departments less feasible, as nearly 70% of IR offices have three or fewer professional staff. Norbut and Glaser (2012) interviewed IR professionals about how their offices fit into the overall structure of their institution. While some respondents indicated reporting lines that connected to the president, provost, or other senior administrator, the following response is more consistent with elaborate profusion:

> IR functions exist separately in most of our schools. We follow a model where the schools are really independent, and act as revenue generating units. Each of the big schools (business school, medical school, and arts & sciences) has its own independent IR functions in place. (p. 70)

Capacity challenges in the IR office have led to many student affairs divisions creating new positions to serve their data and assessment needs. For example, the Association for Institutional Research (AIR) jobs board typically lists more than 150 advertisements for entry level, midcareer level, and senior level IR positions (Association for Institutional Research, 2017). While the majority of the positions are located in a central IR office, some are housed in other departments across the institution. Examples include advertisements for an IR position in a center for research on learning and teaching and an opening in a college of education and human development. The qualifications necessary for these positions included a background in IR as well as contextual knowledge of the program area, which implies that the IR-related activities of the position could be somewhat decentralized from those of the institution-level IR function.

It is reasonable to assume that institutions collect some data that are infrequently used by the IR office simply because of the specificity of the variables. Elaborate profusion exists because departments have uses for their data that vary from those of the campus IR office. As a result, it is more feasible for department-level research to exist in silos across the institution. For example, the number of teacher education program graduates who pass a state licensure exam is an achievement measure that may be collected by a central IR office; however, such data would likely be used more regularly at the department level than the institutional level. Similarly, the rates at which students participate in service activities is a measure that the division of student affairs typically collects for programming purposes.

Academic Culture Versus Administrative Culture

Volkwein (1999) stated that IR operates in two contrasting institutional cultures; activities such as teaching, research, and service are carried out by the academic culture, which places high value on quality and effectiveness, while the administrative culture supplies support services and places high value on efficiency. The pressure from differing academic and administrative cultures appears to magnify the vagueness of the distinction between IR as a practice versus a profession. This ambivalence is particularly relevant to elaborate profusion because while the IR function is present in various campus departments, it may not be referred to as IR. Volkwein and colleagues (2012) acknowledge that there is consensus about the skills needed for IR, but question whether IR is a mature profession. As new people enter the IR field with varied backgrounds, training, and earned degrees, there is no common IR curriculum or accreditation process, and IR career paths and patterns are unclear. This is especially true of the diffusion of centralized IR into student affairs divisions, as many of the professionals who have data-related roles in the division do not have job titles that contain IR but conduct critical analyses to inform the administration of their programs and initiatives.

Those who view IR as a practice may focus on first-tier competencies, which Terenzini (1999) refers to as technical/analytical intelligence, and include tasks such as familiarity with units (e.g., students, faculty, finances, and facilities); familiarity with categories and definitions (e.g., part- or full-time, first-time, credit hours, and class status); knowledge of basic counting rules and formulae; and familiarity with structures, variable names, definitions, coding conventions, and schedules for maintaining institutional data files. These competencies are certainly useful for addressing the administrative goal of department-level efficiencies, and those who have such skills are very knowledgeable of their data. For example, program managers, coordinators, and assistants are likely department data stewards or users; however, without references to IR in their position title, they may be hard to identify as data experts outside of their offices. Their existence in pockets and corners of the institution may be influenced by their perception of IR as a practice, one that they choose to perform in their department rather than in the institution's central IR office.

The academic culture of an institution may persuade those who view IR as a profession to focus on other first-tier skills related to research design, sampling, statistics, measurement, research methods, technical mainframes, and personal computing. Regarding formal preparation for an IR career, elaborate profusion appears most relevant to IR certificate programs which focus on the academic culture of quality and effectiveness. Most certificate programs are housed in an academic department, but not all require students to gain experience in an IR office; some consider the completion of academic courses as adequate to meet certificate requirements. Some certificate programs combine IR with student affairs assessment. For example, Kent State University's Institutional Research and Assessment Certificate is housed in the School of Foundations, Leadership, and Administration and includes interdisciplinary instruction that covers competencies from the Association for Institutional Research, NASPA–Student Affairs Administrators in Higher Education, and American College Personnel Association (Kent State University, 2016).

Institutional Needs Versus IR Professional Needs

Although Swing (2009) suggests that the field of IR is moving toward strategic planning, outcomes assessment, and advocacy for improvement, the function is still ambiguous, as indicated by the challenge of identifying the necessary qualifications to conduct IR activities. Norbut and Glaser (2012) interviewed IR directors about the preconditions of success in the IR role and received varying opinions. Respondents validated the assumption that individuals have largely "fallen into" the field of IR, which Norbut and Glaser

(2012) suggest is because IR is a discipline that institutions have built over only the past several decades. However, the core functions of IR are not new, as offices have been responsible for mandatory reporting and routine data collection and analysis for decades.

Volkwein (1999) suggests that IR professionals often experience tension between their role of being hired to produce accurate numbers and descriptive statistics, which are institutional needs, and their involvement in research and analysis, which are professional needs that could lead to increased job fulfillment. Elaborate profusion is signaled by loosely coordinated, fragmented IR work, which creates the necessity for IR professionals to balance the needs of the institution with their professional needs. As institutional IR priorities are continuously shaped and reshaped, we could see even greater separation of institutional and department-level needs, and as a result, the demographics of IR professionals at both levels will likely shift accordingly. The absence of a clear definition of IR also contributes to elaborate profusion, as decentralized IR activities present an attractive option for department-level IR professionals to tailor their research career. Norbut and Glaser (2012) predict that the IR field will more fully comprehend the requisite skill sets for a successful IR professional as the field matures.

Opportunities

Elaborate profusion supports department-level IR using data that are underutilized by the institution-level IR office. While central IR offices may not make frequent use of these data, IR professionals in various departments and offices would likely use it to inform their decisions. Gagliardi and Wellman (2014) report that the analytic functions in most campuses remain topically stove-piped, with the named IR office focused primarily on student-related research, and reporting and research in other areas, such as resource use and personnel, handled by the budget and human relations offices. They add that campuses have been slow in their use of data to examine cross-cutting issues such as student success. This presents an excellent opportunity for student affairs divisions to conduct their own analyses, and many appear to be doing so. For example, Gagliardi and Wellman (2014) found that only 5.1% of central IR offices reported using data related to learning outcomes assessments in the past three years. This is an area of high importance to student affairs divisions and a priority of their assessment activities.

A decentralized IR function is also leading to more visible department-level data experts. Such stewards are knowledgeable of the nuances in their own data and can provide the department-level context for certain metrics. The change agent role can be shared between data professionals at the department and institution levels, as elaborate profusion would lessen the burden on the central IR office and provide capacity for it to focus on varying institution-level requests from senior leadership and external consumers.

Challenges

One challenge presented by elaborate profusion is a slower development of the institution-level IR function, which could be the result of department-level professionals not moving into central IR office positions. Norbut and Glaser (2012) argue that professionals who make up "typical" IR offices are in those roles because of chance or because they fill a specific technical need required by that specific department. Centralized IR offices may also have difficulty hiring qualified IR professionals with institutional-level experience. Leimer and Terkla (2009) found that training effective IR professionals requires a considerable time investment and institutions may have difficulty finding competently trained staff members. However, Norbut and Glaser (2012) predict that the field of IR will become more widely marketed as a career option and will more deliberately entice college and university students into IR roles.

Another challenge of elaborate profusion is inconsistent data analysis across departments, which could stem from varying data definitions, research questions, and methodologies. While it is expected that departments will develop systems for data collection and analysis that best fit their operations and research interests, the resulting abundance of unique data definitions make it difficult to combine or compare analyses across departments. As elaborate profusion continues to occur, there will likely be new relationships formed between various division-level data handlers and the campus information technology (IT) department. For example, as the division of student affairs builds robust dashboards and other tools for manipulating their data, new relationships with IR and IT could help streamline data analysis and reporting.

Data Analytics in Student Affairs: Four Emerging Areas

Gagliardi and Wellman (2014) found that nearly 90% of IR projects are focused on student outcomes. It appears as though IR offices will be joined in increased analysis of student outcomes as elaborate profusion results in more divisions across an institution engaging in data analytics. It is likely that student affairs professionals are also heavily involved in data-informed decision-making, as Swing and Ross (2016) found several student success data activities for which IR offices are typically not involved or do not have any

ty. For example, their national survey of IR offices revealed that
ٱo responsibility for class scheduling or studies. Several emerging
ٱdent affairs are becoming more reliant on data, and as a result, the
division's data analytics capacity is steadily increasing. Four areas of particular
focus for student affairs professionals are policy, assessment, campus climate,
and predictive analysis of engagement data.

Policy

State and federal policy developments, particularly those that relate to
resource management, are creating opportunities for student affairs professionals to use data to inform their decisions. One example is recent regulatory guidance related to the Fair Labor Standards Act. The U.S. Department
of Labor (2016) considered issuing rules related to overtime pay for sala-
ried employees across all industries, including postsecondary education.
These rules would have increased the annual salary exemption from overtime pay for qualifying employees from $23,660 to $47,476 and included
an automatic update to the overtime salary and compensation levels every
three years. Although implementation of these rules did not occur and may
not take place in the near future, most senior-level student affairs administrators conducted several financial analyses to inform critical decisions
related to how they would need to adjust staffing and operational processes,
both to comply with the new rule and ensure consistent delivery of high-
quality services to students.

Assessment

Several factors, including increased pressure from senior leaders to measure
the return on investment for programs and activities, national discourse on
the value of cocurricular activities, and high expectations for the delivery
of services, have led student affairs divisions to increase their assessment
capacity and embed data analytics in many, if not all, core functions of the
division. As a result, three types of assessment appear critical to the efficacy
of student affairs divisions: needs assessments, which are focused on identifying gaps between current and desired programs, resources, institutional
policies, or support services; process assessments, which examine how programs, resources, institutional policies, or support services are delivered;
and outcome assessments, which measure the results of a program, resource,
institutional policy, or support service to study whether intended objectives
were met. It is not uncommon for these assessments to involve the collection and analysis of various data variables, and as a result, student affairs

divisions are increasing their capacity to conduct studies external to the IR office.

Volkwein (2008) stated that an indicator of elaborate profusion is the development of independent studies that are loosely coordinated, if at all, with the central IR office. An example of this is related to cocurricular learning. There is ample research that suggests that students who are more engaged with their campus have higher rates of persistence (Kuh, 1995; Tinto, 1993). Student affairs divisions are increasingly exploring methods for documenting and assessing learning that occurs in activities that take place outside of the classroom. Service activities, leadership training, and cross-cultural experiences offer students opportunities to strengthen several skills that employers seek in college graduates, such as critical thinking, communication, and problem solving. As colleges explore methods for capturing learning in these settings with tools such as cocurricular transcripts, badges, and portfolios, new opportunities are arising to collect data from cocurricular experiences and assess the influence of such engagement on various student outcomes.

Campus Climate

Amid the changing landscape of college campuses, one that unfortunately includes higher rates of violence and other acts of aggression, student affairs divisions are more closely attuned to the importance of managing campus climate. As a result, professionals are providing data and information to support campus climate surveys, which are critical to assessing the level at which their institution is responding to issues that may create uncomfortable learning environments. This presents another opportunity for IR offices to partner with student affairs to monitor and analyze data trends and develop the necessary interventions and programming to respond to climate shifts.

Predictive Analysis of Engagement Data

In their national research on the responsibilities of central IR offices, Swing, Jones, and Ross (2016) found that many IR offices have limited access to some types of data that are frequently collected and used by student affairs divisions. Such data includes student early warning alerts and academic advising data, for which the researchers found that 49% and 43% of IR offices have no access respectively.

Predictive analysis of data from learning management systems (LMSs) is becoming more common as a strategy to advance degree progress for students. Efforts such as the Predictive Analytics Reporting Network and the Education Advisory Board's Student Success Collaborative are helping institutions identify variables to examine patterns and assist at-risk students. Colleges are also experimenting with projects that examine a range of behavioral data points outside of the classroom experience. Senior leaders and administrators are using new insights from analysis of engagement and involvement data to inform the development of proactive interventions and support strategies to help students succeed. These analyses also provide details that can support the examination of outcomes for student subgroups, such as first-generation and low-income college students. Although the division of student affairs is often the guardian of student engagement data, there is still an opportunity for the IR office to assist in the analysis of key metrics, and doing so will give senior leaders a more robust picture of students' experiences inside and outside of the classroom. As veteran leaders in the use of data to inform decisions, institutional researchers also have a valuable opportunity to engage with the larger campus community as data coaches. Such a role would involve IR offices helping staff and administrators interpret their data and use their analyses to develop and implement strategies in their respective divisions. Another benefit of the coaching role is that as functional units use data to assess the progress of their division-level goals, institutional researchers can help connect those goals to larger, institution-level metrics.

Elaborate profusion may result in some IR offices having concerns about data quality. The often-used reference to a "single source of the truth" in regard to data may be challenged by the emerging role of student affairs professionals as data stewards and consumers. However, considering the need for college administrators to deepen their understanding of students' experiences, it is likely that the benefit of integrating data campus-wide, regardless of its origin, will outweigh the challenges of stewardship.

Conclusion

As elaborate profusion results in the spreading of the IR function across the institution, it will be critical for student affairs divisions to connect their data systems to as many additional campus data sets as possible. Although this will likely create challenges related to identifying common variables to link students' information across systems, it will, in the long run, result in more thorough analyses of student outcomes. Perhaps the process of connecting student affairs data with IR data could be one responsibility of a chief institutional research officer, a new cabinet-level role that Swing and Ross (2015) suggest will perform as an institution-wide connector and coach. Considering the intersection of divisional and institutional mission, it will be imperative that a professional in such a position address not only practical needs, such as consistent data variables across departments, but also professional needs, such as senior-level support for campus-wide data strategies and goals.

While the pressures of internal versus external demands, academic versus administrative culture, and institutional versus professional needs are influencing the decentralization of the IR function, the upside is that elaborate profusion will also lead to the positive outcomes that researchers have argued are the reason why data analytics are necessary. Leimer (2009) contends that IR can contribute to institutional goals by helping to foster a broader organizational view, operating as a connector and facilitator of collaboration and stimulating organizational learning. This chapter has identified several areas for which new collaborations between student affairs and IR can provide such an atmosphere and support a more data-informed culture on our college campuses.

References

Association for Institutional Research. (2017). *Jobs board*. Retrieved from https://www.airweb.org/Careers/Pages/Jobs.aspx

Gagliardi, J. S., Espinosa, L. E., Turk, J. M., & Taylor, M. (2017). *The American college president study 2017*. Washington DC: American Council on Education.

Gagliardi, J., & Wellman, J. (2014). *Meeting demand for improvements in public system institutional research* [Progress report on the NASH Project in IR]. Washington DC: Retrieved from http://nashonline.org/wp-content/uploads/2017/08/Assessing-and-Improving-the-IR-Function-in-Public-University-Systems.pdf

Kent State University. (2016). *Institutional research and assessment certificate program*. Retrieved from http://www.kent.edu/ehhs/fla/eval/institutional-research-assessment-certificate

Kuh, G. D. (1995). The other curriculum: Out-of-class experiences associated with student learning and personal development. *Journal of Higher Education, 66*(2), 123–155.

Leimer, C. (2009). Imagining the future of institutional research [Special issue]. *New Directions for Institutional Research, 143.*

Leimer, C., & Terkla, D. (2009). Leaving the foundation: Institutional research office organization, staffing, and career development. *New Directions for Institutional Research, 143,* 43–58.

Norbut, M., & Glaser, P. (2012). *Association for Institutional Research telephone interview summary*. Retrieved from http://www.airweb.org/Resources/Documents/Report-on-Voice-of-the-Members.pdf

Parmley, K. A. (2009). Raising the institutional research profile: Assessing the context and expanding the use of organizational frames. *New Directions for Institutional Research, 143,* 73–83.

Swing, R. L. (2009). Institutional researchers as change agents. *New Directions for Institutional Research, 143*, 5–16.

Swing, R. L., Jones, D., and Ross, L. E. (2016). *The AIR national survey of institutional research offices.* Tallahassee, FL: Association for Institutional Research. Retrieved from http://www.airweb.org/nationalsurvey

Swing, R. L., & Ross, L. (2016). *Statement of aspirational practice for institutional research.* Tallahassee, FL: Association for Institutional Research.

Terenzini, P. T. (1999). On the nature of institutional research and the knowledge and skills it requires. *New Directions for Institutional Research, 104*, 21–29.

Tinto, V. (1993). *Leaving college: Rethinking the causes and cures of student attrition* (2nd ed.). Chicago, IL: The University of Chicago Press.

U.S. Department of Labor. (2016). *Guidance for higher education institutions on paying overtime under the Fair Labor Standards Act.* Retrieved from https://www.dol.gov/whd/overtime/final2016/highered-guidance.pdf

Volkwein, J. F. (1999). The four faces of institutional research. *New Directions for Institutional Research, 104*, 9–19.

Volkwein, J. F. (2008). The foundations and evolution of institutional research. *New Directions for Higher Education, 141*, 5–20.

Volkwein, J. F., Liu, Y., & Woodell, J. (2012). The structure and functions of institutional research offices. In R. D. Howard, G. W. McLaughlin, W. E. Knight, and Associates (Eds.), *The handbook of institutional research* (pp. 22–39). San Francisco, CA: Jossey-Bass.

5

THE IT–IR NEXUS

Three Essentials for Driving Institutional Change Through Data and Analytics

Timothy M. Chester

While typically viewed as representing separate and distinct professions, both information technology (IT) organizations and institutional research (IR) offices actually have a lot in common. Both require a certain level of specialized skill and expertise to successfully carry out their roles, but the methodology and experience required are not typically well understood by others operating outside these professions. Both have operational responsibilities within the university context that are important and critical—but not necessarily strategic—in that they provide transformational opportunities for reforming the enterprise. In this sense, running servers, operating a network, and facilitating classroom technology all rank up there with producing annual enrollment reports, submitting data to the Integrated Postsecondary Education Data System (IPEDS), or compiling faculty salary information. These are the routine operational responsibilities that must be done well in order for the institution to function, but this work, on its own, is often far removed from activities that can create innovative or transformational opportunities for institutional reform. Today, creating such opportunities is a must for higher education institutions and poses a significant occasion for collaboration between IT and IR organizations.

Nevertheless, when thinking about institutional reform as a necessary, compelling, and desired outcome, both IT and IR can and should have a meaningful role to play in facilitating and supporting institutional change. IT organizations in higher education originally focused on supporting academic and administrative processes with a mainframe, later focusing on supporting desktop computers and connecting them with a network. In the 1990s and 2000s, IT organizations supported the implementation of packaged enterprise resource planning (ERP) systems that replaced homegrown, legacy mainframe systems. Today, better use of these technologies can create efficiencies, eliminate redundant work, and provide greater access and better use of university resources. Stronger understanding and use of institutional data can help the institution deliver better student success outcomes while also improving institutional decision-making. More relevant and timely access to data on the use of institutional resources, facilities, and personnel are critical for reform efforts. IT organizations are typically responsible for championing and supporting the use of academic and administrative information systems that IR offices depend on to provide data, reports, and analyses—data that are produced through the day-to-day business transactions recorded in these systems. Thus, there is tremendous benefit to engaging IR directly in the design, implementation, and ongoing support of these systems. While it remains atypical, my institution (the University of Georgia) is one of the growing numbers of institutions that have brought both IT and IR under the same organizational umbrella, led by the institution's chief information officer (CIO). While sufficient for improving collaboration between IT and IR, such realignment often reflects the CIO's individual expertise and interest in the areas of data analysis and analytics. Yet, it also reflects an understanding by senior institutional executives that better data-informed decision-making must start at the transactional level, where institutional data is first produced. This is the crux of the IT–IR nexus.

The IT–IR Nexus

The IT–IR nexus can be best understood as an opportunity for a series of collaborations around data: data production, use, distribution, and analysis. It can provide an institution's leaders with a critical advantage in the form of timely and relevant analysis that lends previously unknown insights into old problems or new opportunities. Insights from the IT–IR nexus have been critical to Georgia State University as it has nearly doubled its undergraduate graduation rate while simultaneously increasing the numbers of Pell Grant eligible students (Kurzweil & Wu, 2015). Improved use of data and analytics was critical to Arizona State University as it revamped both its administrative and academic programs to build and grow as a twenty-first-century public institution of higher education that engages "the demographic complexity of our society as a whole" (Crow, 2012, p. 19). The same can be said of the University of Kentucky, which has been working over the past several years to improve the institution's retention rates by constantly measuring and closely monitoring a student's engagement with the institution and its resources over the course of any given semester (Straumsheim, 2013).

All three of these examples of institutional reform are made possible by three critical and overlapping activities that allow an institution to make better use of its information resources: standardized *data* elements, informed *analysis* framed by the strategic issues, and *advocacy* for change and reform (see Figure 5.1).

If one takes a traditional view of both IT and IR, these activities are typically siloed apart from one another and are performed by different units within the university. While IT historically is responsible for storing and securing data, it is the business offices producing the data (admissions, financial aid, registrar, etc.) who are responsible for defining it, consistent with their individual business needs. While data analysis is a core activity for most IR offices, identifying and framing strategic research questions more often is performed outside the IR office. Although many IT and IR leaders understand the need for greater advocacy for change and reform, while aspiring to perform such a role, the successful carrying out of this mission is often left to senior executives and leaders who have greater recognition and visibility across the enterprise can play an enhanced leadership role by together facilitating these three activities across an institution.

Because of their core responsibilities, both IT and IR offices are positioned, almost uniquely, to play more strategic roles as agents of reform and change across their institutions. For starters, the work of both offices touches nearly every single part of the institution. Whether providing IT services or

Figure 5.1. Key activities to optimize information resources.

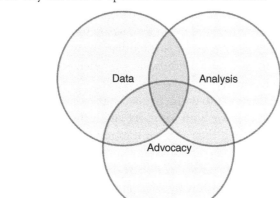

Note. This figure illustrates the three critical and overlapping activities that allow an institution to make better use of its information resources.

facilitating and distributing reports, both IT and IR typically have working relationships with every operating unit. Those working relationships provide both IT and IR with an insider's view on business processes and the strengths and challenges of the major university administrative and academic functions. These insights can provide a foundation for IT and IR leaders who want to take a more aggressive leadership position when it comes to governing data, driving analysis of strategic issues, and advocating for reform and change. Other prerequisites also exist: well-integrated information systems that are shared by all major business offices; a culture of collaboration that facilitates cross-functional collaboration between and among business offices, IT, and IR around the creation and use of data; a strong and well-used technical infrastructure for reports and analytics; and regular access to institutional executives.

The potential of the IT–IR nexus is that it provides a set of regular and continuous collaborations that define and govern the use of data at an institution, it drives the IR agenda to align with an evolving institutional strategy for transformation and reform, and it acts as an advocate for change. It is built on a foundation of strong information systems, cross-functional collaboration, and regular access to institutional executives. These activities and collaboration are what allow an institution to improve its data-informed decision-making. The challenge is how to begin traveling down this road. This history of improving decision-making is one of misstarts, travels down unproductive paths, and initiatives that failed to realize their strategic potential. This is because organizations typically make a couple of false assumptions at the beginning of this type of improvement initiative: (a) that what's missing is the right set of tools and technologies; and (b) that driving better collaborations is facilitated by leadership changes and changes to the org chart. In fact, the more successful organizations are the ones that figure out that tools and technologies are less important than the ways that we use them and that the way individuals and offices work with each other is more important than who they report to.

There are three essentials to doing these things well. These are prerequisites, in the sense that they are both necessary and sufficient to help both IT and IR offices move beyond their regular, rote responsibilities of maintaining systems and producing reports to assume a recognized role as key leaders facilitating institutional transformation and reform. The first is strong data governance, or the cross-functional relationships that allow data and information to be organized and maintained as a key strategic asset. The second is fostering the development of new and different competencies for both IT and IR—competencies that go beyond the traditional technical or statistical skills emphasized in both offices. The third is a promoting a culture of continuous improvement, where the organizational culture itself understands that regular transformation is vital to maintaining and enhancing the institutional mission. These three essentials go to the root of what it takes to develop strong IT and IR collaborations that facilitate greater data-informed decision-making within an institution.

Data Governance

When I arrived at the University of Georgia in 2011, one of the things that I frequently heard was that the institution struggled with data-informed decision-making because it could not get to a "single version of the truth" for key performance indicators. What the admissions office would announce as the benchmarks for the incoming class of freshmen would almost always diverge from what IR would report on regular census days. The same went for enrollment reports from our transactional academic information system, which would differ from the number found in our IR data warehouse. When you hear executives lamenting that they can't get to a "single version of the truth," this almost always indicates that the institution itself has challenges with managing data holistically as an enterprise asset.

Why so? Data themselves have context—they have standards that precisely define what they are, how they were derived, and the rules themselves by which the data were constructed. In large institutions such as the University of Georgia, a lack of a strong, shared understanding of the context behind data (whether in the form of reports, analysis, or analytics) is often the cause of a "single version of the truth" problem. Different data standards and definitions are driven by the distinct business needs of the various business units producing data through day-to-day business transactions. When the admissions office reports on its incoming class of freshmen enrollees, its business purpose is to demonstrate the superior academic qualifications of the class and to portray the academic selectivity of the institution in as positive a light as possible. This is a fundamentally different business purpose than a census-day enrollment report by the IR office, whose business purpose is to support funding and resource allocation decisions. Each of these business needs has different standards for defining what a student is, how students' composite test scores might be computed, and/or how to standardize students' high school GPAs across different schools and types of curricula. The lack of understanding of the types of context behind data reports can typically be traced to a lack of cross-functional collaboration between IR and the offices that produce the data. At the University of Georgia in 2011, the problem was not just lack of collaboration, but a technical disjunction, as each of the major academic offices had its own separate information systems and databases. Collaboration between admissions and financial aid and the registrar only consisted of the routine sharing of flat files of data between these databases. None of these offices had any knowledge of the sometimes dramatically different ways each would define such basic concepts as *an enrolled student*. What's worse, they tended to be unaware that these differences existed.

Data governance is a set of collaborative processes that has the aim of producing well-known standards (context) governing the production of precise and well-understood data. These standards are suited to multiple business purposes and are enforced when data are produced either by data entry or by large-scale importing into institutional information systems. By virtue of these standards, the data become authoritative in the sense that they are trusted and considered reliable. While shared information systems are a necessary component for maintaining authoritative data elements, it is the cross-functional collaboration that is both necessary and sufficient for ensuring successful data standardization and the recognition that authoritative data exists.

The collaborations that comprise effective data governance must be managed as regular business processes of the institution, no different than processes that manage student course registration or the disbursement of financial aid. To be truly effective, data governance needs an owner, and that ownership should not conflict with other regular duties of providing services to the campus community. Many institutions err when they assign the responsibility for stewarding data governance to one of the business offices involved in the production of data, like the registrar. The challenge is that, all too often, the day-to-day effort required to support the delivery of regular services to the campus community will detract from the mission of coordinating and facilitating cross-functional data governance. Data governance becomes something that often falls below the most pressing priorities of the day, and it becomes a second or third priority. Thus, there is the need for an institutional chief data officer—someone whose prime role is to steward and facilitate the cross-functional collaborations necessary for successful data governance; someone who works above the day-to-day fray of delivering regular services to the institution.

The identification and assignment of someone with chief data officer responsibilities cover the "who" aspect of data governance. Next, institutions should consider the optimum time to get started. Lack of consistent data standards doesn't happen overnight, and it almost never represents a conscious choice by the institution to bypass the need for authoritative data.

Data inconsistency occurs because the need of individual business units to meet their unique business objectives first typically outweighs the burden and upfront inefficiencies created when collaborating on good data governance. Good data governance is difficult—it takes time and commitment, and it requires constant vigilance and collaboration; otherwise, it would happen organically across institutions. But it doesn't.

At the University of Georgia, the imperative to create a culture of good data governance was necessitated by the institution's commitment to adopt commercial, off-the-shelf, packaged ERP applications for its major academic and administrative systems. Operating with a shared database, each of the major units at the institution would be working, for the first time, with the same data elements. Therefore, what was generated in the admissions or financial aid office would have dramatic ramifications for downstream users of the system. For institutions that have already implemented packaged ERP systems, major upgrades of those systems will provide similar imperatives to initiate or reinforce strong data governance collaborations.

Cross-functional collaboration requires formal and well-understood organizational structures for effective operation. The collaborating entities should operate with a set of guiding principles and be charged by the chief executive officer and other senior executives of the institution. For our initiative at the University of Georgia, our ERP implementation governance structure resembled the administrative chart in Figure 5.2.

Ultimate success for any good data governance initiative begins with the executive leadership of the institution. Day-to-day executive leadership over the academic, administrative, financial, and technology areas manages the overall scope and direction of the activities, allocates resources, and works to keep the initiative on track. We have found that having an overall chief project officer, who is responsible to the executive leadership, is a very important

Figure 5.2. University of Georgia ERP governance structure.

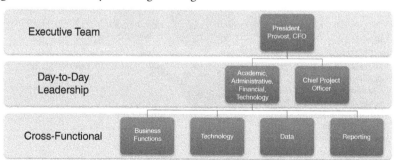

mechanism for ensuring that the executive team receives regular updates and can easily weigh in when necessary to resolve difficult issues or ensure that the initiative remains on track.

The "how" of good data governance revolves around four distinct types of cross-functional activities (see Figure 5.3). Karel (2014) describes these activities as four essential process states of good data governance.

Discovery processes are about assessing the institution's current maturity when it comes to how data is produced through different business transactions, how the units responsible for those transactions collaborate in producing and consuming those data elements, and the current state (cleanliness) of the data itself. Such an assessment is necessary for formulating an overall governance strategy, setting priorities for data standardization efforts, defining supporting business cases for change, and, ultimately, determining where the institution desires to go with its data governance strategy.

Definition processes are a series of collaborations where essential data elements are defined, catalogs of business processes are produced, and glossaries that map data elements to processes are documented. These are the essentials for operationalizing good data governance efforts. At the University of Georgia, this work has created the contextual awareness among cross-functional groups that underlies common and shared data elements, reports, and analytics.

Apply processes occur when technology is used to enforce the data standards, business rules, and associated business processes that are documented in the discovery and definition phases. Apply processes might consist

Figure 5.3. Key activities to optimize information resources.

Discover
- Data discovery
- Data profiling
- Data inventories
- Process inventories
- CRUD analysis
- Capabilities assessment

Define
- Business glossary creation
- Data classifications
- Data relationships
- Reference data
- Business rules
- Data goverance policies
- Other dependent policies
- Key Performance Indicators

Measure and Monitor
- Proactive monitoring
- Operational dashboards
- Reactive operational DQ audits
- Dashboard monitoring/audits
- Data lineage analysis
- Program performance
- Business value/ROI

Apply
- Automated rules
- Manual rules
- End to end workflows
- Business/IT collaboration

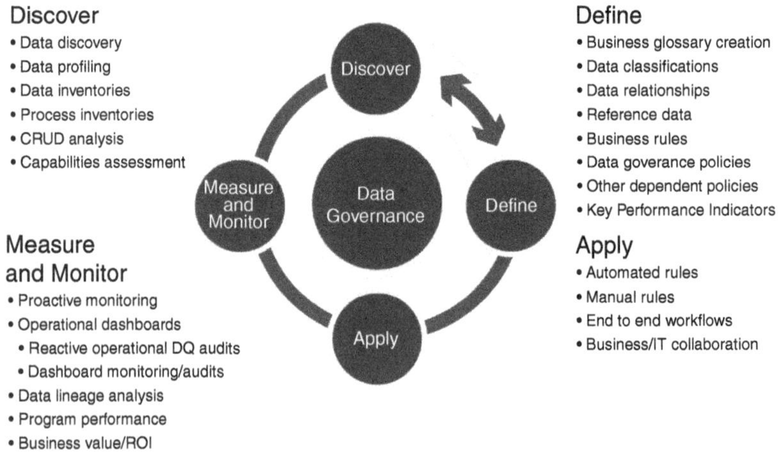

Note. This figure illustrates the four critical and overlapping activities that allow an institution to make better use of its information resources.

of data edits that are enforced on data entry forms used by office personnel, or data rules that are enforced when large batches of data, such as applications for admission or test scores, are imported into shared information systems. Such automation is also critical when exporting or sharing information: Data reported from the University of Georgia to the University System of Georgia is scrubbed by a set of scripts that enforce data standards and flag elements that do not conform. Exceptions must be resolved by cross-functional teams before the data export is completed and the results are shared with the system office.

Measure and monitor processes are about ensuring the effectiveness of the discovery, definition, and apply phases. It ensures compliance with data standards and forces cross-functional teams to review exceptions and work together to resolve issues with data quality as they arise.

Together, these four phases make up the distinct type of activities that constitute good data governance. It is critical to understand that these four phases must operate interactively: Good data governance is not a one-off project, but a series of collaborations that recur over time. For example, the automated enforcement of system-wide academic data elements in Georgia was produced through a similar process of discovery, definition, application, and monitoring. These initiatives were led by the system's CIO and IR leadership, working hand in hand as peers. While the creation of the automated export and data-checking scripts began as a one-off initiative, the processes execute multiple times each year. Each iteration of the process provides the next opportunity for monitoring the success of the program, discovering any exceptions or changes to business practices that require new definitions, and updating tools to enforce those changes to data standards. This cross-functional collaboration across the University system and its component schools has allowed the entire system to be better informed with more timely and relevant data on system-wide academic operations.

Competencies, Not Skills

The long-term success of IT–IR collaborations means that both organizations move beyond the ordinary, regular skill sets that have been their bread and butter in the past. For IT organizations, this requires moving beyond the technical skills necessary to run networks, operate servers, and support desktop computing. For IR offices, this requires moving beyond the statistical and data skills required to clean and validate data and compile reports. In our fast and changing world of higher education—where collaborations around data, analysis of strategic issues, and advocacy for change are the key leadership opportunities—the transactional skills normally sufficient for IT–IR success simply no longer matter to the extent they have in the past.

The traditional, transactional skills emphasized in both IT and IR offices are foundational in the sense that they provide a solid basis for ensuring consistency of data, protecting it, and establishing repositories for distributing it. But these skills are not sufficient for success in leading cross-functional collaborations. When it comes to the types of collaborations outlined here, competencies like strategic planning, business knowledge, and developing relationships are the essential traits that are both necessary and sufficient. The possession and regular demonstration of these types of competencies are the difference makers when it comes to IT and IR organizations performing more than their traditional, transactional roles. For IT and IR leaders, this is an exercise in organizational and professional development, as it requires the identification and promotion of the competencies necessary to support reform and be a recognized thought leader driving institutional change (Chester, 2011).

The concepts of *value* and *versatility* are important for delineating the differences between transactional and thought leadership roles. Value can be best understood as the difference between things (services, deliverables, and outcomes) that are important and things that have transformative potential for the institution. Versatility can be best understood as the difference between the skills required to operate technology or produce reports and those necessary to engage others around the business application of data and analytics. If mapped to a grid, these two concepts form a value curve with the concept of "versatility of performance" mapped along the horizontal axis and "value of contribution" along the vertical axis. Organizational roles,

Figure 5.4. The contribution-performance curve.

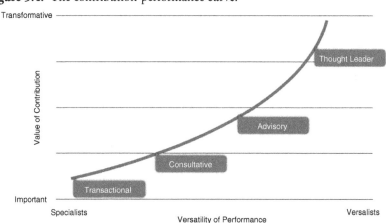

Note. This figure illustrates the three critical and overlapping activities that allow an institution to make better use of its information resources.

understood as different stages of organizational and leadership maturity, are mapped across this value curve in Figure 5.4.

In the lower left-hand quadrant of the curve, the transactional role is understood as a role emphasizing skills-based services that are important, but play less of a strategic role. In the upper right-hand quadrant is the thought leader role, which emphasizes the transformative power of data and analytics made possible through cross-functional collaborations and advocacy for change.

Moving from the transactional role to the thought leadership role is not something that happens overnight, but reflects a maturation of both organizational reputation and individual professional development that occurs through regular and successful demonstration of the mastery of different sets of competencies. These roles reflect the institution's perception of the performance of the IT and IR organizations and their leadership and are not necessarily tied to the role that both IT and IR desire to play within the institution. It's the view of those outside the IT and IR organizations that matters when it comes to maturity and progression in organizational roles.

Successfully performing the transactional role is indicated by consistent, efficient, reliable, responsive, and process-based service delivery. Performing well in the transactional role requires the successful mastery of competencies such as accountability; initiative, technology, or statistical skills; problem solving; teamwork; and thoroughness. When both the IT and IR organizations have developed reputations for being successful in this role, their role performance matures up the value curve into new and broader roles:

- The *consultative role* is about cross-functional collaboration around solving well-understood and well-defined problems. Success with this role is indicated by regularly demonstrating business smarts, communication and project management acumen, and strong relationship management abilities. It requires mastery of competencies such as analytical thinking, business process knowledge, process orientation, and openness to learning.
- The *advisory role* is about having a seat at the table when the institution considers the range of challenges and opportunities before it. It is more about supporting strategic planning and forecasting than about problem-solving; therefore, success in this role is indicated by strong analysis, assessment, and measurement skills and the ability to redesign business process architectures. It requires mastery of competencies such as business enterprise knowledge, relationship building, developing and empowering others, and emotional intelligence.

- At the top of the value curve is the *thought leader role*, which is demonstrated by successfully displaying the ability to build cross-functional alliances and partnerships, exhibiting leadership, and innovating together. It requires mastery of competencies such as change advocacy and strategic planning.

IT and IR leaders both get caught up, on occasion, in determining whether they have the proverbial "seat at the table." Those performing the transactional role typically do not. Those in the consultative role may be called to the table when others feel they can contribute, while those playing an advisory role maintain a regular seat at the table. Individuals and organizations performing the thought leader role are typically the ones charged to lead those meetings.

Both IT and IR leaders know that their organizations can play a crucial role in supporting institutional reform efforts, but successfully moving beyond the transactional role requires a deliberate effort to upgrade the organization's key competencies. The challenge is to move beyond ordinary IT and IR skills and to work diligently with staff to identify and promote those competencies necessary to performing more than a transactional role. There is strong awareness among institutional senior executives that clearly identified leadership is needed for successfully leading change and promoting organizational transformation initiatives. There is also recognition by those same executives that better use of data and analytics is an important tool for doing so. With that in mind, and with the right competencies, there is no reason why that leadership shouldn't come from the IT–IR nexus.

Committing to and Promoting Ongoing Change

There's a saying that "culture trumps strategy every time" (Merchant, 2011). Culture, being the glue that holds organizations and teams together, is made up of the values, beliefs, and expectations shared by the larger community. When continuous improvement is not ingrained within that organizational culture, too many transformation and business reform projects assume a one-off status, whose long-term effects tend to not last. Neither IT nor IR is normally considered a driver of organizational culture. However, they both can become contributors by promoting and advocating a culture of regular, continuous improvement through their support of an institution's processes of assessment, program review, and reaccreditation. For most institutions, these processes can provide some of the best opportunities for institutional change and reform. IT and IR leaders looking to expand their leadership roles should work within these regular processes in a way that sets them up as vehicles for lasting organizational change. Competencies such as relationship building, business enterprise knowledge, and communicating for results are essential.

There is a difference between one-off change projects and a culture of continuous improvement and reform: Only in the latter are institutional leaders regularly held accountable for moving the needle when it comes to advancing the performance of the institution through ongoing transformation. Too many one-off change initiatives fail when regular assessments of both institutional and individual leadership performance are not tied closely to the change agenda. If one truly desires an organization to change, its leadership must regularly be held accountable for initiating and leading that change. Assessment and performance review programs provide the best opportunities for ingraining this type of accountability within an organization's culture, but there are some essential elements:

- *Unit goals that reflect institutional goals.* When the strategic goals for programs, departments, and other business units are not tied directly to the institution's strategic goals, those larger strategic goals either are not well understood or are meaningless to the broader institution.
- *A mix of qualitative and quantitative performance indicators.* Assessment requires evidence, but relying too much on only qualitative or quantitative indicators can be less helpful. Qualitative evidence and assessments of positive change can be too subjective and based on opinion, whereas too great a reliance on quantitative evidence runs the risk of change initiatives that focus too much on gaming the performance indicators. Accountability requires assessment, and assessment of performance goals requires both qualitative and quantitative evidence.
- *Individual contributors know their part in fulfilling strategic goals.* Institutional and organization goals should be operationalized and turned into individual goals for key leaders across the institution. Annual reviews of the performance of these leaders should be largely based on their success in accomplishing these goals. Rewards, bonuses, or salary increases should be largely based on these accomplishments. In this sense, institutional goals are tied to unit goals, which are in turn tied to individual goals and form the primary basis for rewards and advancement. This is the strongest form of accountability for change and reform that can exist within an institution.
- *Regular communications and transparency regarding performance.* Institutional executives, preferably the CEO, must regularly communicate with the broader community regarding progress

toward strategic goals—and this should include reports on progress as well as challenges along the way. Such communication says to the entire institution that the strategic goals are taken seriously and that leaders are held accountable for accomplishing them. These regular communications from the top help cement an expectation of continuous improvement and positive change within an organizational culture.

IT and IR leaders are not typically in positions to drive these sorts of cultural changes. However, they do typically have a seat at the table in supporting regular assessment and review practices where they are most visible. By nudging these processes so that they include these critical elements, IT and IR leaders can take steps to help ensure that change initiatives are not one-off projects. Successfully doing so requires the type of competencies essential for playing a thought leadership role across the institution.

Summary

Change is in the air for higher education, and how this industry evolves over the next decade is very much in question. There is tremendous opportunity for IT and IR offices to play a significant role in supporting change and reform within their institutions. However, performing a greater role requires that IT and IR work together to first change and reform the way that they typically do business. Both must understand that one of their first and foremost missions is to support the institution in its greater use of data to inform decision-making. Second, they must understand that institutional change and transformation require timely and responsive data and analytics analysis and research that bring that data to bear on critical opportunities and challenges facing the institution—and that changes require advocacy. Performing those roles requires IT and IR to collaborate to create and maintain sound data governance practices within their institution, and successfully doing so necessitates the development of competencies that go beyond the traditional skills emphasized in their organization. Third, these opportunities are best realized when continuous improvement and reform are a regular part of an institution's culture—and there is a contributing role for IT and IR leaders to play in these processes. Nevertheless, successfully doing so requires that both IT and IR leaders first reform their practices, then develop their organizations and themselves in ways that prepare them to play greater leadership roles, and finally assume those opportunities by advocating for greater institutional change and reform. Over the coming decade, these are the prime challenges for advancing both the IT and IR professions.

References

Chester, T. (2011, January/February). Technical skills no longer matter. *EDUCAUSE Review, 46*(1), 63.

Crow, M. (2012, July/August). No more excuses: Michael M. Crow on Analytics. *EDUCAUSE Review, 47*(4), 14–19.

Karel, R. (2014, January 2). The process stages of data governance [Web log post]. Retrieved from http://blogs.informatica.com/2014/01/02/the-process-stages-of-data-governance/

Kurzweil, M., & Wu, D. D. (2015). *Building a pathway to student success at Georgia State University* [Case study]. Retrieved from http://www.sr.ithaka.org/publications/building-a-pathway-to-student-success-at-georgia-state-university/

Merchant, N. (2011). Culture trumps strategy every time [Web log post]. Retrieved from https://hbr.org/2011/03/culture-trumps-strategy-every

Straumsheim, C. (2013, October 18). Before the fact. *Inside Higher Ed.* Retrieved from https://www.insidehighered.com/news/2013/10/18/u-kentucky-hopes-boost-student-retention-prescriptive-analytics

6

PURSUIT OF ANALYTICS AND THE CHALLENGE OF ORGANIZATIONAL CHANGE MANAGEMENT FOR INSTITUTIONAL RESEARCH

Angela Y. Baldasare

"At a time when companies in many industries offer similar products and use comparable technology, high-performance business processes are among the last remaining points of differentiation" (Davenport & Harris, 2007, p. 8). Davenport and Harris wrote that sentence more than 10 years ago in *Competing on Analytics: The New Science of Winning* (2007), and the world they described in corporate America has now manifested itself in virtually every domain of our lives. The *Moneyball* approach, using data and analytics to influence outcomes, has become pervasive as corporate giants such as Amazon, Google, and Netflix use analytics to increase profits and personalize our buying experiences. Today, analytics are no longer just for the corporations written about by Davenport and Harris; they are seen as the pathway to optimizing outcomes of all kinds for corporations, institutions, voluntary organizations, small businesses, and individuals alike.

Higher education is not immune to the analytics revolution. As higher education has become increasingly competitive, scrutinized, resource-constrained, and regulated, data within many institutions is becoming more widely available and systematized through data warehouses and business intelligence applications. Campus consumers of that data, no longer limited to the ranks of top administrators, have come to expect on-demand data and sophisticated analytics to inform decision-making. On a managerial level, administrators expect staff members to use data to inform decision-making on a routine basis. Many are hoping to earn or sustain a competitive advantage in the higher education marketplace through analytics, and the pressure is on.

Currently this is one of the hottest topics in institutional research (IR) circles, as these changes have begun to challenge IR offices within colleges and universities in new ways. The position of IR offices as the "one source of truth" on campus over the past 50 years is now fundamentally in flux (Swing & Ross, 2016). The *Statement of Aspirational Practice for Institutional Research* (Swing & Ross, 2016), published by the Association for Institutional Research (AIR), has directly recommended that IR become recognized and nurtured as a dispersed function organization-wide. In this vision, dedicated IR professionals should move toward consultant or coaching roles, guiding new data consumers and decision makers, including students, to help build data literacy and manage data and analytic requirements across the institution (Swing & Ross, 2016).

This chapter will present an up close and personal case study of how this sea change is being grappled with at the University of Arizona (UA), where the IR office and business intelligence team have recently merged and where UA have entered into significant vendor partnerships to accelerate the deployment of action and predictive analytics. To place the UA story in the larger context affecting many IR offices today, this chapter is informed by conversations with numerous IR colleagues from across the country over several months in 2016. While by no means a representative sample, I spoke with colleagues from large and small offices; new IR directors and those who have been at the helm for decades; colleagues from large public institutions, private institutions, and community colleges; and those operating in highly centralized IR offices and those working on campuses with distributed or networked IR functions.

The forces and tensions that led UA to aggressively press forward with analytics through reorganization and vendor relationships are the same as those identified by my colleagues, and the same that are being pointed out in the recent AIR publications. Major changes in our environment over recent years include a wave of new technologies and advanced analytics products, intense regulatory environments, the wider availability of data through data warehouses and analytics systems, challenges in standardization of data across systems and between offices, decentralization of analytic capacity, self-service models for analytics, wide variation in data literacy among our audiences, expectations informed by corporate models and consumer experiences, budget cuts and being asked to do more with less, performance-based funding models, outcomes assessment, media rankings, and intensely competitive environments for research funding and enrollments.

For those of us who have spent our careers cultivating a culture of curiosity and/or data-informed decision-making, many can declare success. This

Figure 6.1. Business intelligence and analytics.

		Analytics
Optimization	What's the best that can happen?	
Predictive modeling	What will happen next?	
Forecasting/extrapolation	What if these trends continue?	
Statistical analysis	Why is this happening?	
Alerts	What actions are needed?	Access and reporting
Query/drill down	Where exactly is the problem?	
Ad hoc reports	How many, how often, where?	
Standard reports	What happened?	

(Vertical axis: Competitive Advantage; Horizontal axis: Degree of Intelligence)

Source: Davenport, 2007, location 222.

brings to mind an old joke: "I've got good news and bad news. The good news is they said 'yes.' . . . The bad news is they said 'yes.'" Data-informed decision-making is now the expectation, and that culture has brought with it a flood of demand for more on-demand data, actionable information, compelling visual formats, and advanced analytics including statistical analysis, forecasting, predictive modeling, and optimization. Figure 6.1 illustrates the progression of analytics delivery and its relationship to the intelligence produced. While delivering analytics in a production environment has been more the domain of business intelligence (BI) units, IR offices have, for decades, been offering many of these forms of analysis as a service. Standard and ad hoc reporting are the bread and butter of IR. Depending on size and capacity, IR offices have also offered statistical analysis, predictive modeling, and forecasting to inform institutional planning and decision-making for administrators. For many IR offices, the pressures today to deliver more advanced analytics is less about capacity to do the analysis itself and more about the ability to deploy it at scale, in self-service and on-demand production environments for campus data consumers.

A Consistent Version of the Truth

Current conversations about how the IR role is changing are appropriately focused on building a more distributed or networked IR function to foster analytic capacity across campus and in broadening the definition of *data consumers* beyond administrators to include faculty, staff, and students. With data accessible everywhere and with an expectation for analytic capacity being increasingly the norm, there is no way for IR offices to be the sole providers of information or for administrators to remain the primary clients.

We should be empowering administrators, faculty, staff, and students to make informed decisions with data. By offering training and serving as consultants, IR professionals can use their analytical skills to build data literacy and strengthen and expand the culture of informed decision-making. What has been lacking in this conversation thus far, however, is sufficient discussion about what a truly functional distributed IR model requires. As Davenport and Harris (2007) noted

> Data for business intelligence originates from many places, but the crucial point is that it needs to be managed through an enterprise-wide infrastructure. Only by this means will it be streamlined, consistent, and scalable throughout the organization. Having common applications and data across the enterprise is critical because it helps yield a "consistent version of the truth," an essential goal for everyone concerned with analytics. (pp. 160–161)

The importance of this "consistent version of the truth" cannot be overstated. On many campuses, data are indeed available everywhere. But often, the landscape is one of siloed data that is collected, stored, and deployed in an array of homegrown and third-party systems that do not integrate. Campuses that have built data warehouses must continually work to ensure that additional data sources are taken in, appropriately structured, accurate, and well-defined in order for them to be useful to amateur analysts across campus. Even for the more advanced analysts, the questions we seek to answer with predictive analytics, forecasting, and optimization usually require data that span financial, student, personnel, research, and other systems. Figure 6.2 depicts five stages of analytics readiness. Working toward a distributed model of analytic or IR expertise without having accurate, systematized, and well-defined data in place is a recipe for frustration.

IR has enjoyed the position of being the bearer of "truth" for nearly half a century, since its inception as a discipline. Today, what campuses require is a "consistent version of the truth," and that is not something an IR office alone can provide. It is a goal that requires an enterprise approach and partnership with information technology (IT) and BI units. It requires a state of analytic and organizational readiness. It is a foundation of data upon which meaning is created, and the creation of meaning out of data is at the heart of IT.

The University Analytics and Institutional Research Story

In July 2014, UA's Office of Institutional Research and Planning Support (OIRPS, the IR office) and the enterprise and information analytics group

Figure 6.2. Stages of analytic readiness.

Data and IT Capability by Stage of Analytical Competition

Established companies typically follow an evolutionary process to develop their IT analytical capabilities.

Stage 1. The organization is plagued by missing or poor-quality data, multiple definitions of its data, and poorly integrated systems.

Stage 2. The organization collects transaction data efficiently but often lacks the right data for better decision-making.

Stage 3. The organization has a proliferation of business intelligence tools and data marts, but most data remain unintegrated, nonstandardized, and inaccessible.

Stage 4. The organization has high-quality data, an enterprise-wide analytical plan, IT processes and governance principles, and some embedded or automated analytics.

Stage 5. The organization has a full-fledged analytic architecture that is enterprise-wide, fully automated and integrated into processes, and highly sophisticated.

Source: Davenport and Harris, 2007, p. 156.

(EIA, the BI team) merged to form University Analytics and Institutional Research (UAIR). Formally, the opportunity for this reorganization of the IR and BI teams was triggered by the retirement of the head of IR, but the impetus for the merger had been building for years. Campus stakeholders were frustrated by conflicting sources of data on campus, and the provost had heard far too many complaints that people didn't know where to go for the "truth." It wasn't uncommon for stakeholders to get different answers to the same questions from OIRPS compared to the self-service analytics environment supported by EIA.

Prior to the UAIR merger, the organizational structure located OIRPS under the provost's office, while EIA reported up through the CIO. Following the merger, the two units responsible for providing data and information to campus were integrated under the provost's office (Figure 6.3).

The emergence and growth of BI on campus is a key part of the UA story that fits into themes of the larger analytics revolution that is confronting other campuses as well. From 2008 to 2012, UA embarked upon a complete overhaul of administrative systems, replacing some that were as much as 30 years old. The project, named Mosaic, greatly reduced the risks associated with the tottering, old systems and resulted in a huge increase in the quality and quantity of data available to campus users, with hundreds of new BI dashboards and reports. While it was a multiyear project that created its own challenges in workflow and data overload, it was a fresh start, a reset button for campus. From this project the BI team emerged, and the reporting environment they built onto the data warehouse democratized access to data for campus in an unprecedented way.

Figure 6.3. UA organizational structures before and after UAIR merger.

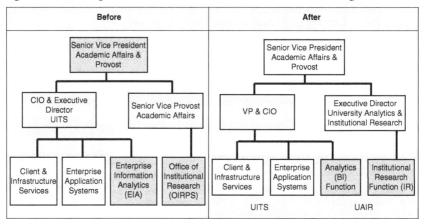

The BI team grew out of operational reporting, but they didn't stop there. They continued to push information out, meeting needs as they arose, growing in a very organic fashion driven by customer requests. The first priority of the BI team was to make the data available, then to automate request fulfillment by building dashboards and reports that empowered users in a self-service model. The BI environment now serves more than 2,000 unique operational users per month, averaging more than 30,000 queries per day. Results to self-service queries often didn't match up with official IR reports because different rules were applied in each, IR census files were not originally integrated into the data warehouse, the IR "secret sauce" for official student census counts was not transparent, and a lack of data definitions left many users frustrated and unable to understand the differences or reconcile BI reports and IR findings.

The IR office retained its longtime focus on rule-based official and external reporting, ad hoc requests, student cohort-based analyses, enrollment management support, and consultation on research and policy questions from administrators. Additional responsibilities came in the tracking and analysis of media rankings, support for assessment efforts, and teacher-course evaluations. IR took a small step into the BI domain by building a set of self-service interactive admissions and enrollment reports for enrollment management and the colleges. Both teams created census files and snapshot data for their own purposes. IR held expertise in student and faculty data, while BI held expertise in financial, HR (including faculty), student, space, and research data.

Over time, data rapidly proliferated on campus, and campus stakeholders were eager to make use of it. The accessibility of data put a spotlight on the separate and often disparate information produced by IR and BI. With the differences between the IR and the BI approaches to data not being easily understood by stakeholders, tensions naturally arose, and the call for a single, unified source of "truth" became a mandate for the two offices to merge.

Larger Context for the UAIR Merger

The emergence of BI and the accessibility of data that it facilitated is an important factor in the formation of UAIR. However, a host of other environmental factors that brought about the IR and BI merger at UA are the same factors pressing on many higher education institutions. Like many other institutions across the United States, state budget cuts have been steep. UA went from 43.3% state funding in 1987 to 22.7% by 2012, with state appropriations for general operating funds falling another 30% since 2008 (Hart, 2015). At the same time, the regulatory environment of higher education continued to intensify, with the state of Arizona moving through multiple iterations of (unfunded) performance funding models, key performance metrics, and increased scrutiny and involvement in university operations by the Arizona Board of Regents. We needed to do more with less, and the call for data-informed decision-making was heard from all sides.

Technology was also advancing with increasing speed, visibility, and influence over daily life, and with that came higher expectations for on-demand data. Senior administrators would sometimes cite Google or Amazon in their ability to track and predict customer behavior, wondering why we couldn't do the same. It wasn't enough to provide raw data and reports on-demand through BI, or to wait days or even weeks for IR analysis. Administrators wanted not only timely decision support data but also more in the way of forecasting, simulations, predictive modeling, and action analytics.

Change Is Hard

As has already been mentioned, IR and BI organizations have historically operated very differently. For a year prior to the formal merger of IR and BI into UAIR, the two teams were asked to work together presenting a seamless front to campus in what our administration informally referred to as a "virtual organization." Although this was easier said than done for two organizations with long-standing unique identities, it was manifested at first through the following key shared projects: (a) the decision support data system (DSDS), a static, public-facing view of 10 years of commonly requested data, drillable to unit and (for authorized users) record-level data; (b) predictive analytics for student success through a third-party vendor partnership; and (c) the development of systems architecture and reports to deploy responsibility centered management (RCM) as the university's new budget model.

Shared projects provided the two teams opportunities to collaborate, share credit, leverage individual strengths, and overcome the shortcomings of either team. IR offered deep content knowledge, particularly in student data analysis and implications, with a long history of close consultation with student affairs, enrollment management, and academic affairs, often working as a partner to inform programs and initiatives to improve student retention, course completion, time to degree, and graduation rates. BI brought strength in its technological expertise, ability to automate and move reports into production, and deep content knowledge in financials, HR, space, and research data. Both teams wanted to play a larger role in policy and programmatic conversations, inform critical decision-making, and expand skill sets to include higher levels of analysis.

Merging two very different organizational units, however, is not for the faint of heart. The teams historically had a somewhat adversarial relationship. IR was always protective of its ownership of "analysis" and the "official" numbers, while BI continued to increase access to data. Mutual trust and respect were low. IR was dependent upon BI for base data and was often treated as any other client on campus rather than as a critical partner and administrative function. BI had the advantage of controlling the data warehouse and was perceived by IR as trying to take over as they moved more explicitly into analysis and service to administrators. The BI imperative to provide open access to data often conflicted with the IR sensitivity to stakeholder's ownership of data, strategic uses of data, and the potential for data to be highly politicized. In addition, within the student and HR data domains, the rules applied by IR in analyses were not always consistent with rules built into automated reports by BI. The two teams needed to collaborate but often were competitive instead. Buy-in of individual staff members to the idea of a merger remained slow and conflicts persisted. Over time, some staff turnover provided the opportunity to hire new analysts and team leads who were not privy to the historical conflict and were willing to approach the merger with open minds.

IR and BI continue to differ in their preferred tools, with some overlap. The IR team works on a SQL server, with Microsoft Access or Hyperion queries, analyses in Excel, SAS, or SPSS, and Tableau for visualization. The BI team works with the Oracle database, Data Stage, and analyses in SQL and OBIEE and has also started to work with Tableau. The topic of visualization has surfaced tensions in who does what, in what environments, for which audiences, and with what tools. Collaborations between the two teams required access to one another's servers, which was threatening, and time-consuming transformations of IR SQL files into the Oracle database continue to be necessary to integrate IR-produced files back into the data warehouse for joint projects. While work is underway to migrate onto a single server environment, toolset preferences and skill sets will take longer to integrate. Debates continue about how the organization as a whole will move forward and enhance the delivery of data to campus and external audiences. The two teams continue to discuss a larger, combined data strategy for executive level dashboards, visual and interactive reporting, and public facing information. Both teams want to participate, everyone wants to be an analyst, and no one wants to be relegated to a purely technical function. It's a great example of individuals needing to remain close to the value of their work, seeking self-actualization and growth.

Staffing efforts have also changed in response to the UAIR merger. IR has made explicit efforts to hire analysts with more sophisticated statistical knowledge, and any experience with Oracle PeopleSoft or other EPM(s) or OBIEE is highly valued. We look now for crossover skills, employees who can work across the divide with empathy for each of the different approaches. The BI team continues to hire both subject matter experts, such as folks from academic affairs units, training them to do the technical work, as well as hiring technical experts who then must learn higher education data. Both teams are interested in additional capacity for higher order analytics, modeling, forecasting, simulations/scenario testing, predictive analytics, and action analytics. And, while some movement in that direction has been possible through hiring, the demands for complex analytics are urgent and not something UAIR can immediately develop from start-to-finish or in a scalable manner. Thus, the subject of vendors enters.

Outsourcing Analytics

The environment described so far at UA is one with a strong administrative appetite for data, increasing scrutiny and regulatory pressures, urgency to inform policy and strategic decision-making, urgency to support student success, increasing competition for enrollments and research funds, democratized access to data through the data warehouse and BI reports, and high variability across campus in data expertise.

External pressures such as state performance metrics, stretch goals, external rankings, fierce competition for student enrollments and research dollars, and deep budget cuts cause urgency in looking for data solutions that will more thoroughly inform decision-making or even prescribe courses of action to become more efficient and effective. The title of this book is *The Analytics Revolution in Higher Education,* and the term *analytics* requires some unpacking as there are many different forms and the distinctions are not always well understood.

Figure 6.4 (Gartner, 2012) illustrates a continuum of analytics, ranging from descriptive analytics that show what has already transpired, to diagnostic analytics that explain why or how it happened, to predictive analytics that show what is likely to happen in the future, to prescriptive or action analytics that compel an informed course of action. Most IR offices, even those like UA's that have merged with BI or who maintain closely collaborative relationships to IT, cannot provide this full continuum of analytics services to campus. Even one sufficiently complex analytics project, as you move through the continuum, can be all-consuming and challenging to deliver in a scalable and sustainable fashion. In response to the demand for more analytics, a significant influx of vendors has arrived on the higher education scene, many promising campus administrators silver-bullet solutions to persistent challenges like student success and growing/maintaining the research enterprise.

Even in the space of predictive analytics, the field can be daunting to understand. Take the sphere of student success analytics, for example. Many

Figure 6.4. Analytics value estimator.

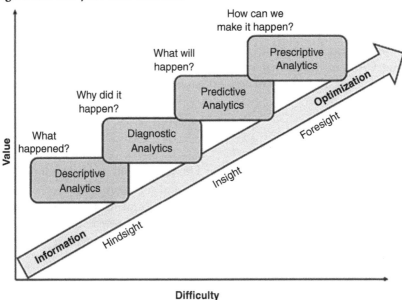

Source: Gartner Pictures (2012), www.flickr.com/photos/27772229@N07/8267855748

so-called predictive analytics offerings are just descriptive reconfigurations of existing student data into friendly user interfaces with visualizations that are filterable by unit or student type to make data more actionable. Some predictive analytics offerings are fixed algorithms based on what is already known about student success from the research literature. In these cases, the 100 or so "usual suspects" of variables are requested and measures of student risk are churned out with very little customization or accommodation of institutional differences. True data science companies, in contrast, compile disparate sources of data, segment data prior to analysis to account for limitations such as data availability and variability by student type, and generate multiple, dynamic, institution-specific models per institution.

Solutions also vary in the extent to which they are *source agnostic*, meaning whether they can work with unique institutional data sets and systems, if they require standardized data elements for their modeling, or if they aim to build entire ecosystems for appointment scheduling and tracking to create data rather than importing it from existing systems. There is also variation among vendor capability for working with data sources that have significant missing data due to variable system usage (e.g., learning management system data).

Wrapped around these different analytic approaches are various degrees of action analytics platforms or integrated user interfaces that bring data to particular audiences, such as administrators, academic advisers, faculty, and students. Feature sets can include appointment scheduling, case management capabilities (note sharing and referrals), campaign and messaging deployment, and even full customer relationship management (CRM) functionality. With all the variation in analytical sophistication and rigor, source dependencies, and user interfaces, the third-party vendor landscape is a challenging one to navigate, even for those who are systems and data savvy.

Managing Vendor Madness

The vendor space for analytics in higher education is still young relative to other industries, with many leading-edge companies being startups only a few years old themselves. It is extremely competitive and growing quickly. The array of offerings from vendors can be overwhelming to administrators who face a continual barrage of solicitations, and it can be difficult to manage or coordinate a process of vetting when looking for a particular solution. RFP processes offer structure to these selection processes but are still time and resource intensive, and procurement practices need to be informed by those who understand the vulnerabilities of the institution when giving outside entities access to and responsibility for their data.

IR shops (and analytics organizations like BI) should play a role in vetting and procurement processes for analytics solutions. IR professionals are aware of the complexities in the data, and most have studied institutional data trends for decades and may be well positioned to assess the extent to which analytics from a third party represent value added or an extension of current in-house capabilities. BI and other IT professionals should also play a role in vetting, since they may be responsible for data transfers, involved in technical issue resolution and systems integrations, and are able to recognize data anomalies. This is not a one-time engagement; it's ongoing, particularly when working with vendors that are continually growing and enhancing their solutions.

At UA, UAIR has voluntarily offered leadership in vetting analytics solutions, understanding the field of offerings, and creating guidelines for procurement processes that protect the institution's interests with respect to data issues. Even for data experts with significant implementation and project management experience, it can be challenging and time-consuming to collect information about these solutions, discern true functionality from smoke and mirrors, assess the quality of the data science, understand what is in production versus what is planned or still under development, estimate startup time and level of difficulty in file transfer or systems integrations, identify required in-house investment and support requirements, and gather feedback from current and past clients about their experiences with the vendor.

UAIR currently works with multiple external vendors for analytics products. There is one to support student success outcomes with predictive and prescriptive analytics that can be deployed to a range of users. A more recent partnership delivers analysis to optimize yield and financial aid packages for enrollment management. Moving outside of student data, the research enterprise is supported by a vendor that provides visual displays of nationally benchmarked faculty scholarly productivity data. Still, with these and other vendor relationships in place, investments committed, resources deployed, and progress being made, "vendor madness" continues. There have been cases where contracts were signed for duplicative services when units felt acute pressure for results and were either unaware or did not think they could wait for current solutions to deliver. In a large, decentralized university setting, there are so many offices looking for their own solutions that it is nearly impossible to keep track or manage centrally.

Change Management: When Did This Become Our Job?

Whether advancement in analytics is something an institution chooses to undertake internally, through partnership with third parties, or both, how does an institution ensure that those analytics are effectively deployed and used in decision-making? How do we assess whether the use of analytics is ultimately leading to better outcomes? Does IR (or IR and BI) simply provide the info and let others run with it? Or does IR (or IR and BI) become a much more activist organization, leading the way?

Take a story from a podcast I recently enjoyed (Gunja, 2016): When electricity was becoming popularized, many factories began replacing their steam engines with electricity. However, it took 20 to 25 years for there to be accompanying increases in productivity. This phenomenon, referred to by economists as the *productivity paradox*, arose from the fact that the factories simply laid electronic wire along the old steam pipe configurations. It took decades before factories began taking advantage of the new configurations of machinery, such as assembly lines, made possible by flexible electronic wiring.

Today, higher education institutions need to adapt and move our "machinery" into more productive configurations. At UA, we have moved more aggressively in the analytics space by merging IR and BI and by partnering with third-party vendors. Both types of efforts landed us squarely in the business of change management. Merging organizations, dealing with historical tensions and differences, and developing new joint approaches to the work has been formidable work in change management, focused largely on overcoming issues of culture and distrust. The strategy of merging the two units was clear but, as the quote attributed to Peter Drucker goes, "Culture eats strategy for breakfast." Without purposeful change management efforts, a merger like this won't be successful.

Change management has also been critical to the deployment of large-scale analytics projects where partnerships with third-party vendors are involved. People have to learn to work differently with analytics technology and the information it provides. Even with user interfaces that present data in easy-to-understand, visual formats, there is no guarantee that users will adopt the technology or know how to use it. Dashboards and user interfaces help to organize data so the results are more easily understood, but the data still do not speak for themselves and a process of interpretation is still required. For instance, at UA our work with student success analytics is generating new insights on student risk at a much more granular level than ever before. We are beginning to identify previously undetectable sources of risk to student course completion, persistence, and graduation. We also now have real-time data that allow us to observe how risk factors shift and evolve throughout the student life cycle, rather than being dependent on static assessments of students' academic preparedness at the time of admissions. The same can be said for our vendor-provided platform for faculty scholarly productivity data, which are generating new insights about risks for faculty attrition and opportunities for increasing research collaboration, funding opportunities, and awards. How do we move from insights to action? How do we empower large numbers of diverse campus stakeholders with this new data in a way that is scalable? Neither set of tools would be adopted in any successful way at UA without leadership and purposeful change management.

As a discipline, IR has a great deal to offer as leaders in this change management processes. Terenzini's (1993) writings on IR intelligence specify three forms of personal competence and institutional understanding: technical and analytical intelligence, issues intelligence, and contextual intelligence. To the extent that IR professionals embrace and embody these forms of intelligence, they are also well positioned to guide others at the institution as analytics expand and challenge the status quo.

AIR's *Aspirational Statement* (Swing & Ross, 2016) advocates for IR offices to adapt to our new environment by moving toward a distributed IR function that serves a larger campus audience with a focus on the student perspective, but the change management that this major shift will require needs to be more explicitly addressed. Figure 6.5 shows how change management processes can go wrong if key elements are missing. Giving users a new set of tools requires not only sensitivity to existing workflow and culture

Figure 6.5. Managing complex change.

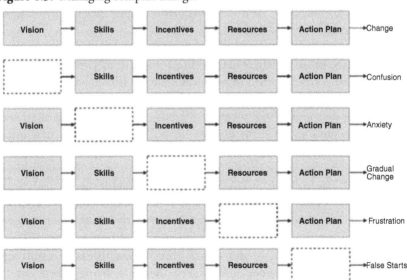

Source: Conejo, 2011. How to support change management. www.theacagroup.com/how-to-support-change-management

but also a clearly articulated vision, skill-building, incentivizing, resources, and an action plan. Campus stakeholders need to understand the vision for how they will advance our mission. Analytics will require investments in new skills so that amateur analysts and experts alike can participate. Analytics may be viewed as creating additional work or, worse, supplanting the expertise of individuals, so it is important to articulate why working with analytics in a new way is actually an added value for the individual. And without the critical investment in resources such as support personnel, technology and infrastructure, common applications, and consistent data, the attempt to deploy analytics will be met with frustration. Finally, action plans are where the rubber hits the road, and there is tremendous opportunity for IR professionals to offer guidance in the process of interpretation, fleshing out implications, prioritization, and action-planning. In the UA case, we found it much easier to implement our major vendor analytics solutions first within UAIR, where our team of data experts could wrestle with data validation and technical challenges, sense-making, and think through use cases. With that experience under our belts, we are much better prepared to then help inform the process of broader implementation and assist campus stakeholders in the adoption of the new tools.

Conclusion

Returning to the visionary work of Davenport and Harris (2007), it's clear that the IR experience in this changing higher education landscape and the recommendations of AIR for a distributed IR function are following a familiar script. Companies will provide greater structure and human capability for strategically important analysis with a variety of tools and approaches: software that guides the analysis process, substantial education to develop more analysts, and a group of "coaches" to help guide more amateur analysts in their work (p. 181). Along with this, many organizations will begin to more formally manage their decision-making processes, expecting managers to have analytical skills, review decisions made in regard to the process used, and evaluate not only on the outcome but also on the processes, information, and analyses used to make them.

Davenport and Harris (2007) also predicted that companies using analytics to succeed will not only eventually move beyond the provision of analytics to drive internal decision-making but also provide analytics to their customers and supply chains as well. Efforts to empower our students with analytics are already underway at many institutions and, as statewide longitudinal data systems continue to evolve, supply-chain data will become a reality as well.

The vision for moving forward with analytics to improve student success and institutional effectiveness in higher education is full of potential and momentum. In order to fully realize that vision, institutions must address this as a change management process first and foremost, with significant investment in enterprise-wide analytics architecture; common tools and consistent data; and attention to the culture, workflow, and needs of a diverse array of individuals who must construct meaning and action from the information provided.

The challenge for institutional researchers is to decide what role they are going to play as data analyses and other IR functions are inevitably distributed. How can we best develop skills and understanding that allow crossover and collaboration with the teams that are also needed in this work, such as BI and IT? How do we support and develop staff members who may feel threatened? In what ways do we need to rearrange our operational machinery? What new skill sets are required? What can we learn from corporate implementations of advanced analytics systems, and how must we adapt those lessons to appropriately serve the mission of higher education? How do we recognize when we should build out complex analytics solutions ourselves, versus partnering with a third party? How can we most effectively help build data literacy and analytic capacity across campus? What do we need to learn in order to effectively serve an expanded audience of faculty, staff, and students?

Despite uncertainty and challenges, the vision for what can be accomplished through advanced analytics remains (in this author's mind) solid justification for sticking it out. At UA, we will continue working to understand and reconcile the IR and BI approaches to data, one subject area at a time, project by project, and relationship by relationship. We must work together to provide campus users with a "consistent version of the truth" rather than competing. Together, IR and BI can automate more of the mundane and routine data processes, freeing up talented analysts on both sides for compelling advanced analytics work and deeper, more fruitful consultation with our campus clients. We will continue to explore how partnerships with third-party vendors can accelerate our progress in deploying sophisticated analytics at scale in a way that empowers daily and strategic decisions. And, if we remain intentional about change management, perhaps we can make the experience more of an evolution than a revolution.

References

Conejo, C. (2011, January 1). How to support change management. Retrieved from http://www.theacagroup.com/how-to-support-change-management/

Davenport, T. H., & Harris, J. G. (2007). *Competing on analytics: The new science of winning*. Boston, MA: Harvard Business School Press.

Gartner Pictures. (2012). *Gartner analytics ascendency model*. Retrieved from https://www.flickr.com/photos/27772229@N07/8267855748

Gunja, A. (Producer). (2016, April 20). How to be more productive [Audio podcast]. *Freakonomics Radio*. Retrieved from http://freakonomics.com/podcast/how-to-be-more-productive/

Hart, A. W. (2015). *Philanthropic partnership and the future of public universities*. Retrieved from http://president.arizona.edu/communications/blog/philanthropic-partnership-and-future-public-universities

Swing, R. L., & Ross, L. (2016). *Statement of aspirational practice for institutional research*. Tallahassee, FL: Association for Institutional Research.

Terenzini, P. T. (1993). On the nature of institutional research and the knowledge and skills it requires. *Research in Higher Education, 34*(1), 1–10.

7

ENROLLMENT TO CAREER

Dynamics of Education and the Workforce

Stephanie A. Bond-Huie

Offices of institutional research (IR), if thoughtfully staffed and strate-gically placed within the institutional hierarchy, are uniquely poised to facilitate data-informed discussions on pathways to promote student success. While the idea of achieving success has not changed much over the years, the way for students to achieve success has.

Faced with a mercurial global economy, as well as increasing tuition and costs related to a postsecondary education, students today are finding that the decisions they make pertaining to their academic career require as much thought and consideration as their postcollegiate professions and other life goals.

As students are faced with more difficult decisions, institutions of higher education need to evolve with them, providing better, more up-to-date resources to improve their experiences and outcomes. This chapter explores the value of IR offices, and how important it is that they are structured in such a way that allows them to evolve with the needs of the student.

UT System's Commitment to Accountability and Transparency

During a time when there were increasing calls at the national level for higher education accountability, and public universities in Texas were asking for more autonomy from the state legislature, leaders at the University of Texas System (UT System) took steps to foster a culture of transparency and accountability. In 2002, the UT System created the accountability and per-formance conceptual framework, which had at its core a call for the central-ized collection, analysis, and reporting of data on the performance of the UT System institutions (University of Texas System Office of the Chancellor, 2002). This was the birth of the IR function at UT System and the seed of what would eventually become the office of strategic initiatives (OSI).

This model of transparency, accountability, and evidence-based decision-making was further solidified in 2011 in the strategic visioning document *Framework for Advancing Excellence*, which called for comprehensive analytics to keep leadership informed and to facilitate effective and substantive decisions (University of Texas System Office of the Chancellor, 2011). As part of the framework, the Board of Regents invested in infrastructure to support the creation of a data warehouse and in resources in support of data collection, research, and analysis. In 2014, the regents formalized their data-oriented approach through adoption of a rule that "recognizes and supports the importance of data collection, retention, and analysis for purposes such as reviewing System operations and policies, guiding decision-making, improving productivity and efficiency, and evaluating performance outcomes" (University of Texas System Board of Regents, 2015).

CRITICAL ELEMENTS: Formalize a data-oriented approach through inclusion in policies and planning; reflect that priority with investment in resources such as a data warehouse infrastructure.

Developing a Data Culture

With the regents' investment to develop a data warehouse, as well as support from the leadership, the infrastructure was in place to develop a culture based on data-informed decisions. A data culture is best developed with two foundational elements: data use and data delivery.

In terms of data use, the evolutionary process toward data-informed decision-making starts with reporting, which typically answers the *what?* question. The next phase of data use is analyzing—transforming data into information to answer the *why?* question. The most advanced phase of data use seeks to address the *what now?* question by transforming data and information into knowledge for planning, predicting, and improving. A data-evolved organization is characterized by a primacy for data within the organization, thus solidifying the role of IR as a key player in decision-making.

Data delivery, the other foundational element, is critical to driving data use. Data and information must be easy to access, relevant to the audience, and timely. Good delivery will foster more use—increasing the demand for data and spurring the need for faster, more sophisticated delivery. To improve its information delivery to internal and external stakeholders, OSI developed the UT System Dashboard. The dashboard is actually a business intelligence system that includes publicly accessible web-based applications for extracting and analyzing institutional data. It provides current data, trends over time, and comparative benchmarking across a variety of metrics in support of better decision- and policy-making (University of Texas System, 2016). The dashboard's goals are to increase transparency; measure more effectively UT System's productivity, efficiency, and impact; and demonstrate more clearly UT System's accountability to its primary stakeholders, including legislators, policy and decision makers at all levels, academic and administrative leaders, as well as students and their families.

Two major components of the dashboard are visualizations, which are varied and compelling, and interactive tables, charts, and graphs, which provide users with customizable and downloadable data. This customization gives users the power to ask and answer many questions on their own, while quality data visualizations are one way to deliver accessible, relevant, and timely information. The increased access, understandability, and relevance all result in increasing demand for IR services.

Even as the dashboard was being created and UT System leaders were forming a culture of data-informed decision-making, concern was growing at all levels about the rising costs of college and the burdensome levels of student debt. UT System recognized the need to build and expand on that foundation of accountability and transparency to address these critical issues.

CRITICAL ELEMENTS: Move beyond answering the what? *to focus on the* why? *and* what now? *questions. Provide interactive and timely data through compelling visualizations.*

A National Problem: Increasing Costs and Rising Student Debt

College is expensive, and the cost to attend is increasing. Compared to 2010, the average published tuition and fees in 2015 increased in inflation-adjusted dollars by 13% at public four-year institutions and by 11% at private nonprofit four-year institutions (College Board, 2015). The average published price for in-state tuition and fees and for room and board in 2015 was $19,550 for public institutions and $43,920 for private nonprofit institutions (College Board, 2015). According to the CIRP Freshman Survey, almost half of the students indicated that the cost of attendance (45%) or an offer of financial assistance (47%) were very important reasons for why they chose the institution in which they were enrolled (Eagan et al., 2015).

As the cost of higher education increases, so, too, does student debt. Between 2010 and 2014, student debt increased 56% to an average of $28,950 for students completing a bachelor's degree (Cochrane & Reed, 2014, p. 2). In addition to the personal impact of debt on an individual student, the impact of student debt on the economy has become a real concern. Recent research indicates that students with student loan debt tend to delay major purchases such as cars and homes (Gallup-Purdue Index, 2015).

Despite rising tuition and debt, more than two-thirds of Americans who recently completed high school or the equivalency attended either a two-year (24.6%) or four-year (43.7%) college (National Center for Education Statistics, 2015). Add to this the fact that the percentage of adults earning a bachelor's degree has risen from 5% in 1940 to 33% in 2015 (Ryan & Bauman, 2016).

Students are attending college and are finding it to be a valuable investment. In fact, more than three-quarters of recent alumni agree (27%) or strongly agree (50%) that their education was worth the cost (Gallup-Purdue Index, 2015). If higher education is an investment, what exactly are students expecting in return? Results from the 2015 CIRP Freshman Survey showed that, while students remained interested in pursuing knowledge and personal interests, students also indicated that the ability to get a good job (85%), receive training for a specific career (76%), and increase earning power (70%) were very important reasons for going to college. Given the evolving dynamics of the global economy, it is not surprising that students are increasingly motivated by employment-focused outcomes.

Increasingly, jobs are requiring different and more complex skill sets to develop, operate, and interact with technology (Metz, 2015). Jobs that in the past have only required a high school diploma are now more likely to require a bachelor's degree (Carnevale, Smith, & Strohl, 2013). Additionally, unemployment statistics provide further evidence of the growing importance of a college degree. In 2015, the unemployment rate for recent high school graduates was 17.9% compared to the unemployment rate for recent college graduates of 5.6% (Kroeger, Cooke, & Gould, 2016).

Research by the U.S. Census Bureau shows that "the impact of degrees, beginning with the bachelor's degree level, are substantial with most of them far larger than any of the other social, demographic, and geographic components" (Julian & Kominski, 2011, p. 13). Over a lifetime (40 years, from age 25–64), U.S. Census Bureau projections find bachelor's degree recipients are expected to earn about $1 million more than those with only a high school degree (Julian, 2012).

Yes, college is a good investment, but institutions need to be mindful of operational efficiency to help control costs while still maintaining academic excellence. However, controlling costs is not enough. Higher education institutions have a responsibility to offer programs, services, and tools to help students make informed choices about cost, debt, and postgraduation income relative to student loan repayment.

A Local Solution: The UT System Takes Action

In 2012, amid the growing concern about the increasing costs of a degree and the burden of student loans, the UT System Board of Regents convened the Student Debt Reduction Task Force to address these critical issues (University of Texas System, 2012). Completion, transparency and decision support, costs and returns—these are all factors that the task force considered during its 2012 deliberations.

A Seat at the Table

The task force included among its membership the vice chancellor for strategic initiatives as the leader of the UT System IR function. Having a seat at the table for this important discussion gave the vice chancellor the opportunity to participate in conversations around the data, provide key points of context, and be included in subsequent policy recommendations. The task force ultimately provided a call to action to control costs, reduce student debt, improve postcollegiate outcomes, and provide better information to help students and families make informed decisions about higher education. The IR function was critical to achieving these objectives, and OSI began to pursue avenues to implement change.

The findings of the task force, combined with the other significant actions taken by UT System leadership in support of accountability and transparency, empowered OSI to collect and analyze data to explore higher education pathways and postcollegiate outcomes and to contribute to executive-level conversations about potential solutions.

> *CRITICAL ELEMENTS: Recognize the importance of direct access and engagement with decision makers. Respond to a call to action that is supported at the highest levels.*

Data Sharing and Collaboration

While the IR office was able to answer many of the questions the task force had, several major questions of the Student Debt Reduction Task Force—and of UT System leadership—remained unanswered: What was happening to students after graduation? Were graduates getting jobs? Were they seeing a return on investment? To answer these questions, OSI engaged the Texas Workforce Commission (TWC) in conversations around matching UT System student educational records with Texas wage records from TWC's unemployment insurance (UI) database. The result was an agreement with TWC to match wage records for graduating cohorts starting in 2001–2002 that continues until either party decides to cancel. This helped answer the question of postgraduation employment, but there were other pieces to the puzzle that remained unfilled. Using the financial aid data set, OSI was able to provide the debt of borrowers at graduation. Additionally, OSI contracted with the National Student Clearinghouse (NSC) to receive data at the system level on students from all UT System institutions. OSI used the NSC data to help account for students who are not found in the wage record due to enrollment in additional education.

> *CRITICAL ELEMENTS: Collaborate beyond institutional boundaries. Create a compelling and dynamic database that has capabilities to examine multiple dimensions of the issue. Recognize the limitations of available data, but don't allow these limitations to become a deterrent.*

The Art of Creating New Tools and Engaging New Audiences

Establishing a partnership with the TWC and other organizations to match student educational records was only a first step of many to follow. The data had to be cleaned and stored in the data warehouse; this process often involved data sleuthing to properly assign information for duplicate social security numbers or other critical missing data fields. Finally, however—with the data collected, cleaned, and stored—it was time to address how the data would be analyzed, displayed, and generally deployed to further the transparency and decision support goals of the task force.

One of the main recommendations of the task force was to provide information for students and parents to make informed decisions about educational pathways, including an understanding of the potential debt and postgraduation income associated with those pathways. In support of this recommendation, OSI staff set out to develop a web-based interactive decision support tool that was geared toward students and their families. However, OSI staff had never created a tool directed toward this particular audience—this was new territory.

The first steps were determining which of the elements in the data set to display, deciding how to display them in a straightforward and nontechnical manner, and designing the user experience, which would be appealing to a young audience used to the pace, ease, and attraction of today's technology. Added to that was one additional requirement: OSI had no application development resources, so it would need to work within the limitations of the tools it already had in place.

With these requirements in mind, OSI staff developed a draft tool that was shown to leadership at the system and campus levels for discussion and feedback. Perhaps the most important feedback came from OSI's collaborative partnership with the UT System student advisory council (SAC), a group of student leaders from each UT System campus that meets quarterly to discuss important cross-cutting issues.

As part of the user testing, OSI staff presented the tool to the SAC with only an overview of the high-level goals of the tool and with no instructions for use. The students were given a questionnaire on how they interacted with the seekUT tool. Then they were asked to answer a series of questions about the ease of use, ease of understanding, appearance, and overall impressions of the tool. The results more often than not challenged the assumptions of the OSI staff, and this iterative process with the students ultimately led to a number of important changes, particularly in the visual presentation and display of the data. Ultimately, the SAC became a critical partner in the implementation and communication about this consumer-oriented tool named seekUT.

> *CRITICAL ELEMENTS: Presentation, display, and usability of the data are just as important, if not more so, than the back-end processes that IR shops typically focus on. Develop vehicles to display data with the end-user in mind. User testing and feedback are critical to successful data tool development. Foster relationships to create support for the work with champions throughout the organization.*

seekUT—A Tool for Students and Parents

seekUT is an online tool that is available on tablets and smartphones and provides median earnings of UT graduates working in Texas by degree levels in 400 areas of study 1, 5, and 10 years after graduation, alongside average student loan debt. It also looks at the debt-to-income ratio—the estimated monthly loan payment as a percentage of gross monthly income. seekUT includes program descriptions, average time to degree, and the percentage of graduates who have continued their education beyond the baccalaureate. It shows the industries where graduates are working by area of study and the anticipated job growth in Texas by occupation through 2022.

Because success comes in many forms, the seekUT website includes profiles of alumni who are saving lives, creating art, educating young people, and inventing the next big thing. The tool also puts data behind the idea that liberal arts degrees do produce living wages, and in many cases these wages exceed popular notions. The purpose is to provide students and their families important information they need to make potentially life-changing educational and financial decisions. A related goal is to help students understand the context and potential outcomes of their decisions regarding loan debt, to encourage timely graduation, to provide realistic expectations about the costs and benefits of a higher education, and to demonstrate that an individual's investment in higher education is worthwhile.

> *CRITICAL ELEMENTS: Deliver interactive data tools with multiple access points (computers, tablets, smartphones), provide information in context—not only salary data but also data on majors and other outcomes such as professions that contribute to the community; provide information to support informed decisions, not to direct actions.*

Beyond the Tool: Using the Data for Advanced Research and Analysis

After building the foundation of the data warehouse and the seekUT tool for students and parents to access the data, OSI had the time, the necessary skill sets, and the demand from the UT System administration and constituencies—as a result of building a data culture—to dig deeper into the data to conduct predictive analyses with the aim of understanding underlying patterns of student outcomes that would ultimately inform policies to support the students. UT System analysts are currently researching the impact on student success of working on campus while enrolled. Recent work in this area finds that undergraduates working on campus while enrolled more than doubled their likelihood of persisting from their first to second year when compared to those working off campus. This could have major implications for institutional and state policy in regard to aid-related work-study programs and student employment on campus in general.

Other analyses using the same data demonstrate the value of earning a degree. Findings indicate that students who enroll and complete their bachelor's degree program earn approximately $71,000 more in the first five years of working in Texas after completion than those who enroll and do not complete their degree. As these research findings demonstrate, workforce data dramatically increases the ability to show returns on a student's educational investment.

A Team of Teams to Get Things Done

As evidenced, revamping and reinventing a traditional IR office can create a resource better prepared to support a data-evolved organization, but it takes a lot more than just data and tools to make the switch. In order for the OSI to become a next-generation IR office, it leveraged existing talent across the organization to increase capacity, adding to and moving beyond the traditional IR data collection and reporting model. These new skill sets included advanced research and statistical analysis and modeling, information technology and application development, communications, strategic relationship skills, and data presentation and visualization.

As part of his vision statement in November 2015, Chancellor William H. McRaven proposed to transform the organization and operations of the UT System with the *team of teams* approach. He defined this approach as

> a formal and informal network of subject matter experts bound together by a common mission, using technology to partner in ways that seemed inconceivable just years before, brought together through operational incentives, bottom-up desire and top-down support to solve the most complex problems. (University of Texas System Office of the Chancellor, 2015, p. 23)

The team of teams concept calls for the establishment of integrated planning teams made up of people from across the organization.

Optimizing the IR Office

OSI had already been operating using a team of teams approach. OSI has five small functional teams: IR and analysis, business intelligence and data warehousing, information technology, communications, and administration. The key to the success of the office is that the members of these teams work together seamlessly, integrating members from across the functional areas based on project needs. In addition, there are strong working relationships with staff from other offices across the system, including those offices that OSI serves (by providing data and information) and those—there is crossover—that OSI partners with on projects.

Of these functional areas, probably communications and information technology are least frequently found in IR offices. However, since those two areas go hand in hand with better data delivery and are more effective together, having communications experts and information technology professionals in IR offices is critical to telling a complete and compelling story. Although the ideal model is to house this expertise within the IR office, budget constraints may not support hiring these individuals, so strong partnerships and regular meetings with these professionals in other parts of the organization are recommended.

> *CRITICAL ELEMENTS: Organizational structure needs to support the skill sets necessary to implement a data-informed decision model—communications, information technology, and research and analysis.*

Leveraging Your Entire Organization

Not all education organizations are financially positioned to invest in the infrastructure to create a data warehouse, to acquire visualization software, or to hire staff within the IR office to focus on communications, information technology, data visualization, and research and analysis. However, these skill sets and tools can be harnessed from the larger organization by taking a team of teams approach. While UT System OSI has been in a process of transformation—including staff skill sets and the role of the office—since 2010, this concept of a team of teams will take the office to the next level and allow us to serve the organization more and more effectively.

An IR office can apply this concept to establish collaborative relationships to support functions such as communications and technology support for data storage, processing, and display. Critical to the success of these types of cross-cutting collaborations are a few principles: foster a sense of ownership by bringing collaborators in on the process early and consistently seeking their suggestions and input, work together toward a shared goal or vision for the project or perhaps the larger organization, and remain open to new ideas and ways of approaching a project.

> *CRITICAL ELEMENTS: Leverage skill sets across the organization through the creation of collaborative cross-disciplinary teams.*

The Big Picture

Whether for reasons of accountability, transparency, decision-making, policy-setting, student support, or other, IR is recognized for its value in "telling the data story" and is being used more than ever before.

This chapter has explored the critical elements in the UT System example that led to the transformation of its traditional system-wide IR office to a next-generation IR office with resulting competencies, services, and products. But these processes are not unique to the UT System; any organization can optimize its IR function and capabilities to create a strong data culture.

For an institution to effectively expand data capacity and sophistication, there are some critical components that can play a major role—with or without major investment—in the successful transformation of a traditional IR office to a next-generation IR office.

Critical Components for Organizational Change

Adopting internal policy of a data-oriented approach through the strategic visioning process

- Creating a data culture by moving beyond answering the *what* question as in reporting, but looking forward to the *why* and *what now* questions
- Providing direct access to and engagement with decision makers
- Collaborating beyond institutional boundaries

- Fostering relationships to create support for the work with champions throughout the organization
- Ensuring that organizational structure supports the skill sets necessary to implement a data-informed decision model—communications, information technology, and research and analysis
- Leveraging skill sets across the organization (including student workers) through the creation of collaborative cross-disciplinary teams

Critical Components for Data Processes, Communications, and Display

Creating a compelling and dynamic database that has both the data and the power to allows analysts to examine multiple dimensions of the issue. Critical components of the database include the following:

- Recognizing the limitations of available data but not allowing these limitations to become a deterrent
- Developing vehicles to display data with the end-user in mind; user testing and feedback is critical to successful data tool development
- Delivering interactive data tools with multiple access points (computers, tablets, smartphones)
- Providing information in context—not only salary data but also data on majors and student debt
- Providing information to support informed decisions, not to direct actions

In Closing

It is important to note that as organizations expand in the IR area, many will face budget constraints, staffing challenges, and other hurdles in improving data literacy and increasing buy-in to a data culture. To overcome these challenges, it is important for organizations to employ creative strategies capable of effecting change, keeping in mind that expansion does not happen in a vacuum. Successful change requires a number of components—from the organization as a whole to the actual products offered—working in partnership with one another to achieve the desired outcome.

References

Carnevale, A. P., Smith, N., & Strohl, J. (2013). *Recovery 2020: Job growth and education requirements through 2020.* Center for Education and the Workforce, Georgetown University. Retrieved from http://cew.georgetown.edu/recovery2020

Cochrane, D., & Reed, M. (2014, October). *Student debt and the class of 2014.* The Project on Student Debt, The Institute for College Access and Success. Retrieved from http://ticas.org/posd/home

College Board. (2015). *Table 2A: Average tuition and fees and room and board in 2015 dollars, 1975–76 to 2015–16, selected years.* Trends in Higher Education. Retrieved from http://trends.collegeboard.org/college-pricing/figures-tables/tuition-and-fees-and-room-and-board-over-time-1975-76-2015-16-selected-years

Eagan, K., Stolzenberg, E., Bates, A. K., Aragon, M., Suchard, M., & Rios-Aguilar, C. (2015). *The American freshman: National norms fall 2015.* Higher Education Research Institute, UCLA. Retrieved from http://www.heri.ucla.edu

Gallup-Purdue Index. (2015). *Great jobs, great lives.* Washington DC: Gallup, Inc.

Julian, T. (2012). *Work-life earnings by field of degree and occupation for people with a bachelor's degree: 2011.* Department of Commerce, American Community Survey Briefs. Washington DC: U.S. Census Bureau.

Julian, T., & Kominski, R. (2011). *Education and synthetic work-life earnings estimates.* U.S. Department of Commerce, American Community Survey Reports. Washington DC: U.S. Census Bureau.

Kroeger, T., Cooke, T., & Gould, E. (2016). *The class of 2016: The labor market is still far from ideal for young graduates.* Washington DC: Economic Policy Institute.

Metz, C. (2015, August 24). Robots will steal our jobs, but they'll give us new ones. *Wired.* Retrieved from http://www.wired.com/2015/08/robots-will-steal-jobs-theyll-give-us-new-ones/

National Center for Education Statistics. (2015). *Table 302.10. Recent high school completers and their enrollment in 2-year and 4-year colleges, by sex: 1960 through 2014.* Digest of Education Statistics. Retrieved from http://nces.ed.gov/programs/digest/d15/tables/dt15_302.10.asp

Ryan, C. L., & Bauman, K. (2016). *Educational attainment in the United States: 2015.* Washington DC: U.S. Census Bureau, U.S. Department of Commerce.

seekUT: search + earnings + employment = knowledge. (2016, August 10). Retrieved from seekUT: http://www.utsystem.edu/seekut/

University of Texas System. (2012, December 5). *College credit: Reducing unmanageable student debt and maximizing return on education.* Student Debt Reduction Task Force. Retrieved from http://www.utsystem.edu/documents/docs/publication/college-credit-reducing-unmanageable-student-debt-and-maximizing-return-e

University of Texas System. (2016, August 10). *UT System dashboard.* Retrieved from http://data.utsystem.edu/

University of Texas System Board of Regents. (2015, September 28). *Rule 10801: Policy on transparency, accountability, and access to information.* Regents' Rules and Regulations. Retrieved from http://www.utsystem.edu/board-of-regents/rules/10801-policy-transparency-accountability-and-access-information

University of Texas System Office of the Chancellor. (2002, November 27). *University of Texas System accountability and performance conceptual framework.*

Board of Regents Meetings. Retrieved from http://www.utsystem.edu/sites/utsfiles/offices/board-of-regents/board-meetings/agenda-book-items/12-13accountabilityframework.pdf

University of Texas System Office of the Chancellor. (2011, August 25). *Framework for advancing excellence: Action plan.* A Framework for Advancing Excellence. Retrieved from http://www.utsystem.edu/chancellor/framework

University of Texas System Office of the Chancellor. (2015, November 5). *Leading in a complex world: Chancellor McRaven's vision and quantum leaps for the UT System 2015–2020* [prepared remarks]. Retrieved from http://www.utsystem.edu/offices/chancellor/chancellors-vision-university-texas-system

8

STATE SYSTEM RESEARCH

Increasing Products, Data, Roles, and Stakeholders

Angela Bell

Much of the discussion around higher education data analytics and its impact on institutional research has focused on the campus level, but this chapter focuses on changes in functions of state system research offices. The trend in institutional analytics is shaped by increasing calls for performance and the completion agenda and is facilitated by vast amounts of information generated by learning management systems, student portals for administrative functions, and digital mechanisms to facilitate payments, access to buildings and events, and so on. System offices have the same performance and completion pressures, and though they rarely have access to institutional real-time student interaction data, many systems have long had access to a different type of "big data" and leveraged it in ways to add value in reporting and research.

In this chapter I explore recent trends in system research office products with an eye to the stakeholders these products serve and the unique data available. System offices are positioned at the intersection of the public, campuses, and state government and are thus called to serve a broad range of stakeholders. These demands for traditional reporting, accountability products, policy analysis, and information for administrative decision-making are more than sufficient to keep a system research office busy. But the completion agenda and the imperative to utilize data and analytics effectively to achieve it add additional opportunities and challenges. I will discuss system office roles and initiatives in this environment and how we are undertaking an analytics initiative to meet stakeholder needs.

Changing Products and Publications at State System Research Offices

State system research offices, like campus research offices, have traditionally produced retrospective descriptive reporting products and conducted research and analyses. It is an expectation that these offices synthesize normalized system-wide data into useful information about the institutions under their purview as well as conduct research on educational issues from a state policy or practice perspective. Over time these products have evolved in keeping with higher education trends and changes in technology and data availability.

A historical role of the system research office has been to compile a sort of system-level fact book that reports information such as enrollment, tuition and fees, retention and graduation rates, faculty salaries, and so on, for all institutions. These publications primarily were aimed at high-level stakeholders such as the members of system boards/commissions and state legislative and executive branches. These documents provide a cogent summary of the state of the system and its institutions and as such are a tangible expression of the value of a system-level office. Another audience is education professionals both inside and outside of the state seeking to compare performance between institutions and systems. These publications also serve the general public, but less so, as there was no public distribution method for paper copies prior to the Internet age and, even with the Internet, the general public is less likely to know the state higher education governance structure to access this information. Stakeholders were fairly limited.

These documents have shifted over time, with an increasing focus on accountability, from merely providing information about the higher education system (e.g., the University System of Georgia's *Information Digest* produced up to 2007) to providing progress of the system in meeting strategic plan goals or other key performance indicators. Examples here would be more recent versions of West Virginia's *Higher Education Report Card* or the *Texas Public Higher Education Almanac*, where information is organized around, and provides outcomes on, the system's strategic plan. In some cases, this is benchmarked against peers or regional and/or national data. Notably, these publications convey the values of the system through what they count. For example, some publications shifted to not only providing student outcomes overall but also disaggregated outcomes for underrepresented populations such as low-income or racial/ethnic minority populations. Another less explicit value displayed is a focus on the student and the state, as opposed to the institution, through reporting on student outcomes at any system institution or, in some cases, at any institution in the country via the National

Student Clearinghouse. This capability for states to report on students in a variety of ways as they move throughout a state system not only is necessary to capture the increasing mobility of students (Hossler et al., 2012) but also illustrates an important state system capability to add analytic value through its enhanced access to system- and state-level data resources. It isn't big data, but it is bigger.

While these publications have evolved, the larger evolution, of course, is toward provision of data about higher education systems, not in finite publications with a narrative, but through a large variety of online resources. Like campus institutional research websites, the information ranges from static reports to dashboards to very sophisticated interactive data portals. While other authors in this volume speak to other aspects of these advances in data delivery, I want to focus on two. First, these broad online resources serve a wider range of stakeholders. Dashboards might be thought of as the digital corollary of report cards as they focus on key performance indicators and therefore similarly serve high-level stakeholders such as legislators and education professionals looking for comparative progress data. But their accessibility broadens their potential reach to the general public. While dashboards provide succinct high-level information, system research office websites, through a dizzying array of other reports and data portals that disaggregate information in innumerable ways, speak to a larger set of stakeholders. These reports and drill-downs enable staff and faculty at system institutions easy access to granular information on the activities and progress of other institutions and the system as a whole that can inform and guide their work. This information also serves the information needs of a larger external audience of education researchers and advocates with granular, normalized data on system institutions.

The second aspect of these web resources I want to emphasize is how they leverage agency-level relationships to access and incorporate external data resources to more comprehensively answer questions about the state's educational system. The examples are many but I point to a few for illustrative purposes. The Texas Higher Education Coordinating Board utilizes K–12 student data to provide education feedback information for cohorts of eighth grade students disaggregated by county, gender, race/ethnicity, and socioeconomic status (Texas Higher Education Coordinating Board, 2016). A growing number of systems are now publishing wage information for graduates derived from state unemployment insurance records (e.g., Minnesota Office of Higher Education, 2016). It has also become commonplace to include completions at any institution in the country, via a National Student Clearinghouse contract, when reporting on student outcomes (e.g., State Council of Higher Education for Virginia, 2016). Historically these data would have been procured through direct agency relationships but increasingly are available through the state longitudinal data systems that integrate data from a number of state agencies ranging from early childhood services through secondary and postsecondary education to the workforce. These online resources and tools that integrate data beyond the higher education system push systems in the direction of big data and provide at least the potential to conduct broader education pipeline analytics. They also expand the stakeholders served beyond traditional postsecondary ones to researchers, administrators, and leaders in other agencies and sectors seeking to understand how their domains intersect with higher education. Broadening data sources serves a wider host of interested stakeholders by answering more comprehensive questions about the state's education, economic, and societal ecosystem.

Another way of tracking these trends in system office research functions is to examine presentations at the annual Association for Institutional Research (AIR) Forum. Presentations on this national stage may not be representative of all state office work but do provide some evidence of trends. Furthermore, they may include ad hoc research projects that might not be featured on a system website. I analyzed conference programs for the 2005, 2010, and 2015 forums and looked for trends in the focus of state office presentations (AIR, 2005, 2010, 2015). Not surprisingly, the majority of these presentations reflect state- or system-wide analysis. Related to this focus is a strong presence of presentations about policy at the state or system level; about one-third of presentations addressed system- or state-level policy. Student success also figures prominently among the presentations (27%) but interestingly, the number of presentations in this area declined over the three years. Importantly for this chapter, the attention to new and external data sources increased markedly in 2015, being featured in two-thirds of state office presentations. These included sessions focusing or relying on state longitudinal data systems, data mining techniques, and most commonly, workforce outcomes data. Another notable trend was a higher share in 2015 of proposals explicitly attending to stakeholders of research projects (50%). The potential for broadening stakeholders as disparate data sources are merged seems to be playing out in system conference presentations as well.

Increasing Roles Amid the Completion Agenda

I turn now from this panoramic view of system products to a more focused look at how one state office is evolving amid the trends outlined elsewhere in this book. I lead the University System of Georgia's (USG) division of research and policy analysis (RPA), which is tasked with the functional side of system academic, financial aid, and human resources data collection; data governance; standard and ad hoc reporting, support for system initiatives, planning, and policy development; and research on higher education and related topics. In fall 2015, USG enrolled about 318,000 students in 30 institutions, all of which offer four-year degrees, though some institutions in our "state college" sector predominantly award sub-baccalaureate degrees. This chapter is not meant to exhibit best practices; rather, it explores the work one system office is doing amid the current higher education trends and more specific institutional research changes and challenges. I argue that system offices are being asked to take on new roles, ranging from actual implementation of initiatives to facilitating and equalizing campus analytic capability.

USG, like many state systems, is engaged heavily in the work of the completion agenda. Governor Nathan Deal launched Complete College Georgia in late 2011, and Georgia became a Complete College America (CCA) state, embracing CCA's central strategies of reforming remedial education, encouraging full-time attendance, guided curricular pathways, and development of performance-based funding. USG has pursued other completion strategies including better articulation with the Technical College System of Georgia (TCSG), bolstering the systems online general education curriculum (eCore), and undertaking a state reverse-transfer initiative by which students transferring from an associate-granting institution to another system institution without the associate degree are awarded that degree once requirements have been met. RPA has been called on to serve this agenda in multiple ways.

Traditional Reporting and Analysis

RPA has continued its traditional role of providing information and conducting research. RPA provided descriptive baseline information that established the need for initiatives. Examples are the share of students enrolling and succeeding in remedial education or taking the recommended 15-hour credit load necessary for on-time graduation. On the other end of the initiative, RPA has played a vital role in providing data and research on the outcomes of the educational initiatives. One example is data on students passing remedial and gateway courses prior to and after the transformation of remedial placement and delivery. Another example is research comparing outcomes in subsequent courses between students who took introductory courses at a technical college versus at the USG institution, or who took introductory courses via eCore versus in face-to-face courses. While this research is ongoing, findings to date suggest these alternate pathways are not disadvantaging students, even when employing matching mechanisms to reduce selection bias. This RPA work is playing an important role in allaying fears among faculty and others that educational quality is being sacrificed in efforts to promote completion. RPA also serves on and provides data to a hierarchy of committees developed to examine and update system policies and procedures that are serving as obstacles to student completion or are otherwise out of step with current higher education practice.

It should be noted that providing accurate data and conducting meaningful research on the multiple initiatives and reforms occurring as a part of Complete College Georgia requires ensuring that system data collection captures these changes. For example, we must be able to identify eCore courses and distinguish reverse-transfer associate degrees from regular associate degrees. The system functional data governance committee I oversee has been kept very busy reviewing, analyzing, and approving changes to system data collections and working with the system's technical data governance committee to identify how to collect the information. Collection is complicated by the fact that most campus data are submitted via direct extracts from institution transactional systems. We have to find or create a place in the transactional system to store new data elements and then develop training for personnel at campuses entering information into the systems. This role is not new, but the pace of change under Complete College Georgia requires a high volume of data governance work that must proceed quickly to capture information on changes as they happen.

Growing Grant Data Submission Responsibilities

My division has also been called on to expand its role in providing data to external entities for Complete College Georgia. RPA has historically collaborated with the system's information technology services (ITS) to report on behalf of system institutions to entities such as the federal Integrated Postsecondary Education Data System (IPEDS) and the Southern Regional Education Board. This role is increasing, however, with the growing role of philanthropic organizations fostering and shaping the completion agenda (Hall & Thomas, 2012). The USG has received grants to support its completion efforts from CCA, the Lumina Foundation, and the Bill & Melinda Gates Foundation and, like most grants, these require data submission about grant efforts. The system office is submitting these data. This alleviates the reporting burden on campuses, freeing them up to devote resources to the activities of the grant or other analyses; it ensures consistency in reporting across campuses; and it achieves efficiencies of scale as the system office programs what once would have to be done at each individual institution. What is notable about this work, however, is the changing role and nature of data in these grant efforts and what that has meant for the scope of data submissions. Jennifer Engle, senior program officer at the Gates Foundation, noted this shift as part of the panel "Using Data to Change the World" at the 2016 AIR Forum (Brown, Engle, & Miller, 2016). She argued that the role of data in grant efforts has shifted from support and compliance to a central focus of the work. Data requirements are speaking to the values of the grantor, elevating the role of data analysis in the grant's work, and even changing the landscape about what is measured. For example, the CCA submission requires aggregate data on a host of progress and success metrics. These are disaggregated by various demographic groupings to focus attention on achievement gaps and explicitly track part-time and transfer students, populations historically not tracked. These disaggregations move the field forward, but also expand the initial reporting burden as well as the need for resolution of data flagged as problematic due to anomalies in small populations.

The submissions for the Lumina Credit When It's Due reverse-transfer grant and Gates Institutional Partnership Grant take the focus on data a step further. They require deidentified student-level information on background, financial aid, college progress, and outcomes on not only students participating in the grant's activities but also entire cohorts of entering or transfer students. This granularity provides grantors not only with data on prespecified outcomes but also flexibility and power to analyze the data themselves, including sophisticated comparisons of students who do and do not participate in the grant's work. In the case of the Gates grant, the use of this data from the beginning to establish baseline and develop key indicators is an explicit part of the system's grant work. These expansions in granularity and scope of grant data submissions will indubitably facilitate rigorous research and are intended to foster better practices, but it must be noted that they require extensive reporting resources. Converting system data to grant specifications and investigating issues where files violate assumptions and rules built into the data collection (that may not violate our system data integrity checks) take a large investment in time.

Information in Implementation

In addition to the traditional ways the USG research division has supported initiatives through data provision and research, we have also been called on to assist with actual implementation. This is beyond Swing's discussion in "Institutional Researchers as Change Agents" (2009), where research personnel use information about a domain to encourage change or guide the direction or method of implementation. Here, the information we produce *is* the actual means of change—it is part of the administrative process. The transformation of remediation in the USG has included both the transition to corequisite remedial courses and improvement in placement methods. Consistent with findings from national research (Scott-Clayton & Stacey, 2015), the USG undertook to utilize multiple pieces of information to place students, as opposed to one data point, such as a placement test. RPA used historical data about student SAT scores; ACT scores; high school GPA; and, if other data were missing, Compass test scores to develop formulae for math and English placement indices. The indices are based on the historical probability of passing gateway courses in these subjects, and formulae to calculate the indices are different depending on what measures are available. All campuses were required by January 2017 to utilize these indices in their placement of students in traditional remediation, corequisite remediation, or college-level math and English. At that point RPA has returned to a more familiar role of analyzing the endeavor's outcomes to guide future refinement.

Another example of RPA assisting in implementing the completion agenda is the USG's reverse-transfer initiative. The process of awarding the reverse-transfer degree begins with RPA identification of students potentially eligible for the award: enrolled students seeking a bachelor's degree, who transferred from an associate-granting institution without the associate's degree, and who have earned 60 credit hours, with at least 15 of those at the associate institution for residency purposes. Of course, campuses could pull these data themselves, but to alleviate institutional burden and ensure consistency in operationalization (and thus opportunity for the award), the decision was made for RPA to use system enrollment data to identify students and provide the lists of those potentially eligible to campus personnel responsible for contacting the students for consent. Once consent is obtained, the student transcript is sent to the associate-granting institution for audit and then awarding of the degree if requirements are met. A key difference between this effort and the development of the learning support indices is that our role will be ongoing; RPA will identify potentially eligible students every fall and spring.

A final example of the RPA role in Complete College Georgia implementation is the initiative to adopt a performance-based funding formula. The effort ultimately stalled, but the role we played in development was substantial and resource intensive. Discussions with research staff at other system offices corroborate this level of effort and emphasize the ongoing responsibilities if such a formula is adopted. RPA involvement began in 2012 with a place on the working group that advised the Higher Education Funding Commission. The commission ultimately approved the proposed system, but it was the working group of staff from USG, the TCSG, and various governor's offices that provided and analyzed background data, developed a framework, proposed weights, and recommended metrics and their definitions.

In 2013 and early 2014, the work devolved to the separate education systems to develop their specific formula and produce the metrics data to be used in an initial revenue neutral pilot for fiscal year 2015. The division of fiscal affairs and RPA performed this work at USG. Metric data were produced in an iterative process through collaboration of RPA with the USG's information technology arm; changes to metric definitions were recommended by RPA and approved by the governor's office of planning and budget. In June 2014, a process of data validation with system campuses began. This proved to be exceedingly time-consuming and difficult, as the method of system data collection at the time lacked transparency. Also, some metrics relied on system-level data that institutions could not see; for example, extra points for successes of Pell Grant recipients were based on an indicator for Pell receipt at any system institution. Even data points that had been in published reports for years became the subject of intense scrutiny as dollars were attached. Two employees in RPA spent virtually all of their time on this endeavor for about six months. Lessons were learned and presented at the 2015 AIR Forum to help other systems facing this challenge (Bell, Bhatt, & Donoff, 2015). The system research office isn't merely a data provider; it has the unique knowledge about system data and dynamics reflected in that data that should guide a performance-based funding model. In Georgia's process, that expertise was incorporated.

Further political negotiations around the formula resulted in additional metrics, a delay for a further year of study, and, seemingly, abandonment at the present. While RPA is not operating under a performance-based funding model, discussions with my counterpart at the Florida Board of Regents, Jason Jones, suggest that the intensive work does not end with adoption. He indicates that one of his staff spends roughly six months annually working on data production and responding to institutional questions about the metrics data. This is another example of a research office being involved in implementation with ongoing responsibility to sustain the initiative. The research office is functioning less as a reporter or analyst of data and more as a data processor in an administrative function. This is a substantive shift in the roles of state system research offices.

System Research Office Analytics

Most of the RPA work described in conjunction with the USG's completion efforts would not qualify as *analytics* in the strict sense of the term. It is largely retrospective rather than predictive; it is not dealing in the megabytes of big data; and, in most cases, it involves little merging of separate data domains to create boundary spanning knowledge. But these activities, along with routine data provision and analysis, keep my system research office occupied. A very informal canvassing of colleagues currently or recently in state system research shops suggest that many of them also struggle to move beyond the incessant demands of data governance, routine and ad hoc reporting, regulatory compliance, and requests for analyses of a more pedestrian nature. So how can a system research office elevate its game?

Partnering to Get in the Game

The final part of this chapter describes how the USG is elevating its game. In early 2014, prior to my tenure at USG, system office leadership identified a need for better ways to utilize the vast amounts of data collected from institutions to guide system planning and decision-making. Historically, RPA had provided voluminous retrospective reporting as well as in-depth sophisticated analyses. But even these capabilities were truncated at the time as a result of lingering understaffing from the recession, leadership transitions, and a series of incomplete data warehousing projects. These challenges were being addressed, but leadership wanted analytics to guide the system faster than internal resources could provide. USG decided to partner with the University of Georgia's Carl Vinson Institute of Government (CVIOG), an organization that provides training, research, policy analysis, and so on, to assist public officials. This decision to engage an outside entity is consistent with literature recommending use of consultants in institutional research when there is an immediate need that can't be met or a new technology that cannot be leveraged (Milam, 2008). The collaboration began just as I and the new head of Business Intelligence came on board, and we were tasked with providing guidance and data access respectively. Also, the project convened a subject matter expert team consisting of system and campus research and administrative personnel to inform the work and provide feedback.

Over the next 18 months, CVIOG marshalled the expertise and time of staff with varied backgrounds to advance the analytic capacity of the USG, focusing on student data in keeping with the system's Complete College Georgia efforts as well as the large role of enrollment in system funding. CVIOG transformed the system's semester snapshots of student demographic and enrollment data into a clean master longitudinal research database for years 2002 to 2012 that was analysis ready. This data set removed the necessity of pulling, merging, and cleaning data from disparate tables each time a new research question arose and reduced the time and effort from question to answer. The data set was enhanced with a custom database on Georgia high school information, U.S. census data through geocoding of student permanent addresses, and National Student Clearinghouse records. Capitalizing on staff backgrounds in demography, geographic information systems, and data science, CVIOG proceeded to develop analytic tools including social network analysis of high school to college feeder patterns, visualizations of student transfer using means developed for population migration, and distillation of student enrollment behaviors over time into character strings to draw out patterns and facilitate analysis.

The subject matter expert team and USG leadership reviewed the products as they were developed and provided feedback. It became clear that the visualizations appealed to the researcher and leadership stakeholders alike, but for different reasons. For leaders, the visualizations conveyed large amounts of information simultaneously, succinctly, and dynamically in ways tables of numbers could not. Leadership saw power and utility in more effectively communicating complex phenomena to facilitate decision-making. Researchers saw these benefits but immediately began asking questions about the data; the visualizations were portals to further inquiry. The visualizations drew out relationships that would take them back to the raw data for research.

The project was rolled out to the larger USG community of stakeholders at a January 2016 USG Board of Regents meeting with similar success. The regents were impressed but had little followup; this isn't surprising given the very high level of information with which they usually engage. Personnel in the various USG divisions clamored to get access to the data set and tools to inform the work of their division. Presidents at a number of campuses immediately reached out to USG staff asking how they, too, could gain access for their campus. They articulated that they lacked analytic tools, their research staff were stretched too thin to develop them, and, in some cases, no data warehouse existed and reporting occurred from transactional systems. Like many institutions across the country, these leaders aspire to analytics, but data use is mostly limited to reporting (Bischel, 2012). These conversations mirrored discussions several months prior at a Complete College Georgia summit of campus leaders. While some campuses like Georgia State University and Valdosta State University have advanced analytics to support their completion efforts, other campuses didn't. These tended to be our state colleges and state universities, where the access mission makes data-informed completion efforts especially critical. A tectonic shift in the USG/CVIOG analytics project occurred: It was not just for system decision-making; it needed to enhance the analytic capacity of institutions lacking in this critical tool for decision-making and student success. The project would try to close gaps in analytic capacity across campuses much like the completion agenda seeks to close gaps in student achievement.

The Analytics Project Moving Forward

The success of the project thus far led to a focus on providing campus access via a secure web portal to two of the project tools (visualizations of intra-system student transfer and first-time freshman high school to college feeder patterns). Moving forward, campus feedback would be solicited to prioritize future data packages to be delivered. By providing these analytic packages, efficiencies are realized through one-time development of tools for all 30 campuses. And even for campuses with advanced analytic capacity, the data packages add value through their ability to track enrollment throughout the system, a key system data advantage (Lane & Finsel, 2014). These first packages relied on Family Education Rights and Privacy Act (FERPA)-exempt directory information, but protocols and agreements will have to be developed as future packages include student progress and outcomes. The provision of these packages will be accompanied by training on use and potential applications. While we recognize that other factors shape effective analytics use, such as leadership, culture, and processes and policies (Norris & Baer, 2013), the project is lowering barriers to entry through provision of tools and training.

The next phase also includes updating the longitudinal data set, adding data sources like financial aid information, and transitioning the data set to RPA staff for maintenance, governance, and use. Most importantly, this phase moves the analytic tools developed from demonstrations to actual implementation. Analytics on high school feeder patterns and characteristics of students and their community background will be utilized to target for enhanced outreach to Georgia high schools less well connected to USG institutions. Here, analytics akin to those institutions employed to market to and enroll students (Goff & Shaffer, 2014) will be deployed at a system level with a different lens of better service to the state. A predictive model of student success of first-time freshmen based on student, high school, and community characteristics will be deployed to identify entering students in need of additional support. Similarly, system-wide historical enrollment patterns and probabilities of dropout and success will be utilized in sensitivity analysis and simulations to model financial aid gap funding and other retention strategies. Pilots will be developed with institutions to target finite student support resources to students in need with strategies likely to be effective. The aim will be to ameliorate the condition of unfocused support systems not engaging with students identified as struggling

(Wildavsky, 2014). Also, student groupings derived from a random forest model in conjunction with clustering and outlier analysis will be utilized to develop and deploy policy analysis modeling tools. Finally, RPA staff will receive intensive training on the project's analytic tools; this will be critical to the long-term integration of the project into USG operations.

In summary, the USG/CVIOG project is advancing the USG footprint in analytics at a pace that never could have been achieved by internal resources consumed with routine operations and making infrastructure investments. Furthermore, the application of staff with varied disciplinary backgrounds enriched the approaches and types of tools developed. The creation of one analysis-ready, system-wide longitudinal data set enhanced with robust external data sources will support not only the project's analytic tools but also more traditional academic research. The analytic tools in the second phase will be deployed on system-level issues, such as better outreach to the state, as well as distributed to campuses to jump-start their use of analytics in decision-making and success efforts. The campuses were not initial stakeholders of the USG analytics work but have been included to address their needs.

Conclusion

This chapter has traced briefly some changes in system research products noting the obvious changes in technology but emphasizing how websites can accommodate and make accessible innumerable data sources. Both the platform and the proliferation of products expand the audience for research. These products have come to incorporate data from external entities and in doing so also broadened stakeholders of the work. Integration of external data with our own student data positions us well to do more sophisticated analytics. At the same time, the completion agenda has brought further changes to system research offices, and at USG it has expanded the traditional roles of reporting, analysis, and data provision with the latter qualitatively changed by grantors' demands for more granular data. We are serving a new function in facilitating the grantors' research. We are also serving a new role in actual implementation of system completion initiatives due to our comprehensive data as well as the efficiency and consistency of conducting the work at the system level. These demands leave little bandwidth for advances in analytics and resulted in a partnership with a campus institute to meet leadership demands for decision-making analytics. The CVIOG partnership is meeting system office needs with tools incorporating different disciplinary approaches and USG data merged with valuable external sources. But the project highlighted needs at many campuses for similar capacity, and so the project is pivoting to serve our campus stakeholders. This shift is perhaps a state corollary to the vision expressed in the AIR *Statement of Aspirational Practice for Institutional Research* (Swing & Ross, 2016). We are meeting local campus need, and enhancing overall system capacity, for data-driven decisions through distribution of analytic data tools and training. All of these projects point to an expanding role for system research offices through the proliferation of available data sources, the varied demands of the completion agenda, and the pressures to escalate traditional reporting and research to analytics. These expanded roles are simultaneously broadening the stakeholders that system research offices serve and how they serve them. It is a demanding but exciting time to work in a state system research office.

References

Association for Institutional Research. (2005). *AIR annual forum program book and schedule.* Retrieved from https://www.airweb.org/EducationAndEvents/ AnnualConference/Documents/2005finalpgm.pdf

Association for Institutional Research. (2010). *AIR annual forum program book and schedule.* Retrieved from https://www.airweb.org/EducationAndEvents/ AnnualConference/Documents/AIR_2010_Program_Final_lowres.pdf

Association for Institutional Research. (2015). *AIR annual forum program book and schedule.* Retrieved from: https://www.airweb.org/EducationAndEvents/ AnnualConference/Documents/2015%20Forum%20Program%20Book%20 Web.pdf

Bell, A., Bhatt, R., & Donoff, S. (2015). *Opening the black box: Development of Georgia performance funding metrics.* Presentation at the Association for Institutional Research Forum, Denver, Colorado.

Bichsel, J. (2012). *Analytics in higher education: Benefits, barriers, progress, and recommendations.* Retrieved from https://library.educause.edu/resources/2012/6/ 2012-ecar-study-of-analytics-in-higher-education

Brown, C., Engle, J., & Miller, E. (2016). *Using data to change the world.* Plenary at the Association for Institutional Research Forum, New Orleans, Louisiana.

Goff, J. W., & Shaffer, C. M. (2014). Big data's impact on college admission practices and recruitment strategies. In J. E. Lane (Ed.), *Building a smarter university: Big data, innovation, and analytics* (pp. 3–25). Albany, NY: SUNY Press.

Hall, C., & Thomas, S. L. (2012). *"Advocacy philanthropy" and the public policy agenda: The role of modern foundations in American higher education.* Paper presented at the annual meeting of the American Educational Research Association, Vancouver, British Columbia.

Hossler, D., Shapiro, D., Dundar, A., Ziskin, M., Chen, J., Zerquera, D., & Torres, V. (2012). *Transfer and mobility: A national view of pre-degree student movement in postsecondary institutions* (Signature Report No. 2). Herndon, VA: National Student Clearinghouse Research Center.

Lane, J., & Finsel, B. (2014). Fostering smarter colleges and universities: Data, big data, and analytics. In J. E. Lane (Ed.), *Building a smarter university: Big data, innovation, and analytics* (pp. 3–25). Albany, NY: SUNY Press.

Milam, J., (2008). The role of consultants in institutional research. *New Directions for Institutional Research, 139,* 27–45.

Minnesota Office of Higher Education. (2016). *College graduate outcomes.* Retrieved from https://www.ohe.state.mn.us/mPg.cfm?pageID=2119

Norris, D. M., & Baer, L. L. (2013). *Building organizational capacity for analytics.* Retrieved from https://net.educause.edu/ir/library/pdf/pub9012.pdf

Scott-Clayton, J., & Stacey, G. W. (2015). *Improving the accuracy of remedial placement.* New York, NY: Columbia University, Teachers College, Community College Research Center.

State Council of Higher Education for Virginia. (2016). *Retention and graduation rates.* Retrieved from http://research.schev.edu/apps/info/Reports.Guide-to-the-Retention-and-Graduation-Reports.ashx

Swing, R. L. (2009). Institutional researchers as change agents. *New Directions for Institutional Research, 143,* 5–16.

Swing, R. L., & Ross, L. (2006). *Statement of aspirational practice for institutional research.* Tallahassee, FL: Association for Institutional Research.

Texas Higher Education Coordinating Board. (2016). *8th grade cohorts tracked through higher education.* Retrieved from http://www.txhighereddata.org/index.cfm?objectId=F2CBE4A0-C90B-11E5-8D610050560100A9

Wildavsky, B. (2014). Nudge nation: A new way to use data to prod students into and through college. In J. E. Lane (Ed.), *Building a smarter university: Big data, innovation, and analytics* (pp. 143–158). Albany, NY: SUNY Press.

9

MOVING FROM DATA TO ACTION

Changing Institutional Culture and Behavior

Desdemona Cardoza and Jeff Gold

For many years, the California State University (CSU) system office has collected large amounts of data on the students who pass through its 23 institutions. Student information related to high school preparation, socioeconomic status, major declaration, credit accumulation patterns, year-to-year retention rates, and time to degree has been amassed in highly structured ways with the goal of coordinating the timely reporting of a variety of federal, state, and public compliance requirements. These data collection and reporting efforts were originally established to answer questions like "Who is attending the CSU?" and "How many students are graduating?" without focusing on "Why are some students graduating and others not?" and "How can the system encourage higher success rates?" As a result, CSU campuses were largely left to their own devices to analyze how student behavior and institutional practices affected academic progress and degree completion.

In recent years, there has been growing attention to the need to increase postsecondary degree attainment, resulting in much public discourse in state and national circles. The traditional emphasis on access and enrollment has expanded to emphasize student progress and degree completion (Yeado, Haycock, Johnstone, & Chaplot, 2014). In light of this new focus, often referred to as *student success*, the CSU introduced the 2009 Graduation Initiative. This initiative strived to raise the freshman six-year graduation rate and reduce the existing gap in degree attainment by underrepresented minority (URM) students by 2015. Involving all 23 campuses, the Graduation Initiative required all campuses to set degree completion targets comparable to the top quartile of national averages of similar institutions and to close the URM achievement gap through a series of carefully planned activities.

119

With the launch of this initiative, the CSU system realized that it was critical to reframe the strategic use of student data in a way that provided a clear indication of whether or not a campus was on track to meet its graduation goals, and more important, what specific actions could help more students succeed. The CSU Student Success Dashboard was developed to serve as a central resource to assist all campuses in identifying and dislodging barriers to student success. From the beginning, our vision was to create a tool whose value would far surpass that of a traditional dashboard, by leveraging historic data to identify opportunities for increasing student success. Typically, business intelligence dashboards display the current status of key performance indicators for an enterprise. Most higher education dashboards have been positioned to present historical data and outcome measures, but they frequently lack predictive analytical models that can identify opportunities for meaningful change.

Initially, the primary focus of the CSU Student Success Dashboard was to provide campus presidents and administrators with information regarding their campus's progress toward meeting graduation and gap-closing goals. Using historical data as well as current retention data, prediction models were developed to determine whether or not campuses were on track. We realized that although the potential consumers of this information covered a wide array of constituencies, our initial target audience for the dashboard was campus presidents, provosts, and vice presidents for student affairs. These were the individuals who ultimately would be held accountable for whether the goals were met. Serving these audiences made the visualization of the dashboard extremely important; campus leadership had to be able to see quickly and clearly how their institution was progressing and understand whether they needed to make changes to meet their goals. Therefore the first dashboard view that campuses saw was of their progress toward meeting their completion and gap-closing goals. This analysis was updated annually, using predictive modeling to provide campuses with on-track indicators of their progress.

Upon the launch of the initial dashboard, it soon became clear that campuses required more granular and actionable information to begin to identify obstacles to timely degree completion. In response, we added a new set of predictive models focusing on specific student academic behaviors and CSU campus support programs. We conducted a series of analyses that implemented different types of statistical modeling. We examined the impact of a set of first- and second-year academic behaviors on the timely completion of a degree (e.g., completing 24 or more units in the first year, completing college-level English and math by the end of the second year, completing lower division general education requirements by the end of the first year).

We also explored the efficacy of various support programs (e.g., Summer Bridge, Learning Communities, First-Year Experience) using propensity score matching to create meaningful control groups. This allowed us to estimate the effect of the intervention by accounting for the covariates that predict receiving the treatment.

Additionally, we felt it was important for users to be able to interact with the data. Using predictive modeling, we introduced a "what if" analysis. This tool allowed users to manipulate the data and see the potential impact on retention and graduation rates based on changes in the predictor variables. Users could also create visualizations showing how future graduation rates at their campus might be impacted by increasing the number of students who meet various academic milestones.

The CSU Student Success Dashboard has undergone significant changes since its inception. The lessons learned will, we hope, assist other institutions as they move toward developing more actionable, data-driven resources in support of their student success efforts. What follows is a set of 10 recommendations to facilitate campuses and systems in the implementation of a student success dashboard that motivates action and supports a culture of data-driven inquiry and discussion. It is important to note that this is an evolving process driven by user feedback.

Develop a Student Success Framework

To be meaningful, your institution's dashboard must be more than a compilation of loosely related data tables and explanatory charts. To set the appropriate context, ensure relevance, and generate user buy-in, it is critical to tie the dashboard to your campus's most important strategic initiatives. Student success must be seen as an institutional priority, and stakeholders must commit to the goals of gaining a true understanding of why students are not succeeding and developing a set of strategies to address the underlying factors.

Historically, many colleges and universities have focused on getting students in the door and meeting their revenue and enrollment targets. Whether students succeeded once they arrived on campus was seen as the responsibility of the academic departments and individual faculty. But as more and more student data have become readily available, many postsecondary institutions have begun to investigate why students leave before they graduate, and those institutions are looking for ways to improve retention and completion rates (Chronicle of Higher Education, 2015).

Figure 9.1 is an example of the initial framework we developed at CSU as part of the 2009 Graduation Initiative to guide campuses in the strategic use of data to support their student success plans. This illustration was used to identify broad areas where students might be experiencing barriers to achieving their academic goals and suggest data sources that could be used to improve understanding of how to address these limiting factors.

This preliminary framework helped campuses understand the connections among various programs and reinforced the strategic centrality of the student success mission. We have since made a number of changes to this structure as we have learned more about what impacts student success.

As you develop your own dashboard and expand your user base, you're likely to have many discussions about the inclusion of additional data. If the requests do not fit within the strategic vision of your dashboard, feel comfortable saying no. Over the years, we have added a number of analyses and visualizations based on user feedback, but we have also declined requests that didn't fit the dashboard's objectives.

Exploring strategically aligned, context-rich analyses in the dashboard has helped CSU faculty, staff, and administrators gain a deeper understanding of why some students are making good progress toward a degree while others are not. As a result, the dashboard has stimulated evidence-based conversations and created a culture of measurement and improvement on many CSU campuses. We have seen that changing culture in this way has been most successful on campuses where decision makers have positioned the strategic use of data as an integral part of daily campus business.

Enlist the Support of Top Leadership

Campus and system leaders play a critical role in promoting student success in higher education. They are the ones responsible for setting and implementing the strategic direction for their university. Over the past decade it has become clear that data play an essential role in developing impactful institutional policies and practices. Postsecondary institutions that have improved student success often do so through a focus on data (Yeado, Haycock, Johnstone, & Chaplot, 2014).

Soon after we developed the initial version of the Student Success Dashboard, we were able to demonstrate its strategic value at a meeting with the 23 CSU presidents. This orientation was very well received and generated dialogue that helped us to frame the next phase of development. Due to the high level of interest, the chancellor asked each executive leader to participate in a customized demonstration of the dashboard with our team to underscore the value of the tool for their campus. Although this was a time-consuming process for us, the results were well worth the effort, as they led to

Figure 9.1. Framework for guiding campuses in developing their Student Success Strategic Plans.

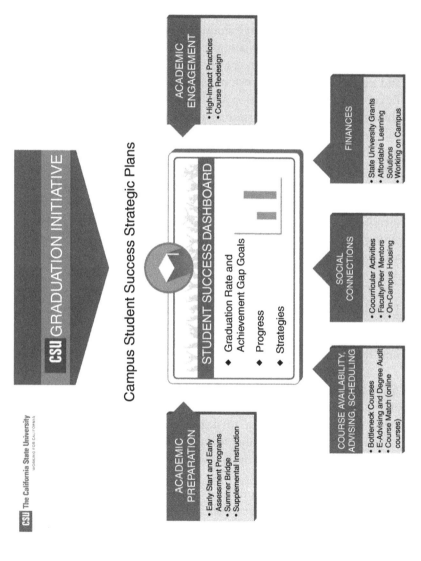

strong buy-in from campus leadership. These meetings also set the precedent for regular discussions with campus provosts and vice presidents for student affairs about how their campus culture, policies, and programs were impacting student success. These conversations led us to explore additional data sets that included actionable variables allowing us to address increasingly sophisticated research questions using predictive analytics.

Although we collect large amounts of data centrally, there is a wealth of information that campuses compile that does not come to the CSU system office. For example, course grades, participation in high-impact practices, and student course-taking pattern data all reside exclusively on the campuses. By combining this information with our larger system-level data sets, we were able to develop more sophisticated analyses, identifying a number of actionable areas for improvement. At first, obtaining these data from the campuses in a timely manner proved to be challenging. Our requests to the campus institutional research (IR) offices were sometimes ignored or delayed because they were not seen as high priority. However, as the presidents became aware of the dashboard's value in applying models to produce actionable recommendations tied to their campus's student success efforts, many became strong advocates of the dashboard and helped to significantly increase our access to their data while also promoting campus usage of the tool.

Develop a Data Analytics Model that Focuses on the Actionable

To make our data actionable and relevant, we began by conducting research into the field of predictive analytics. Predictive analytics has been used as a management tool for many years, but higher education has been a relatively late adopter of these techniques. Still, many colleges and universities are finding tremendous value in their ability to determine which students are at risk of leaving prior to degree completion. Using historical data, institutions of higher learning are able to design, develop, and implement retention strategies that keep students on the optimal path to graduation (Eduventures, 2013).

Students come to the university with a variety of characteristics known to be correlated with degree completion. Research has demonstrated that certain demographic variables as well as experiences prior to attending college are closely tied to persistence and completion. These include race/ethnicity, socioeconomic status, level of college preparation, and college-going generation (Dennis, Phinney, & Chuateco, 2005). Typically, students who come from lower socioeconomic backgrounds, who are first-generation college students, and who are not "college-ready" have more difficulty completing college than their counterparts who come from more privileged backgrounds (Terenzini, Springer, Yaeger, Pascarella, & Nora, 1996; Zalaquett, 1999).

While it is important to understand the relationship of these variables on the college experience, these characteristics are certainly not actionable. However, if we shift our focus to variables over which we *do* have some influence, we can make a significant impact in a short time. With this focus, a campus can implement policies, practices, and other changes to help students achieve important milestones and ultimately complete their degree in a timely manner.

Institutions routinely track and collect data on course-taking patterns and program participation. There are several important milestones and on-track indicators that can be used to predict retention and graduation (Offenstein, Moore, & Shulock, 2010). On-track indicators include

- completion of college-level math and/or English in the first two years,
- completion of a college success or first-year experience program,
- completion of 20 to 30 credits in the first year,
- full-time enrollemnt, and
- maintenance of an adequate grade-point average.

Using this information to predict graduation can be very powerful in molding and modifying student academic behaviors.

The CSU Student Success Dashboard uses several of these indicators in what we term the *leading indicator* analyses. By controlling for student characteristic variables known to influence degree completion, we were able to determine the impact of the several leading indicator variables for each campus. For example, our analyses revealed that for one campus, the first-year retention rate for students completing college-level math and English within the first two years *and* completing 24 or more units in the first year was 82% as compared to 31% for those students who did not meet these milestones (see Figure 9.2). Results like these may lead an institution to make changes in policy and advisement practices, as well as other institutional procedures.

Many of the CSU student support programs are limited to freshmen and focus entirely on the first year. Although these programs may produce high initial retention rates, this does not always result in increased graduation rates. One of the student support programs prominently featured on our dashboard is Summer Bridge. Nearly all CSU campuses have a summer program that provides educationally disadvantaged incoming freshmen an introduction to collegiate life. These programs vary in length, content, and structure, but share the common goal of better preparing disadvantaged students for both academic and social success.

Figure 9.2. Dashboard view of the impact of 3 of the leading indicators (completing 24 or more units in the first year and completing the general education math and English requirements in the first 2 years) on the 6-year graduation rate for a large urban CSU campus.

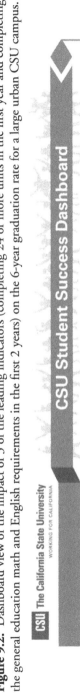
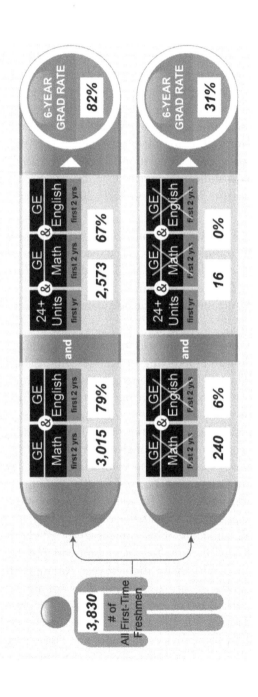

By presenting retention and graduation rates for Summer Bridge students across campuses, we were able to identify one campus in particular where the retention and six-year graduation rates of participating students were not only higher than the comparison group but also higher than the campus as a whole. This trend held up over multiple years. By seeing these results in the appropriate context, cross-campus discussions are now taking place and additional research is being conducted to determine why certain programs have achieved such impressive outcomes.

In addition to identifying high-performing programs, the dashboard provides several analyses related to the number and types of course units that students take on their path to a degree. In examining the data for the CSU, we discovered that a substantial number of students were not completing 15 credit hours per semester in order to stay on track to a degree. This was particularly true for URM students. In examining the historical graduation rates for the CSU system as a whole, it is interesting to note that the seven-year graduation rate for Latino students exceeded the six-year completion goal. In other words, many of these students persisted, but took seven rather than six years to graduate.

Figure 9.3 shows how we implemented an interactive analysis in the dashboard to allow users to combine a variety of student characteristic variables and see the impact on semester-to-semester unit load.

Don't Worry So Much About the Tool

A common point of stress for those developing a dashboard is the selection of a software platform to best provide a series of easy-to-use templates that organize data and display it graphically. Important stories live in our data and graphic visualization is a powerful means to discover and understand these stories and explain them to others (Few, 2016). The business intelligence and data visualization market continues to experience tremendous growth, resulting in a robust product offering that includes everything from simple graphic interfaces to complex data visualization tools that require specialized expertise. While functionality, scalability, cost, usability, and sustainability are key considerations, the adaptability of the tool is critical.

Throughout the creation of the CSU Student Success Dashboard, we have maintained a flexible approach to selecting the most appropriate tools.

Figure 9.3. Dashboard view of unit-taking patterns for students graduating within six years.

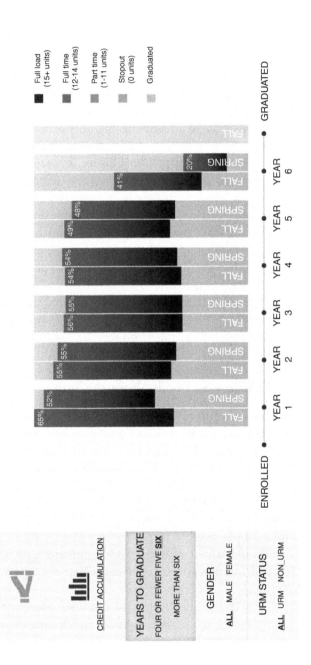

We opted to implement SAS Enterprise Business Intelligence software along with a variety of open source JavaScript libraries to create a highly engaging, dynamic, and scalable set of visualizations that can be readily developed and sustained by CSU staff. For example, we employ the Google Charts library throughout the dashboard and have used this resource to develop time-series graphs and interactive "what if" analyses that allow campuses to interrogate the data and create regression-driven simulations that quantify the potential impact of their graduation rate improvement efforts. These templates are freely available, user-friendly, and easily customizable by programmers with moderate JavaScript expertise.

One of the most frequent questions we get when we present the CSU Student Success Dashboard relates to our choice of products. In response, we typically explain the rationale behind the tools we selected and underscore the importance of aligning product choice to an institution's strategic objectives and resources. At the same time, we are quick to point out that while tool selection can be a critical factor, those just beginning this work should consider leveraging commonly available products such as Microsoft Excel to launch prototypes that enable them to better understand their audience, define their needs, and rapidly develop low-cost prototypes.

Analyzing the wide variety of data visualization tools can be overwhelming, especially for nontechnical staff who have never explored this market. This speaks to the importance of involving stakeholders from campus information technology (IT) and IR departments. Cross-divisional collaboration will greatly increase the likelihood of a successful implementation.

Partner With IR and IT Services

Most colleges and universities underutilize their data and analytical resources. Even though they may have large amounts of data, they often lack the specific information needed to identify the variables that truly matter to them and their constituents. What's more, these performance variables are not necessarily captured in the routine data collection efforts of the institution (Norris, Baer, Leonard, Pugliese, & Lefrere, 2008).

The responsibility for overseeing student success initiatives frequently falls to a committee or an area of the university outside of IR. Although IR offices are typically the "official" keepers of the data, they are regularly tasked with reporting responsibilities to federal, state, and local agencies. The CSU campuses that have been most successful in leveraging data to improve student success outcomes have a collaborative, synergistic relationship between the IR office and the student success team.

In the various iterations of the CSU Student Success Dashboard, we have relied on campus IR directors to ensure the integrity of the data, scrutinize the analyses, and identify areas for increased clarity. This is the group that is most familiar with the data. They can tell us if there is something that does not appear correct and help us understand data anomalies. Including IR as a part of the student success team is essential.

Partnering with IT is also critical, particularly if you are choosing to host your dashboard locally. In our case, we met with the CSU system's IT leadership team early and often to review technical requirements and determine the needed service agreements. As a result of this collaboration, our IT partners created an automated data encryption service and facilitated agreements for us to host the dashboard through Amazon Web Services. Additionally they implemented a Single-Sign-On (SSO) application that allows the CSU's more than 49,000 faculty and staff to access the dashboard using their local campus credentials. The stable server environment and customized views of the data have helped support a growing number of users across the CSU system. With this expanded audience, we have been able to increase the breadth of our analyses by incorporating a wider variety of new data sets.

Use External Data Sources

To promote a context-rich understanding of student success, your dashboard should reach beyond campus and system boundaries to identify relevant data sets. Data coming from the campus is more fine-grained and easily customized than outside sources of data. This facilitates an institution's ability to ask and answer campus-specific questions on an ongoing basis. Few institutions, however, take advantage of compiling and analyzing a wide breadth of data sources to take a deeper look at what actually influences student success (Chronicle of Higher Education, 2015).

There are many robust sources of information that can inform your understanding of student behavior. These include student satisfaction surveys, exit surveys or interviews with nonretained students, analyses of academic performance in gateway courses, and analyses of course-scheduling optimization. Other efforts involve technologies that allow advisers to predict student behavior as a way to steer students to more appropriate courses and majors that can reduce their time to degree. Additionally, incorporating cross-institutional comparisons into solutions can be very helpful to institutions, particularly for benchmarking purposes.

The CSU Student Success Dashboard uses various external data sources to enrich users' understanding of how their students are succeeding. One resource that our users have found to be particularly valuable comes from College Results Online (CRO). CRO applies an algorithm comparing the chosen university to all other public and private not-for-profit institutions in the CRO database and creates a customized peer group. Each comparison receives a *similarity score* based on how alike the peer schools are in terms of a series of institutional and student characteristics. These data allow users to compare their institution with similar national peer institutions (see Figure 9.4).

Another external data set we use is the National Student Clearinghouse (NSC) database. These data allow campus stakeholders to quantify how many of their nongraduates received a degree from another institution. The NSC data provide a glimpse into the successful outcomes of students who graduate from a university other than the one in which they first enrolled and provides details about the names and locations of these degree-granting institutions. For example, one CSU campus that interrogated these data in our dashboard discovered they were losing students to nearby CSU campuses and to local for-profit institutions. This began a series of discussions that resulted in an examination of the adequacy of their course offerings. The campus saw that many students were not able to enroll in needed classes, forcing them to go elsewhere. As a result of these findings, the school has begun to make changes in course scheduling patterns, increasing the availability of their most popular general education classes and providing similar solutions to course offerings for high-enrollment majors.

Employment data can also provide valuable insight. Research on student retention and graduation has identified student employment as a factor that can significantly impact timely degree completion. Recognizing that this is a difficult variable to measure systematically, we decided to look to the CSU faculty for expertise in this area. Drawing on the work of a group of labor economists at one of our campuses, we were able to use California Employment Development Department earnings data to examine the impact of student employment on retention and graduation. Although this work is still in development, we hope to expand these analyses to understand the relationship between working on campus and time to degree.

Engage the Faculty

For any student success initiative to be successful, it is essential that there is cooperation at all functional levels of the institution. There are many stakeholders involved in ensuring student success, and faculty are at the top of the list. After all, these are the individuals who connect with students on a daily basis and at every critical milestone in their academic careers.

Figure 9.4. Dashboard view of peer benchmarks, comparing freshman 6-year graduation rates at CSU Long Beach with those at 11 peer campuses.

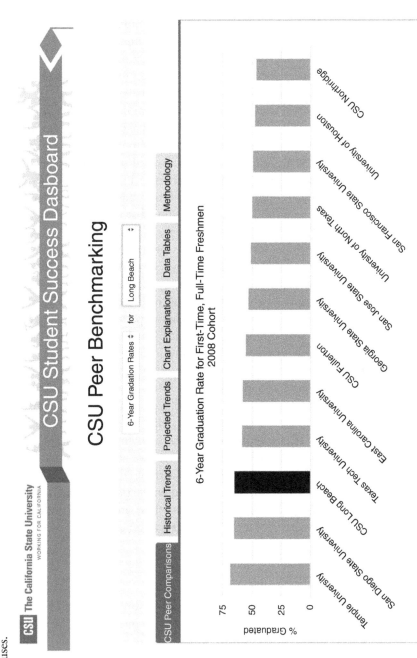

Having data available at the system and campus level is important, but providing college, major, department, and course-level details highlights patterns of student behavior that aren't always visible in the aggregate. Faculty must be able to see information about their students and understand who they are. They need to be able to understand how students are performing in the courses they teach and become familiar with the paths students take in regard to average unit load.

To meet these needs, we created a faculty section in the Student Success Dashboard. This focuses exclusively on major and department-level data. Throughout the development process, we relied on the expertise of several faculty members to help us identify and organize the statistical analyses that would help them and their colleagues gain a better understanding of where students are succeeding and where they were encountering difficulties.

Based on this collaboration we developed a time-series graph showing the credit accumulation patterns of students by major, an interactive graph illustrating major-changing activities of students in each major (see Figure 9.5), and various charts highlighting student characteristics and academic outcomes by major.

Engaging faculty with analyses at the major level has given them a better understanding of their students' progress toward degree, while at the same time identifying areas where increased research is needed to better understand the root causes of the findings. To support these efforts, every page of our dashboard contains links to relevant research, as well as tips for interpreting and applying the data.

Fund Experimentation

To make student success a core part of the institution's focus and mission, it is essential to develop organizational capacity and change the culture to encourage evidence-based behavior and action-focused research to improve performance. This cultural shift must cut across all levels of the institution. On many campuses, it is the administrators and staff who are tasked with determining the student success research questions to be asked and identifying the relevant analyses to answer these questions. However, it's essential to also get faculty involved. There is a wealth of research expertise and first-hand knowledge among the faculty, who, in many ways, are uniquely qualified to complete this important work.

With this in mind, as a part of our Student Success Strategic Plan, we allocated funds for faculty-led action research projects. Campuses submitted proposals in which they used the dashboard to identify impediments to student success on their campus or in their college, department,

Figure 9.5. Dashboard view depicting the various majors declared at entry for students graduating with a degree in biochemistry.

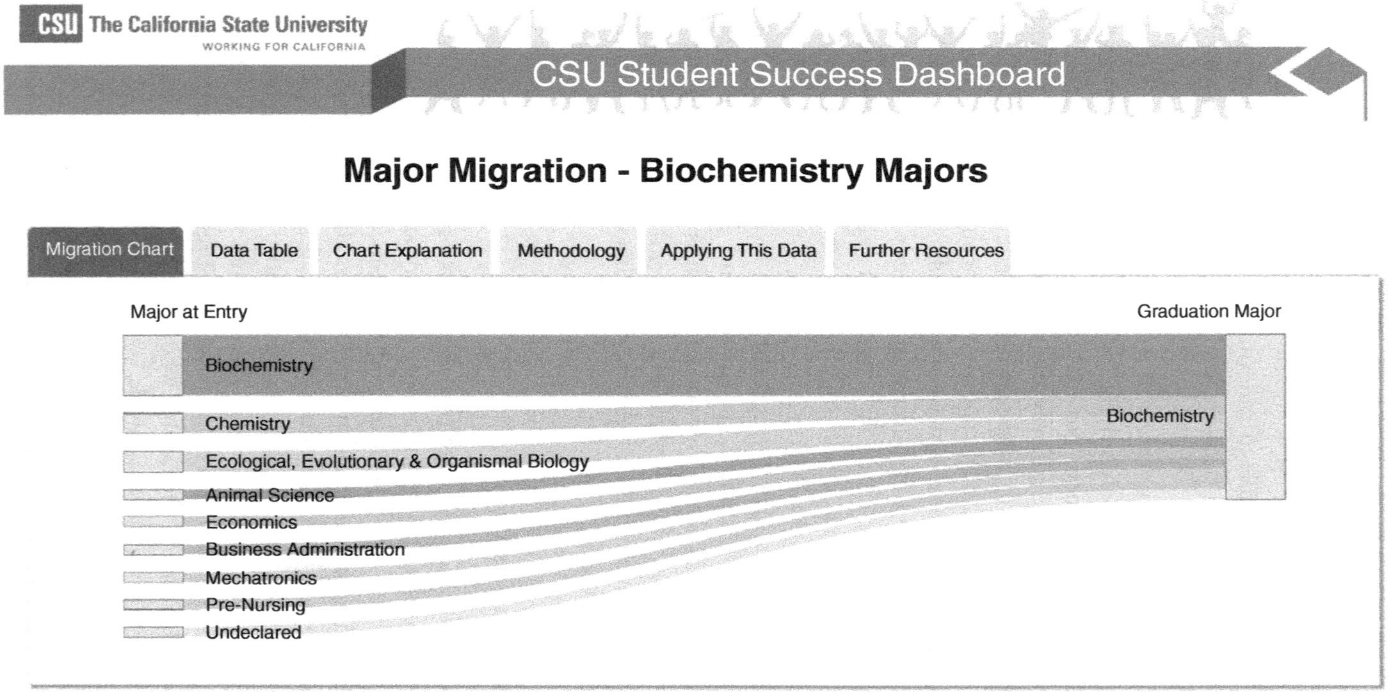

and/or major and proposed solutions to remedy the problem in clearly measurable ways. Through this project we funded a variety of action research projects, including adding supplemental instruction to a high-failure-rate math course, launching a peer-mentor program aimed at disadvantaged students, and mining social media to understand the relationship of noncognitive factors on persistence rates.

Although many of these action research projects are still in progress, we have included a summary and evaluation of completed projects in the Research section of the dashboard. It's worth mentioning that while many of these interventions were successful, some were not, but we share both types of outcomes on the dashboard. We do this to emphasize the importance of experimenting, learning from your mistakes, and collaborating across the system.

Consider Your Audience and Highlight the Most Salient Issues

Analytical practices are advancing in sophistication and proliferation, aided in part by a host of new software and professional services. These new offerings have the potential to determine the efficacy of institutional interventions that result in timely progress to degree, while providing levels of measurement that have not been readily available previously (Norris et al., 2008).

As a result, roughly two-thirds of CSU campuses have developed their own dashboard, which functions at a very granular level. These tools are generally used by campus advisers, allowing them to get detailed information at the individual student level for the purpose of reaching out and assisting students in navigating their academic path.

Part of our communication plan to the campuses involved educating them in how our Student Success Dashboard could work synergistically with their local dashboards. For example, one campus reported that analyses in our dashboard indicated that a number of their students were not being retained after their sixth year. Using their local dashboard, they were able to identify each student, leading to the discovery that many were only one or two classes short of graduating. An adviser then contacted the students and was able to ensure that the students were either able to enroll in the requisite course(s) or obtain course substitutions.

Another important aspect of our communication plan involved the use of textual call-outs next to many charts and graphs. These short messages use algorithms to analyze the data and highlight important takeaways in a direct, easily understandable way. This allows busy individuals to see and interpret the data very quickly and helps them focus on strategies for compiling additional information and deciding what action to take.

Figure 9.6. Dashboard view of call-out text that summarizes the results of the leading indicator predictive analysis for one CSU campus.

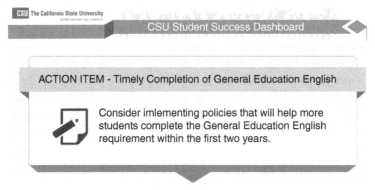

Figure 9.6 shows an example of how we use this text to call out the impact that early completion of the General Education English requirement has on graduation rates.

Stay in Contact With Your Users and Commit to Continuous Improvement

Presentations to various campus groups have been an essential component of our communication plan. As a result, we are able to get feedback on the Student Success Dashboard and hear directly from our users about future development requests. Many of our analyses begin with data from just one or two CSU campuses. However, through these presentations, we have been able to secure data from multiple campuses to conduct analyses. An example of this is work on the impact of Summer Bridge programs on retention and graduation. We began with a handful of campuses providing us with their program information; this allowed other CSU campuses to see the value in our work. Eventually, they requested that their Summer Bridge data also be added to the analysis.

To maintain open communication with our users, we have implemented a feedback button that has generated requests—particularly from faculty—for additional data. One of our challenges had been deciding the strategic value of these requests and determining our role in providing this information. For example, we've been asked many times to provide data at the student level. We feel that our role is to develop and share insightful aggregate analyses, but that individual, student-level research should be conducted at the campus.

Conclusion

Data dashboards will most likely play a major role in helping colleges and universities make evidence-based decisions about a wide variety of issues impacting the student life cycle. For campuses that have made the decision to implement data dashboards designed to help them understand and improve student success at their institutions, there are many factors to consider. This chapter has outlined a number of these issues, including developing a student success framework, gaining support from top leadership, using data analytics with a focus on actionable variables to better understand influences on timely degree completion, and catering to a wide variety of campus stakeholders. Campuses that are on sustained improvement trajectories have often made the transition from seeing the demographics of their students as destiny to understanding that they can reshape their student success rates. The recommendations made here are designed to facilitate the development of a dashboard that engages users, identifies salient issues, fosters a culture of inquiry, and encourages targeted action to improve student success.

References

Chronicle of Higher Education. (2015). *Student success: Building a culture for retention and completion on college campuses.* Retrieved from https://www.pdx.edu/president/sites/www.pdx.edu.president/files/The%20top%20trends%20and%20practices%20for%20college%20student%20retention%20and%20completion.pdf

Dennis, J. M., Phinney, J. S., & Chuateco, L. I. (2005). The role of motivation, parental support, and peer support in the academic success of ethnic minority first-generation students. *Journal of College Student Development, 22*(3), 223–236.

Eduventures. (2013). *Predictive analytics in higher education: Data-driven decision-making for the student life cycle* [White paper]. Retrieved from http://www.eduventures.com/wp-content/uploads/2013/02/Eduventures_Predictive_Analytics_White_Paper1.pdf

Few, S. (2016). Data visualization and human perception. In M. Soegaard & R. F. Dam (Eds.), *The Encyclopedia of Human-Computer Interaction* (2nd ed.). Retrieved from https://www.interaction-design.org/literature/book/the-encyclopedia-of-human-computer-interaction-2nd-ed/data-visualization-for-human-perception

Norris, D., Baer, L., Leonard, J., Pugliese, L., & Lefrere, P. (2008). Action analytics: Measuring and improving performance that matters in higher education. *Educause Review, January/February,* 42–67.

Offenstein, J., Moore, C., & Shulock, N. (2010). *Advancing by degrees: A framework for increasing college completion.* Retrieved from http://edtrust.org/wp-content/uploads/2013/10/AdvbyDegrees_0.pdf

Terenzini, P. T., Springer, L., Yaeger, P. M., Pascarella, E. T., & Nora, A. (1996). First-generation college students: Characteristics, experiences, and cognitive development. *Research in Higher Education, 37,* 1–22.

Yeado, J., Haycock, K., Johnstone, R., & Chaplot, P. (2014, January). Learning from high-performing and fast-gaining institutions. *The Education Trust: Higher education practice guide.* Retrieved from http://edtrust.org/wp-content/uploads/2013/10/PracticeGuide1.pdf

Zalaquett, C. P. (1999). Do students of noncollege-educated parents achieve less academically than students of college-educated parents? *Psychological Reports, 85*(2), 417–421.

NEW AND EMERGING FRAMEWORKS FOR DECISION ANALYTICS

A Data Governance Perspective

Ronald L. Huesman Jr. and Steve A. Gillard

Completing *US News* and Integrated Postsecondary Education Data System (IPEDS) surveys, responding to internal ad hoc requests for data, and developing accountability and accreditation reports are among the more standard "bread and butter" activities of most institutional research (IR) shops. These traditional IR compliance/reporting activities have a common theme: To be completed well, they require a solid foundation of data sources, analytic skills, and the right tools to access and query the institution's data systems. These same data sources, skills, and systems form the foundation for *effective analytics*, defined as the marriage between "large data sets, statistical techniques, and predictive modeling. It could be thought of as the practice of mining institutional data to produce 'actionable intelligence'" (Campbell, DeBlois, & Oblinger, 2007, p. 42).

Why Decision Analytics?

Institutions are faced with the daunting task of meeting growing demands for data, information, and analytics from across the institution. While there has been measurable growth on the demand side for actionable insight, so too have there been changes in the scope, volume, and complexity of reporting and analytical needs from all levels of the organization. These changes have been fed by the evolution of a slowly changing institutional culture that is steadily moving to an evidence-based and data-supported mode of operation. This evolution to an evidence-based culture has passed the tipping point in higher education and is now part of the institutional fabric seen through the integration of decision analytics with existing management processes that include resource allocation, program review, strategic long-term planning, and day-to-day decision-making.

The evolution to a data-driven culture has placed enormous pressure on institutions and the units within them to more fully integrate data, reporting, and analysis into management and evaluation processes. This type of data-informed decision-making that leads to action is a higher order progression of IR functions—where data are turned into meaningful, useful, and relevant institutional knowledge through analysis and interpretation that can be provided to decision makers (Leimer, 2012). Figure 10.1 illustrates this ideal strategic institutional knowledge superstructure: The foundation not only allows the institution to be effective in complying with basic institutional data needs but also expands beyond to conduct analytics that support institutional effectiveness and planning efforts.

Traditional IR activities have formed the foundation of this superstructure; however, it is no longer sufficient to simply conduct compliance reporting. With increasing frequency, IR staff are called upon to assist in developing research questions and goals, identifying and developing multiple data sources, and conducting the necessary studies needed to turn data into actionable information and institutional knowledge (i.e., decision analytics).

Figure 10.1. Ideal institutional knowledge strategic superstructure.

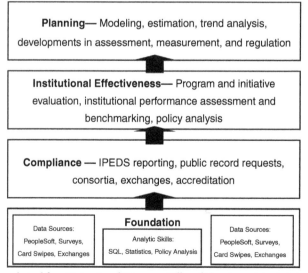

Source: Structure derived from University of Minnesota Office of Planning and Analysis internal strategic planning memo (Internal demo, August 2012).

One example of this work includes examining the effectiveness of transfer student orientation on students' sense of belonging and using those findings to help inform program revisions. Another example includes conducting analyses of exposure to high-impact educational practices (e.g., a writing-enriched curriculum program) as it relates to undergraduates' development of critical thinking skills and then highlighting those efforts in deciding to expand the program across the campus or not. Both are examples of the types of institutional program and initiative assessment work that IR staff encounter in this arena. These studies may access existing data sources from traditional sources (e.g., central records); however, more often than not, these efforts also incorporate nontraditional, large, and structurally complex data sources (e.g., card swipe data, advising systems, learning assessment results, etc.) into these analyses. The complexity and breadth of questions facing institutional decision makers in this age of diminishing public resources and increased accountability requires collaboration; therefore, the old saying "many hands make light work" holds true here.

While that "someone" is often an IR representative, another "someone" has entered the picture. As more and more data become available and as the tools and technology become easier to use, nontraditional players in this space can more easily access, manipulate, and present data, reporting, and analytics within their own unit or program. This evolution has opened the space to new and nontraditional producers as well as consumers of reporting and analytics. The change in supply of unit level reporting and analysis has significantly increased the demand within units across the institution and the expansion of nontraditional decision makers is changing the landscape as it challenges the traditional service model for those units and groups initially charged to own and support this space. These changes are the source of organizational friction that can be seen through the emergence of new structures and organizational models that more effectively align with a new class of producers and consumers of decision analytics.

In such a decentralized environment of IR functions—to the extent that institutions have a uniform understanding of data definitions, access to data sources, and a global understanding of the mission and goals of the institution—the entire organization should move more coherently toward meeting its missions and goals. Swing and Ross (2016) described this shift as a *federation network* model of IR whereby IR plays a crucial leadership role in making certain this understanding occurs, groups are working in tandem, and other units within the institution are contributing to the whole in a strategic manner. But, just as "many hands make light work," the saying "too many cooks spoil the broth" could apply as well: To the extent that data definitions are not well defined, rules around appropriate usage are ambiguous, and there is a lack of coordination among analyses and units, the institution will not progress toward meeting its goals in the most effective and efficient manner. A "head cook" from central IR or a similar office is needed to keep the broth from being ruined.

The reduction in barriers to institutional data used in reporting along with the availability of effective, easy-to-use analytic tools has led to the establishment of distributed data shops across the institution that continues today. It is important to recognize that this distributed nature of data, reporting, and analysis is part of a natural maturity continuum that organizations need to go through. Until this process is complete, organizational redesign will be a source of ongoing institutional stress. This institutional stress continues through the emergence of a new organizational model that at its core seeks to foster a culture of active participation and shared responsibility throughout the university community.

Emergent organizational models tend to expose where the gaps and critical unmet needs in systems, process, and skill sets exist. A more distributed model of decision analytics is no different, and its development has associated risks that require attention. For example, simply providing access to raw data fails to address the downstream needs of practitioners who are working to address the needs of those they support. Developing the institutional capacity for a shared understanding about data, what is available, how to request access, how to use the data, and who to contact for help are all part of the landscape for effective distributed decision analytics. These data governance aspects are only one part of the host of implications of distributed analytics. There is also the need to develop and support people as well as groups who work in reporting to ensure an effective foundation of core services and systems exist for developing a community of data practitioners.

The tools we use to create these analytics—whether arising from basic pivot tables, reports, or dashboards created by the newest data visualization tools (e.g., Tableau) or by analytics created by IBM's Watson artificial intelligence algorithm utilizing big data—all require the ability to capture data from heterogeneous sources; therefore, having the frameworks in place to reliably curate said sources is essential. The adage "garbage in, garbage out" from first-year statistical courses still applies today with decision analytics.

In order to reduce the garbage and increase the likelihood that information will be used, it is imperative to develop an intentional structure around the data that includes how it is used and prioritized on campus. The process of getting good data into the system, maintaining those data once captured, identifying data to collect, operationalizing data definitions, and then making data available through analytical communities of practice for the common good is the essential foundation for institutional and student success.

The following example highlights what our institution, the University of Minnesota, has done to provide governance, create a system for oversight, and build the necessary support structures for an emerging community of data and reporting practitioners at an enterprise level. The example is intended to illustrate how our institution has positioned itself to capitalize on its significant investments in data management and reporting infrastructure.

The University of Minnesota

The University of Minnesota has developed an enterprise data management and reporting (EDMR) strategy for the institution. The primary focus of this strategy is to address administrative and operational data management and reporting needs, including issues of data quality and integrity. The primary audiences are the producers of data, reports, and analyses, as well as the consumers of data assets (e.g., raw data, reports, charts, analyses, dashboards, and visualizations). These primary audiences include faculty, staff, and students who have direct access to university systems. Secondary audiences include those who have indirect access to university data, such as external agencies and the public.

This effort is led by the university's data custodian and director of the analytics collaborative (AC), who provides leadership for data governance and develops collaborative analytic capacity across the university. The AC engages in making significant advancements in reporting and analytic capabilities, sharing knowledge, skills development, and identifying new analytical tools and techniques. The AC is focused on meeting the many and varied needs of a traditional data-rich and information-poor end user base.

In order to integrate decision analytics as a discipline and have it succeed across campus, it is necessary to imagine a new framework. Enterprise-wide data management and collaborative analytics as an organizational structural framework fulfills that need. Having such a framework in place provides the underlying structure for any effective decision analytics on our campuses. Although perhaps not as exciting as the new emerging analytical tools, it is an essential and a key component to increase the use of analytics to inform decision-making that yields resource optimization and allocation.

Working collaboratively to bring together disparate but functionally aligned groups across campus to leverage information assets, share results, and disseminate best practices with analytical communities improves confidence and collaboration that supports the institution's efforts to achieve the *full* value of the organization's data. Such a culture change provides the ability to turn data into actionable information and institutional knowledge used in decision analytics; however, before we can get to operations, it behooves us to create a structural foundation in order to increase the chance of success.

Organization and Governance Framework

The drive to address the need for the right information to the right person, in the right format, at the right time has led to innovations contributing to the emergence of a new organizational and governance model for effective data management and governance framework (see Figure 10.2). This model consists of multiple levels, with each having a specific purpose contributing to the overall framework. This organizational and governance structure is foundational to achieving a shared vision around successfully delivering decision analytics to institutional stakeholders. The same model is also extended to address the information needs of key external stakeholders, which is accomplished through a self-service model for reporting that is considered public and delivered through the IR office. Figure 10.2 is an example of an organization and governance structure that lays the foundation for effective data, reporting, and analysis activities that support decision analytics across the enterprise.

This organizational structure enables the execution and support of decision analytics strategies by taking in projects and moving them through the development life cycle to the end delivery state, steps that require a shared development and delivery strategy for enterprise reporting and analytics.

Figure 10.2. EDMR framework.

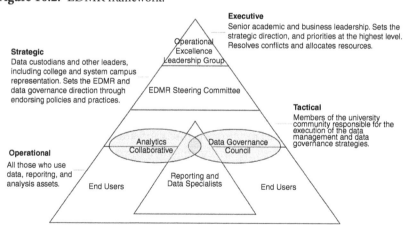

Building such capacity takes time and the formation of key foundational layers. The layers, as shown in Figure 10.2, are highlighted in this organizational structure:

1. *Executive or enterprise oversight layer.* Made up of senior academic and institutional leadership, this layer is involved with setting the strategic direction and priorities at the highest level. This group resolves conflicts and allocates resources.
2. *Strategic layer.* This layer is composed of thought leaders across the university, institutional unit leadership, and others, including college and system campus representation. This group sets the decision analytics and governance direction through endorsing policies, establishing practices, and setting operational priorities.
3. *Tactical layer.* This layer includes members of the university community responsible for the execution of the decision analytics strategies through building and supporting the core enterprise processes, building and supporting the community, and by advancing project work through the analytics pipeline.
4. *Operational layer.* This layer of the model is where consumers of all types connect with reporting and analytics solutions to address their decision-making needs. Consisting of members of the community as well as users and practitioners of decision analytic assets, this level is where decisions are made and where the cumulative effect of those decisions begin.

Each of the layers outlined in the EDMR framework in Figure 10.2 requires planning, oversight, targeted communications, and training.

Groups Within the Organizational Structure

The Operational Excellence Leadership Group provides the campus-wide leadership role and includes the university president; chief of staff to the president; and the senior leadership of human resources, health sciences, academic affairs and provost, research, internal audits, budget and finance, information technology, and facilities.

The role of the EDMR Steering Committee is to provide overall direction and strategic guidance to the university's EDMR efforts, including setting the overall direction and approving the mission, scope, and core components of the AC and general data and reporting agenda. In addition, this group is tasked with setting the data governance direction by endorsing policies and practices that affect the production, quality, usability, and security of data used throughout the university. The group has strategic responsibilities to approve university data definitions, data governance program decision-making, and issue resolution. The EDMR Steering Committee consists of 15 members of the university community that includes representation from the controller's office, registrar, human resources, university services, research, information technology, general council, and representatives from system campuses and colleges. All members of the Committee have a voice in decision-making, which impacts the direction and focus of the institution's data management and reporting strategy.

The AC provides operational oversight and coordination for the EDMR initiative and support and structure for the university's data community, including analysts and end users. The university has an opportunity to capitalize on its significant investment in data management and reporting technical infrastructure. To translate this opportunity into practice, the university established the AC. By facilitating EDMR initiatives and providing a consistent support model, the AC serves a critical quality control and coordinating function by ensuring that information and best practices are maintained, communicated, and shared throughout the university.

The mission of the AC is to inspire innovation, cooperation, and collaboration of data management and reporting to advance the university's commitment to excellence by leveraging the full value of its data, reporting, and information assets. Totaling roughly 50 people, the membership of the AC consists of a blend of those from central offices as well as those who work in units across the university as practitioners of reporting and analytics. While AC membership includes volunteers from across the university, it is important that those with information technology skills, analytic skills, and business skills are represented. Specific competencies and experience include knowledge of data analysis, tools, and business needs; coding and data modeling, data integration skills, documentation skills, understanding of the data and statistical analysis; and subject matter expertise in finance, human resources, and student, research, or physical assets. The AC advances its agenda through monthly meetings as well as participating in projects that have been endorsed by the EDMR Steering Committee.

The data governance council (DGC) is made up of 16 people and is charged to operationalize the university's data governance program and contribute to the mission, strategies, and objectives of the university by helping to transform data into a valuable institutional asset used for planning, decision-making, and meeting operational needs across the university. This is done by improving the availability, understanding, and usefulness of data used throughout the university.

The DGC mission is to develop and foster a culture of active participation and shared responsibility among members of the university community to establish a unified, enterprise-wide view of the understanding, usability, quality, availability, and security of university data.

Members of the DGC are selected and approved by the EDMR Steering Committee and are made up of data stewards and subject matter experts from each of the core business verticals of the university (e.g., central finance, human resources, student, research, facilities) including central information technology and with representation from the office of IR. The skills helpful for members to take full advantage of their participation include understanding of data structures and their use, subject matter expertise, knowledge of the legal implications of sharing data, familiarity with policies and practices related to sharing and managing data, and cross functional understanding of institutional data.

Reporting and data specialists (RADS) are members from across the university located in administrative and collegiate units (e.g., budget managers, data analysts, information technology professionals, and key contacts for student, human resources, and finance) who are key personnel responsible for building, leading, maintaining or providing data management, and reporting services to others in their respective units. Due to the diversity of units and their respective needs for reporting services, members of the RADS group will likely be members of other groups under the EDMR umbrella as well.

The purpose of the RADS network, which consists of roughly 150 people with representation from every unit and campus across the university, is to develop an active and engaged membership that is representative of the university community empowered to help achieve EDMR-related objectives. RADS network members are the first point of contact for data and reporting activities in their respective unit and as such provide communication updates to members of their local unit. Specific goals include alpha/beta testing of reporting and analytics content, providing the voice of the community on data and reporting issues, participating on project teams related to integrating reporting standards within local units, and helping identify local resources to bring to specific projects. This growing network of practitioners and key contacts should be viewed as an extension of existing EDMR groups (e.g., AC and DGC) in that they are an important component of advancing the goals of EDMR.

Foundational Processes

For an institution's decision analytics strategy to succeed, there are several core foundational processes that need to be established. Following is a list of processes that need to be developed and supported through the organizational and governance structure already described. These foundational processes need to be effective and adequately supported to provide the necessary enabling capabilities to ensure ongoing success of the decision analytics strategy, and include

- governance and oversight (e.g., project prioritization, direction setting);
- a full range of data governance initiatives;
- project intake and prioritization;
- thought leadership for the decision analytics;
- standard process for development and delivery of analytics solutions;
- training and knowledge transfer;
- community building, support, and stakeholder management;
- communications-related support structure;
- development and ongoing attention to key partnerships and relationships; and
- project management and oversight.

Developing a Shared Vision

A clear vision for enterprise decision analytics is essential for long-term success. This vision statement should describe the desired end state, a single sentence describing the clear and inspirational long-term desired change resulting from the institution's work in the decision analytics space. The vision statement should set the direction for driving the work necessary to define the concrete institutional goals resulting from implementing the vision. An example of a vision statement developed for EDMR might be "To develop an enterprise information management capacity that can deliver the right data, at the right time, for the right decision." The vision statement articulates the high-level concrete institutional problem to solve along with an associated institutional outcome highlighting how institutional value will be generated. In addition, initiatives and efforts coming from executing the vision should contribute to organizational goals and address several key areas, including adapting over time to changing institutional and/or higher education conditions, clarifying what improvements the institution will see after the decision analytics change, and illustrating how accrued institutional outcomes will align to the mission, goals, and strategy of the institution over time. In general, initiatives that align to the vision should contribute directly to the institution's mission and goals.

Developing a Strategy

Once the shared vision has been refreshed, an executive planning team should develop an enterprise strategy for achieving the vision. The decision analytics strategy answers the questions of who will be involved, what they will accomplish, and how it will be accomplished. The *who* refers to the leadership, governance, and supporting organization of the decision analytics strategy. The *what* refers to the institutional objectives that will be addressed by executing the strategy, and the *how* highlights the structural and technical aspects of the strategy that defines the systems, standards, policies, procedures, processes, and organizational structure needed to execute the decision analytics plan. An effective decision analytics enterprise strategy will address these three critical points and enable the program planning phase to be fully informed.

The enterprise-wide strategy is critical as it provides the framework for the institution going forward and describes how an enterprise will leverage the benefits of decision analytics leading to the success of the institution. In addition, the decision analytics strategy will outline how an enterprise can achieve its institution goals by maximizing the benefits to the institution.

A necessary part of the strategy includes a three- to five-year plan or roadmap that illustrates the multiyear expansion of the decision analytics program, focusing on the build out and delivery of critical program infrastructure and capabilities in addition to the delivery of prioritized projects to the institution.

Identification of Focus Areas

Once the foundational work is complete, including the creation of the vision, strategy, and the organizational and governance structures to support and sustain the decision analytics program, it is necessary to build the capacity to determine high-value focus areas. These efforts to identify focus areas are what make the planning around decision analytics come alive and are essential for creating organizational momentum. The identification of high-value focus areas is an exercise facilitated by both institutional stakeholders and the technical team that develops decision analytics solutions for the institution. A repeatable, consistent, systematic process is needed to determine projects that offer the best institutional value that are also feasible from a technical and resource perspective.

The following steps highlight the process for the identification of focus areas that lead to achievable (feasible) high-value projects.

1. Conduct strategic sessions with institutional stakeholders (process owners) to determine
   a. High-value processes that are good candidates for decision analytics
   b. A high-level institutional case for potential projects
   c. A use case grid to identify the most common or high-value projects

2. Conduct technical sessions to frame the required work to achieve the outcomes from strategic sessions

3. Map out all steps of delivering the solution (the end-to-end process-development model)

   a. Define institutional needs to easily visualize the end state and the path to achieve goals

   b. Combine the results of the strategic sessions with the technical sessions to determine

      i. The institutional (business) impact score

      ii. The feasibility (time and feasibility) score

4. Based on the results of the scoring in #3, complete the business/institutional impacts versus feasibility matrix, as shown in Figure 10.3

5. Develop a project prioritization portfolio to be presented to the institutional sponsor and/or a decision analytics leadership team or steering committee for approval

This process would be driven and supported by a decision analytics project review team appointed by either the decision analytics institutional sponsor or a leadership team for decision analytics. The outcomes of these efforts produce a prioritized list of projects to be reviewed and approved through the governance structure put in place for enterprise decision analytics. Examples of priority projects identified through this process as shown on the matrix in Figure

Figure 10.3. Business impact versus feasibility of decision analytics recommendations (EXAMPLE ONLY).

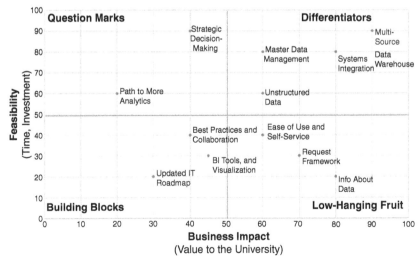

10.3 include the multisource data warehouse, information about data, and updated information technology roadmap. While these are all important projects, the matrix clearly illustrates the differences in business value versus feasibility of each project. This visual analysis allows for decision makers to more easily make an informed decision about project priorities for the institution.

Figure 10.3 (based on the matrix in Goldner, 2016) illustrates the results of the strategic sessions conducted by our institution to determine organizational value and the technical sessions conducted by the technical service team charged to deliver the solution. The intent of the matrix is to provide the decision analytics project review team with an easy way to assess tradeoffs between institutional value and the feasibility of delivering a given solution.

Opportunities and Challenges

The challenge is ensuring coordination of efforts and continuous monitoring to promote efficient usage of resources that maximize effectiveness of the institution's analytic efforts that align with institutional goals and objectives. The sustainability of such efforts is likely to fail in the long term without the appropriate organizational structure and leadership in place.

There are a number of issues that need to be considered in assessing the opportunities and challenges of working toward an effective and sustainable enterprise decision analytics strategy. Those range from access to data to whom to call for help with reporting questions. The following outline lists factors to be considered when institutions are contemplating a path toward enterprise decision analytics. The items on this list should be viewed as foundational capacity areas that need to be addressed through the planning process to ensure the opportunities they present do not turn into challenges down the road.

Access to Data

One of the fundamental challenges institutions face is ensuring that access to data is opened effectively in a way that does not cause unnecessary delays or barriers, while at the same time preserving the necessary security. Balancing costs with risks and productivity with security are key considerations in this area.

Communicating What is Available

The data, reporting, and analytics landscape is broad and often complex, which offers opportunities to those charged as stewards in this space to share what is available with the community they serve through effective communications. These communications or knowledge transfers can take many forms (e.g., e-mail, workshops, campus labs, knowledge base content).

Understanding of What is Available

Data, reporting, and analysis assets are available to people who do not fully understand what they have access to or how best to use it. This scenario is a training opportunity to help the community more fully understand what is available and how best to use what is available.

Whom to Call For Help

Systems and processes need to be put in place to address people's need for a support or help line when they have questions. The challenge is to offer an effective, scalable service that addresses the issues and questions people have around analytics.

Thought Leadership

Developing and sustaining thought leadership around enterprise decision analytics is essential for successful strategy creation and execution. It is also critically important to organizations in making the inevitable adjustments in midflight to keep an analytics strategy on track and moving forward.

Democratizing Decision Analytics

There are several organizational challenges when embracing a decision analytics strategy that involves a federated model of support, usage, and content creation. This is a great opportunity to build a foundation that allows data service providers and consumers to not only get their respective work done but also enrich their own efforts through awareness and collaboration with others across the institution.

Innovation of Decision Analytics

One of the great opportunities of a federated model for analytics content development that extends to consumer self-service is the nurturing, identification, and advancement of the innovative work units from across the university, which are developing through a distributed development model. These steps enable the best ideas from every corner of the institution to potentially advance through the governance process to be scaled up into an enterprise solution.

Prioritization Process for Decision Analytics

Establishing an enterprise prioritization process for data, reporting, and analytics projects is a necessary core function that enables projects to be identified, collected, reviewed, and prioritized for inclusion into the work plans of project teams charged to develop and deliver the solutions.

Alignment With Institutional Goals, Strategies, and Objectives

Long-term program success is largely dependent on how well the analytics strategy, goals, and deliverables align with and/or complement those of a given institution. The key outcomes of analytics must have a positive impact on the mission of the institution (e.g., student success) and address concrete institutional outcomes to be successful.

Reaching Critical Mass of Analytical Capabilities

Achieving the tipping point in the institution's decision analytics strategy related to critical mass of analytics capabilities is one of the greatest opportunities for fully embracing the distributed model for analytics content development.

Building in Process Assessment

Determining if a given initiative or set of initiatives is working, along with making the appropriate adjustments, is part of the function of the organizational structure that advances the work of decision analytics.

Overcoming Organizations in Transition

Most organizations and universities are in the middle of some type of transition, which could be a huge enterprise upgrade project, major changes to core services, or executive-level strategic planning. Any number of things could distract the institution from focusing on decision analytics and affect the cycle time to get the job complete, which is why it is necessary to deliver some early wins (e.g., getting key content to the desktop) at the same time the core foundation is being built.

Disincentives Caused By Organizational Structure

For a federated model for decision analytics to work, it is necessary to understand that ongoing collaboration and engagement by contributors are needed. It is essential for ongoing success of the overall strategy that a culture of active participation and shared responsibility throughout the organization is established and supported. In general, from our experiences, the organizational structure currently in place across many institutions of higher education is not set up to reward individuals who participate on cross-functional teams. An individual on a cross-functional team very often does not officially report to the manager of that team. Rather, the reporting lines and thus the reward structure for an individual is through the home department and not the cross-functional work team. To enable nontraditional work teams to fully engage, it will be necessary to address the disincentives that exist for those who participate on cross-functional teams. Finding ways of changing the current organizational structure to allow participants to be rewarded or incentivized will be necessary for long-term success.

This list offers a set of key points to consider when assessing both the opportunities and challenges of a federated model for enterprise decision analytics. To support a successful strategy in this area, it is essential to develop a governance and supporting organizational structure that addresses these opportunities and challenges. In many ways, these could be considered success measures or criteria for your distributed enterprise decision analytics program.

Summary

The EDMR framework as outlined could fill its own volume; the brief version provided here is intended only to give the reader a high-level overview. This is one institution's understanding of the foundational role data governance plays in good decision analytics and that broader analytical collaboration aligned with the institution's goals and objectives should be embraced. It is a work in progress and our understanding is evolving, but we recognize that in an environment of diminishing resources and increased accountability, our abilities to efficiently utilize existing resources, work collaboratively, and identify high-value analytic projects in a systematic and structured manner are critical. The process as outlined is flexible in that it allows for individual units and programs to determine their own data, reporting, and analytical needs. At the same time, it provides a structure for the institution to create a collaborative analytical environment. This is one institution's approach for marshalling central efforts as well as aligning unit and program efforts toward a cohesive whole.

References

Campbell, J. P., DeBlois, P. B., & Oblinger, D. G. (2007). Academic analytics: A new tool for a new era. *EDUCAUSE Review, July/August*, 40–57.

Goldner, J.(2016). *BI prioritization matrix*. Retrieved from http://www .universebridge.com/insights/your-consultant-and-you

Leimer, C. (2012). Organizing for evidence-based decision making and improvement. *Change: The Magazine of Higher Learning, 44*(4), 45–51.

Swing, R. L., & Ross, L. (2016). A new vision for institutional research. *Change: The Magazine of Higher Learning, 44*(2), 6–13.

EXAMINING HOW THE ANALYTICS REVOLUTION MATTERS TO HIGHER EDUCATION POLICYMAKERS

Data Analytics, Systemness, and Enabling Student Success

Jason E. Lane

A multifaceted tidal wave of data is quickly approaching higher education. Significant resources are being dedicated to linking together once-siloed data sets. Institutions are working to link data across administrative departments such as human resources, finance, and the registrar. Multicampus higher education systems are working to aggregate data across multiple sites. Some states are stitching together statewide longitudinal data systems (SLDS), combining data from K–12, higher education, and labor agencies. Much of this effort is being driven by a federal ban on creating a student unit record (SUR) system, forcing states and other entities interested in understanding the lived experiences of students from cradle to career to create their own SURs.

In addition to the move toward SUR systems, traditional data about students are also being augmented with a student's digital footprint, which can include information about the student's online behaviors, interactions with online course materials, and even how often students enter certain buildings or attend student activities. This data collection means that student profiles will no longer be based only on historic data, but increasingly on real-time information harvested daily from nontraditional data sources such as social media sites, course management systems, and student ID databases (Fonseca

& Marcinkowski, 2014; Lane, 2014; Wildavsky, 2014). Expanding access to new types of data and better linking of existing data will transform the work of institutional researchers and is already proving to have an influence on institutional decision makers and state-level policymakers.

The reality is that this tidal wave of data is approaching as many institutional research (IR) offices remain underfunded and focused largely on data reporting, not data analytics. And while IR offices struggle to adapt to this data analytics revolution, policymakers, at the institutional and state levels, are demanding more—more data and more insight from the data already available. Descriptive data that explain what happened or why it may have happened are no longer sufficient. Now, institutional leaders want to understand in real time how a student is faring from cradle to career and are increasingly expecting their institutions to provide interventions to help struggling students before they fail.

This chapter unpacks the ensuing tension that exists between the data world and the policy world—exploring how the availability of data is pushing development of better policies, understanding how the demand for data by policymakers is forcing IR offices to expand their data warehouses and analytics capabilities, and looking at how to leverage data to create policy environments supportive of student success. The chapter presents the argument that the historic focus on the institution, rather than on the student, creates a spiderweb of policies that at best fail to effectively support the success of modern college students and, at worst, actively inhibit their success. The intention here is to provide a high-level overview and introduction of the topic at hand, as it is not possible within the boundaries of this chapter to thoroughly address all the issues associated with the changing data landscape.

Five Types of Data Available to Policymakers

The types of data available to IR offices dictate the types of questions that can be answered, which in turn influences the types of policies that are created. We are now very much in a transformational period for IR as new types of data and data analysis are becoming available. Figure 11.1 provides the five primary types of data that can be produced by IR offices and made available to policymakers. The two boxes in the gray area to the left represent the data types widely available from IR offices presently: descriptive and diagnostic. The backbone of many IR offices is the descriptive data that is collected, much of it about students—demographic as well as academic performance details. Much of the analysis of these data is based on the institution or aggregated student numbers rather than the individual student. Such descriptive

Figure 11.1. Types of data available to policymakers.

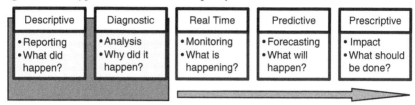

data can then be used, at least in part, to analyze a myriad of diagnostic questions such as why certain students complete a degree while others do not. This type of data was incredibly important in the 1980s and 1990s as modern IR functions were beginning to be developed because it allowed administrators and policymakers insights about their institution and the students they were serving. In many ways, these data were revolutionary at the time, as prior to their development almost no institution-wide data were available to decision makers.

The descriptive and diagnostic data led to better policies, but policies that were based on the past and did not necessarily reflect the current or future needs of students (Jones, 1996; Rice, 2011). Reflective of a growing demand for more real-time data to actively monitor progress, new communication platforms such as data dashboards[1] emerged in the 2000s to help public sector organizations more effectively measure and manage performance against goals as well as respond to accountability concerns (Eckerson, 2010).

The idea behind the dashboards was simple: to make data more easily accessible and more current in order to increase organizational transparency among a broad array of stakeholders. IR offices were largely the backbone of these efforts in higher education, providing the data that made the dashboards possible. The early dashboards opened up access to information to many who did not previously have it, but the data remained static and mostly historic. This limitation, in turn, drove demands for more real-time (e.g., monitoring) data, forcing institutions to find new ways to track, cost of attendance, first-year retention rates, enrollment numbers, diversity of matriculated students, and so forth. Ongoing concerns about the lack of data transparency as well as growing pressure to measure the value of higher education led the report of the Spellings Commission (Secretary of Education's Commission on the Future of Higher Education, 2006) to call on the U.S. Department of Education to

> collect data and provide information in a common format so that interested
> parties can create a searchable, consumer-friendly database that provides

access to institutional performance and aggregate student outcomes in a secure and flexible format. (pp. 20–21)

Many aspects of the Spellings Commission failed to gain political traction, but the creation of easily accessible data displays to monitor progress in higher education emerged in piecemeal fashion across the nation. Higher education systems in Minnesota, Kentucky, and Georgia, for example, took the lead in publishing user-friendly performance data online (Aldeman & Carey, 2009), and in 2015, nearly a decade after the Spellings Commission report, the U.S. Department of Education launched a college scorecard to provide students and parents with easy access to information about an institution's average annual cost, graduation rates, and salaries of alumni. This idea of making data public and transparent has now come to permeate the higher education ecosystem, raising the expectations on IR shops across the country.

The monitoring movement was only the precursor to the larger tidal wave that is approaching. Now that the higher education sector has been able to more effectively monitor its progress, the expectation is shifting toward prediction. As the concept of *big data* overtook many industries, some in higher education began to wonder how all these new data points could be used to predict the behavior of students—not at the aggregate level, but at the individual level (Lane, 2014).

Access to these new data and new analytical methods has led many organizations to rethink basic assumptions about how they do business. For example, Netflix, which was a pioneer in studying user data to predict which movies its subscribers may like to see next, filed a patent for anticipatory product shipping. This process uses an algorithm to predict which movies users would be likely to select to view next and then shipping it to them before they actually make the selection (Matyszczky, 2014). Such analytic-driven strategies are not limited to the business sector. Predictive analytics are now being used to target how to distribute resources to the homeless (Harkinson, 2016), predict where fires may start (Rieland, 2015), and improve traffic flow (Hungerford, 2016).

Some context is required to understand the size of this oncoming tidal wave of data. According to Miller and Chapin (2013), the world produced about five exabytes of information from the dawn of civilization to 2003. At the time of this writing, humans produced that same amount of information in less than two days. One exabyte is roughly equivalent to 4,000 times the entire content of the Library of Congress (Manyika et al., 2011). These data include everything from Twitter tweets to student usage of online learning platforms. This amount of data provides fertile ground for better understanding of how to improve institutional effectiveness and student success, and many other sectors have already used it transform how they operate. In fact, we now commonly hear about *smarter cities, smarter hospitals*, and even a *smarter world*, yet there has been little attention given to how this analytics revolution could support the creation of a *smarter college*, a *smarter university*, or a *smarter higher education system*.

An early example of the predictive analytics in higher education came from Arizona State University, which developed an eAdvisor program to monitor student progress by using data from social networks, learning management systems, student ID usage, and other data sets to identify patterns of behavior that might indicate a student being at risk of not completing a course and/or not returning the next semester and then initiate interventions intended to help keep the student on track toward graduation. In the first three years following eAdvisor's launch in 2008, first-year retention increased from 76% to 84% (Marcus, 2012). Many other campuses and systems have developed similar analytic-based advising opportunities, and many companies have rolled out a range of analytics programs that campuses can now purchase.

This idea of predictive data, which will be followed by prescriptive data, seems to be the leading edge of the tidal wave that is now crashing upon the IR world. To take a step back, it is important to remember that most IR shops continue to be based upon the need to understand historical patterns. Now the shift is to see if those historical patterns can provide a level of prediction of the future. And once there is a general comfort level with prediction, the push will be for prescriptive data that will guide the actions of faculty and staff, as well as institutional policy creation, based upon what the data predict the student might do in the future and what the data suggest might be the best path forward for the student. There are critics of such efforts, and some of the relevant concerns are discussed later in the chapter. However, given the push to move in this direction, particularly given the apparent positive impact on completion rates, it is unlikely that many institutions will be able to resist adopting at least some of these practices.

The move toward prospective data is just beginning, and it is difficult to know its exact implications. What is clear is that both institutional decision makers and policymakers are viewing this type of data as a possible game changer in terms of student success, and early analysis has suggested positive results (see Goff & Shafer, 2014; Rivers & Sebasta, 2016; Wildavsky, 2014). However, there may also be a downside to the growing prevalence of this type of data, and it is important for those using it to be aware of both the potential positive and negative implications. Toward the end of the chapter, I examine some of the potential areas of concern surrounding the use of these new data, particularly as they are used to guide student behaviors. Many of these concerns can be abated if those using the data are aware of the concerns and act to deal with them in the future.

Added Complexities of the Data Tidal Wave: Scope, Scale, and Student Focus

Another important change in the type of data available to institutional researchers and of interest to policymakers (and increasingly demanded by them as well) is being able to link data from individuals across sectors and institutions. This capability means that both the scale and scope of data are changing in such a way that it is increasingly possible to track students from cradle to career, as well as their mobility within sectors. Much of these data are not new data; rather they are being linked in ways that allow for new insights. In addition, these linkages provide a foundation for a new era of analytics focused on individual students, not institutions.

An important piece of the backdrop is that in 2008 the U.S. Congress passed an amendment to the Higher Education Act that blocked the creation of a student unit record (SUR) system at the federal level.[2] This ban works to keep different agencies from linking together data gathered about individuals. For example, agencies such as the Internal Revenue Service (IRS) and Veterans Administration (VA) have detailed information about those filing taxes and serving in the armed services, but this information cannot be linked to information that the U.S. Department of Education has collected about students. Advocates of the ban have raised concerns about a potential breach of privacy, should any or all of this information about an individual be stored in one place and then illegally accessed by hackers. Colleges and universities have also raised concerns that linking information about a student's educational performance and income might create inaccurate or inadequate assessments of the return on the investment made in an individual's education. Such assessments may then be used to unfairly evaluate the value of a college or university.

Because of the federal ban, many states and higher education systems, with the support of the U.S. Department of Education, have been working to create their own SUR systems. The goal of these systems is largely to better understand how students actually experience higher education, unpack the effects of the K–12 experience on their higher education success, and link higher education performance to employment.

The basic idea, as presented in Figure 11.2, is to be able to track individuals across the cradle-to-career pipeline from when they enter school, through a postsecondary educational experience, and into the workforce. Of

Figure 11.2. The cradle-to-career data pipeline.

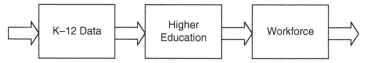

course, for many people, their pipeline is not as linear as the idealized version presented here. We know that there is a great deal of interplay, particularly as individuals move back and forth between higher education and workforce experiences (or pursue both at the same time). However, linking such data together does allow for a more focused analysis of how a student's educational experience impacts his or her success later in life in further educational experience or in the workforce. That said, merely linking the data together is not a silver bullet; the data must be used and used effectively. Many institutions and systems fail to effectively use the data they currently have, let alone figure out how to use an even larger set of data.

It is important to note that gainful employment should not be the only means by which the value of a college experience is evaluated. However, at the moment it is the only unit record data point available in many states and does indicate a certain level of measurable outcome following an educational experience. Should other information become available, such as that collected by the IRS, other variables, such as marital status and charitable giving, could also be analyzed as outcome data. But this information will remain out of reach as long as the federal ban on SUR is in place.

Readers should be aware that creating a state-level SUR is not always easy, either. Many states have also banned sharing data among agencies and, as was the case in New York, higher education leaders first needed to create a legislative and policy environment that supported the sharing of data among agencies. Once the legislative environment was in place, a data sharing agreement needed to be created that would dictate who had access to the shared data, how and for what purposes the data would be used, and what protections were required to safeguard the data. In New York, it took longer to work out an agreeable data-sharing agreement with other agencies than it did to get the legislation changed. Finally, the data infrastructure needs to be created to warehouse the shared data and link the data in a way that matches the individual records together (see Prescott, 2014, for an analysis of efforts to create individual state and multistate SURs.).

Data barriers are being broken down not only between sectors but also within sectors. Let us take the higher education sector as an example. Those working in IR know that higher education is actually full of its own sectors.

We group institutions by level of degree awarded, academic focus, selectivity of student admissions, location, and so forth. Higher education is a sector of sectors. Within those sectors, data are further segmented by institutions, and within institutions, data can be segmented by departments. The new reality of higher education is for those data barriers to be broken down.

The aggregation of data across campuses has been led by multicampus systems and universities. With a single governing board overseeing multiple campuses, the aggregation of data across multiple campuses has long existed. For example, within SUNY, the Office of Institutional Research has collected SUR data for decades. Therefore, in a single location, we annually have data on more than 600,000 students attending 64 campuses—including community colleges, comprehensive colleges, research universities, and a host of specialized institutions such as the Fashion Institute of Technology (FIT) and SUNY Maritime.

These data provide a snapshot into the larger higher education ecosystem as we are able to track students down to their performance in a given course section and across any SUNY institution from the moment they enter SUNY until they leave or graduate. For much of the time these data were collected, it was significantly underused. The data were reported to the Integrated Postsecondary Education Data System (IPEDS) and then sat dormant until a system official or state policymaker asked a question that required analysis of those data. However, over the past decade, this data repository has become a treasure trove of information that we have increasingly used to tell our story, hold campuses accountable for their outcomes, and create a policy environment more conducive to student success.

For example, being able to track students across multiple institutions led SUNY to create a student success metric that followed students no matter where they went in the system. Unlike federal retention and graduation metrics, these measures tracked all students, not just those who started as first-time, full-time students. Also, in the federal measures, if a student leaves the institution prior to graduation, he or she is counted as a failure. In the SUNY student success metric, credit can be given to an institution if the student transfers to another SUNY institution and graduates (rather than drops out entirely). A drawback of the SUNY metric is that it is limited only to SUNY institutions. At the same time SUNY was working to develop its metric, the Association of Public and Land-grant Universities (APLU) created the student achievement measure (SAM) which "tracks student movement across postsecondary institutions to provide a more complete picture of undergraduate student progress and completion within the higher education system" (SAM, 2013). This metric, similar to SUNY's student success metric, merges institutional data and data from the National Student Clearinghouse to track a student's path through all higher education institutions, public and private, two-year and four-year, to determine if the student

1. is still in school at the original institution,
2. completed a degree at the original institution,
3. is progressing toward a degree at another institution,
4. completed a degree at another institution, or
5. exited the higher education pipeline.

Neither SAM nor the SUNY metric is focused on what a student does at a single institution. Rather, they measure performance of a student anywhere in the given data coverage area—giving credit to each institution for its contribution to the student's overall educational performance and not penalizing it for any student who chooses to leave the institution.

SAM and the SUNY metric provide a more holistic understanding of how an institution contributes to a student's academic progression and does not penalize a college or university for students' transferring to other institutions and continuing to make progress toward a degree. Being able to understand the more holistic picture of how the institution is situated on a student's pathway toward degree completion allows institutional policymakers to create environments that support those students, even if they the institution is only a part of the student's overall educational experience.

The Policy Benefits of a SUR Within the Higher Education Sector

The majority of IR offices, and therefore the data they collect, tend to focus on the institution they serve. An inevitable result is that too often we understand only the student experience when the student exists within the boundaries of our institution. However, an increasing number of students are earning credits toward their degrees at more than one institution. In fact, data from SUNY's Office of Institutional Research and Data Analytics reveals that, across the SUNY system, about half the bachelor's graduates and a third of associate's graduates in any given year attend at least two institutions before completing their degree. At the national level, of the 3.6 million students who entered higher education in the United States in 2008, more than one-third (37.6%) attended at least two institutions, and almost half (45%) of those students attended at least three institutions in the subsequent six years (Shapiro, Dundar, Wakhunga, Yuan, & Harrell, 2015).

In recognition of the growing number of student transfers, colleges and universities have implemented articulation agreements in order to stream-line the transfer process from one institution to another. However, these agreements tend to be institution specific, if not program specific, and have resulted in a complicated web of transfer agreements across the nation. For example, since at least 1988, SUNY has required that approval of all new associate and baccalaureate programs across the system have at least two articulation agreements in place. While such agreements are not continually tracked, one can only imagine the number of such agreements, given the more than 7,000 academic programs offered across the system's 64 campuses.

This environment has led to a complex and complicated situation for students. Depending on the articulation agreement, some institutions would accept Biology 100 from one campus but not from another. For those campuses accepting transfer credits, it was up to individual advisers to determine whether the credits would actually count toward the student's degree. This situation resulted in students who had completed 60 hours of credits still needing around 90 to graduate, which meant that a four-year degree turned into a five-year degree. These barriers, and others, often made it difficult for students to transfer and continue successfully toward achievement of their educational goals.

Moreover, when a campus was asked whether its students were transfer-ring, the response was often affirmative; but rarely did the institution know where or whether the students eventually completed their degrees. This lack of knowledge also led to an assumption that most transfer movement was upward, progressing from a community college to a four-year institution. But no one knew for sure. This situation led SUNY officials to ask the IR office for the answer to a very simple question: What is the pattern of student transfer within SUNY? This question could not be answered by any one campus.

The answer to the question, illustrated in Figure 11.3, was quite sur-prising and challenged many assumptions about student mobility. First, the population of students who transfer to a SUNY institution is large, about 60,000 a year. Second, the number of students who transfer within SUNY, more than 30,000 in any given year, exceeded the size of the student body on our largest campus. Third, student mobility is multidirectional, with both community colleges and four-year institutions serving as receiving and sending institutions. In fact, more than 4,000 students each year transfer from a SUNY four-year institution to a community college, and more than 10,000 students transferred horizontally, either from one community col-lege to another community college or from one baccalaureate institution to another baccalaureate institution.

Figure 11.3. Student transfer flows in SUNY.

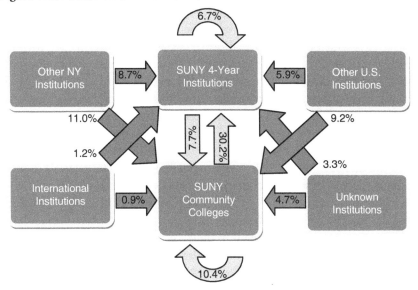

When SUNY policymakers began to realize both the quantity of students transferring within the system and the multidirectional nature of their transfer activity, it became clear that a new policy framework was needed to normalize the transfer process across institutions and enable students to move more seamlessly throughout the system. Using the data gathered about student transfer and evidence-based best practices, the SUNY Board of Trustees passed a new policy that required all institutions to ensure that their academic programs had to

1. be within the designated credit cap limit (i.e., 64 credits for associate's programs and 126 credits for baccalaureate programs),
2. ensure that students were able to complete 7 of the 10 required SUNY general education requirements in their first two years, and
3. design the curriculum so that students can complete a certain number of foundational courses in the major in the first two years.[3]

These curricular revisions were completed prior to the fall 2015 semester and are now available to all students. Sufficient time has not lapsed to allow for analysis of the impact of the policy change, but there already are results from the effort. On many campuses, although programs must be revised periodically, faculty had rarely undertaken a curricular review that focused on ensuring that the curriculum was designed in a way that would encourage success for the growing number of transfer students. In addition, the redesign of the curriculum occurred at the same time as the implementation of a system-wide degree audit platform. As a result, SUNY worked with the platform provider to create a new software module, Transfer Finder, which helps students actively chart their transfer path within SUNY and know exactly what requirements will remain after they transfer. Finally, it fostered new dialogues among faculty from different institutions to share their thinking about curricular design and find areas of commonality.

Much more can be said about SUNY's seamless transfer initiative, but what is important here is that it is a policy framework designed to support student success, enabled and shaped by cross-campus data analysis that is only possible when one has access to a SUR system that tracks students among multiple campuses. Moreover, data served not only a foundational role in the creation of the enabling policy environment but also as a focal point from which to discuss with faculty and others the need for such a policy and the need to redesign the curriculum to support transfer students. Only by showing that the transfer population was so large and demonstrating that many assumptions about transfer patterns were false were we able to implement the new policy.

The next step in the process will be to link student record data from SUNY to data that we are acquiring from the New York State Department of Education and Department of Labor to analyze how K–12 experiences influence students' postsecondary success.

Concerns and Obstacles

This chapter has described the changing data environment in higher education and briefly examines why this changing environment is important for both institutional and state-level policymakers. However, such efforts are not without their detractors, and it is important for anyone associated with efforts to create SURs and embrace predictive and proscriptive analytics to understand these concerns.[4]

Privacy and Security

A fundamental issue that led to the passage of the federal ban on SURs concerns the ability to protect individual data, particularly when it is combined in one location. The use now of a student's digital footprint to augment traditional data makes this concern even more pressing. Data breaches are common occurrences, and all entities that collect and store individual data have an ethical and legal obligation to protect these data to the fullest extent possible. However, disclosure of the type of personal data (e.g., sexual identity, location of employment, patterns of behavior) now being collected and combined could not only put individuals at economic risk but also create significant safety concerns.

Data Integrity

IR offices should consider several data integrity issues. First, unless a common data dictionary is shared by institutions, aggregating student information from multiple campuses may result in combining data that appear similar but are measured differently. Second, the use of data from a student's digital footprint needs to be approached carefully. There is a difference between *generated data*, which are data that represent what an individual does online (e.g., how often he or she logs onto Blackboard), and *volunteered data*, which are the information that students reveal about themselves through social networking sites such as Facebook and Twitter. The problem is that with volunteered data, individuals choose what data they make available to others, and that may represent an "inauthentic digital representation of themselves" (Lane, 2014, p. 19). Third, there are multiple limitations associated with the data sets being tracked by other sectors of which IR practitioners should become aware in the same way that they are familiar with the limitations in their own data sets.

Data Matching

Creating SUR systems necessitates combining data sets in such a way that one can match individual records across the data sets. Unless there is a common unit record identifier, this task can be a daunting process of matching names, addresses, and other information to ensure that matched records are for the same person. Social security numbers (SSNs) are a possible workaround, but not everyone uses them, and sharing them adds a level of security risk if a data set is breached. Indeed, many state regulations still restrict the sharing of SSNs for just this reason. Even within a higher education system, matching records can be difficult if campuses use different identifiers, and no system-wide identification system exists.

Profiling

The ability to track and predict student behavior has both positive and negative implications. For example, microtargeting for the purposes of recruitment may lead institutions away from contact with traditionally underserved populations (Goff & Shaffer, 2014; Rivard, 2013). An attempt to more effectively use limited resources could lead an institution to disengage from outreach to populations that may have not historically attended college but that could benefit from higher education. This type of profiling activity could inadvertently have negative consequences on these underserved populations by making college seem even further out of reach than already perceived. Likewise, new data modeling efforts are being developed to determine which students, once they enter college, are likely to be successful and which are not. The idea is to strategically deploy resources to those students who need them to be successful. However, acting on a prediction that a student may be at risk could lead to less positive actions, such as faculty members not engaging with students they believe will drop out or inappropriately labeling students as at risk and, as a result, having them begin to doubt their abilities to succeed. These examples are broad brushstrokes of potential behaviors, and no concrete data suggest that these behaviors are happening, but such consequences are possible.

Conclusion

Higher education policy is increasingly about what happens to students in the present and not-too-distant future, yet our IR offices have been built to focus on institutions and analyze historical performance of students within those institutions. In part, this is because structures are often shaped by revenue streams, and Title IV funding (federal financial aid) still represents a significant portion of institutional budgets. Therefore, IR offices have largely been structured to respond to federal mandated reporting around institutional data and only a certain cohort of students. This approach, however, has led to a policy environment that is fragmented, too often inhibiting student success rather than enabling it.

So a question remains about how much the oncoming data tidal wave, which is broadening the scope and scale of data now available to IR offices, will push IR offices toward a real focus on organizing data around students rather than institutions. The digital tidal wave is certainly transforming the type of data that are now available to IR offices and policymakers—shifting from descriptive data based on historic patterns to real-time data that allow for active monitoring of activities and eventually to predictive data that will enable campuses to identify potentially at-risk students and actively target interventions to support student success. What remains unseen is whether funding providers, such as state and federal governments, will shift the stipulations around data reporting associated with the receipt of their funding.

The analytics revolution provides opportunities to make microlevel decisions that can improve the success of each student as well as to unpack macrolevel trends that can support the creation of better policy environments. At the macro level, analyzing data gathered from the lived experiences of many students across the educational pipeline has made us more aware that, for example, students now swirl through higher education, increasingly bumping between institutions and accumulating credits that they hope will eventually lead to a degree. These lived experiences of students are now running head-on into postsecondary degrees, institutional policies, and data infrastructures designed for a different era, when students rarely moved between institutions and usually progressed in lockstep from freshman orientation to commencement. In fact, the focus of IR shops on a single institution can leave academic leaders and policymakers with an incomplete view of the myriad ways many students experience higher education and paint an incomplete picture of what student success looks like in higher education. This incomplete view in turn leads to an inadequate policy infrastructure that is unable to create effective policies to support students as they traverse higher education, very often in ways that differ dramatically from how we believe or assume they should experience higher education.

Due to the congressional ban on a federal-level SUR system, states and higher education systems are stepping in to create their own SUR systems—linking data from multiple campuses and across multiple sectors. As demonstrated in the SUNY case, such linked data can challenge existing assumptions about student behavior, in this case about the magnitude and direction of student mobility, as well as challenge the perception of an institution as an isolated island instead of part of a more codependent network. In turn, the information gleaned from the data created an opportunity to adopt and implement a new policy framework that enabled students to transfer more seamlessly between campuses. This example illustrates how the linking of data can create a more holistic understanding of how students actually move through the higher education landscape. In some states that have already linked data from K–12, higher education, and labor, higher education leaders and state policymakers currently can track students from cradle to career. However, at this point, state-level SUR systems are only able to track those students who stay within the state.

Questions from institutional decision makers and state policy leaders are increasingly sophisticated and data-focused. If they have not already, IR offices will be called on to provide more real-time data and learn how to support data-based interventions for student success. IR offices do need to be aware of the concerns around privacy and security as well as data integrity when they are establishing and working with such data sets. They also need to develop the infrastructure to support the data revolution and the analytical capacity necessary to respond to needs of internal and external stakeholders.

Notes

1. For the purposes of readability, I use the term *dashboard* in this chapter as a shorthand for a variety of communications mediums intended to make data more public and transparent.

2. Recent bipartisan efforts in the House and Senate have sought to overturn the federal SUR ban, but the ban remains in place as of this writing.

3. These courses were developed by multi-institutional faculty working groups. The resultant transfer paths are available online at www.suny.edu/attend/get-started/transfer-students/suny-transfer-paths/

4. Lane and Finsel (2014) provide a more in-depth examination of the concerns associated with predictive and prescriptive data.

References

Aldeman, C., & Carey, K. (2009). *Ready to assemble: Grading state higher education accountability systems.* Washington DC: Education Sector.

Eckerson, W. W. (2010). *Performance dashboards: Measuring, monitoring, and managing your business.* San Francisco, CA: Wiley.

Fonseca, F., & Marcinkowski, M. (2014). The big data student. In J. E. Lane (Ed.), *Building a smarter university: Data, big data, and analytics* (pp. 121–142). Albany, NY: SUNY Press.

Goff, J. W., & Shaffer, C. M. (2014). Big data's impact on college admission practices and recruitment strategies. In J. E. Lane (Ed.), *Building a smarter university: Data, big data, and analytics* (pp. 93–120). Albany, NY: SUNY Press.

Harkinson, J. (2016, June 29). Could this Silicon Valley algorithm pick which homeless people get homes? *Mother Jones.* Retrieved from http://www.motherjones.com/politics/2016/06/homelessness-data-silicon-valley-prediction-santa-clara

Hungerford, K. (2016, July 1). Never say die: KC forges ahead with bold transportation plan. *Startland.* Retrieved from http://www.startlandnews.com/2016/07/never-say-die-kc-forges-ahead-bold-transportation-plan/

Jones, L. G. (1996). A brief history of the fact book as an institutional research report. *New directions for institutional research,* 3–26. doi:10.1002/ir.37019969103

Lane, J. E. (Ed.). (2014). *Building a smarter university: Innovation, analytics, and big data.* Albany, NY: SUNY Press.

Lane, J. E., & Finsel, B. A. (2014). Fostering smarter colleges and universities: Data, big data, and analytics. In J. E. Lane (Ed.), *Building a smarter university: Data, big data, and analytics* (pp. 3–6). Albany, NY: SUNY Press.

Manyika, J., Chui, M., Brown, B., Bughin, J., Dobbs, R., Roxburgh, C., & Byers, A. H. (2011). *Big data: The next frontier for innovation, competition, and pro-*

ductivity. McKinsey & Company. Retrieved from http://www.mckinsey.com/business-functions/business-technology/our-insights/big-data-the-next-frontier-for-innovation

Marcus, J. (2012, November 13). Student advising plays a key role in college success—just as its being cut. *The Hechinger Report.* Retrieved from http://hechingerreport.org/student-advising-plays-key-role-in-college-success-just-as-its-being-cut/

Matyszczky, C. (2014, January 19). Amazon to ship things before you've even thought of buying them? *CNET.* Retrieved from http://news.cnet.com/8301-17852_3-57617458-71/amazon-to-ship-things-before-youve-even-thought-of-buying-them/

Miller, K., & Chapin, K. (2013, February 15). *How big data changes lives* [Audio file]. WGBH. Retrieved from http://www.wgbhnews.org/post/how-big-data-changes-lives

Prescott, B. T. (2014). Big data and human capital development and mobility. In J. E. Lane (Ed.), *Building a smarter university: Data, big data, and analytics* (pp. 263–289). Albany, NY: SUNY Press.

Rice, G. (2011). *The Association for Institutional Research: The first 50 years.* Tallahassee, FL: Association for Institutional Research.

Rieland, R. (2015, March 2). How data and a good algorithm can help predict where fires will start. *Smithsonian.com.* Retrieved from http://www.smithsonianmag.com/innovation/how-data-and-good-algorithm-can-help-predict-where-fires-will-start-180954436/?no-ist

Rivard, R. (2013, October 24). Micro-targeting students. *Inside Higher Ed.* Retrieved from http://www.insidehighered.com/news/2013/10/24/political-campaign-style-targeting-comes-student-search

Rivers, C., & Sebasta, J. (2016, July 11). Competency-based education and predictive analytics: Learning from transfers. *EducauseReview.* Retrieved from http://er.educause.edu/articles/2016/7/competency-based-education-and-predictive-analytics-learning-from-transfers

Secretary of Education's Commission on the Future of Higher Education. (2006). *A test of leadership: Charting the future of U.S. higher education.* U.S. Department of Education. Retrieved from: http://www2.ed.gov/about/bdscomm/list/hiedfuture/index.html?exp=0

Shapiro, D., Dundar, A., Wakhungu, P. K., Yuan, X., & Harrell, A. (2015). *Transfer and mobility: A national view of student movement in postsecondary institutions, fall 2008 cohort* (Signature Report No. 9). National Student Clearinghouse Research Center. Retrieved from https://nscresearchcenter.org/signaturereport9/

Student Achievement Measure. (2013). *What is SAM?* Retrieved from http://www.studentachievementmeasure.org/about

Wildavsky, B. (2014). Nudge nation: A new way to prod students into and through college success. In J. E. Lane (Ed.), *Building a smarter university: Data, big data, and analytics* (pp. 143–158). Albany, NY: SUNY Press.

12

EVOLVING FROM REFLECTIVE TO PREDICTIVE

Montgomery County Community College and Analytics

Celeste M. Schwartz, Kent Phillippe, David Kowalski, and Angela Polec

C ommunity colleges, often referred to as "democracy's colleges," have historically served the role of providing open door access to anyone who wants to pursue postsecondary education (Boggs, 2010). As a result of their open door policies, community colleges often serve a more diverse student population than other sectors of higher education on dimensions such as race/ethnicity, age, academic preparation, and income. Concomitant with such diversity are the myriad academic and nonacademic supports necessary for students who enroll at community colleges to succeed.

While the demands of meeting the needs of such diverse student populations are significant, community colleges offer lower tuition and fees than other higher education institutions, despite generally receiving significantly lower appropriations per student than other publicly funded institutions (Desrochers & Kirshstein, 2012). As a result, community colleges do not have many degrees of freedom when determining how to allocate their limited financial and human resources.

Community colleges are also quite diverse in terms of size and structure. Enrollments at these institutions can range from fewer than 500 students to over 80,000 students. In regard to structure, some community colleges have local elected or appointed boards, whereas others are governed by a single statewide board.

Yet, despite the diversity of the students and institutions, all community colleges are united in their mission to help their students successfully meet their educational goals. It is within this context that the role analytics can play in helping community colleges must be considered.

Analytics that sit on top of a college's enterprise resource planning (ERP) system or state longitudinal data system (SLDS) provide a powerful tool for driving increases in student success. Indeed, the ability to more accurately iden-tify students or practices in an institution where intervention can increase stu-dent success is an invaluable tool. However, without an ability to interpret and act on the data and information provided by such a system, the data are useless.

The initial investment in analytics tools is not insignificant for many community colleges, which are, as noted, extremely resource constrained. However, without also investing in the related services and resources neces-sary to act on the investment in the software, efforts to drive increases in student success will not be successful.

For example, if a college can more accurately identify students who would benefit from additional resources or advising, but the college does not have those services available, then the power of the analytics is dimin-ished. Or, if early warning systems are reliant on faculty providing data into a system, the college needs to provide resources to train the faculty on how to input the data in order to adequately predict and support at-risk students.

This chapter will provide a road map of one college's successful trip toward adopting and using analytics in a community college. It is important to note, however, that the success of such an initiative in a community col-lege requires a commitment to institutional change in order to leverage the analytics and improve student success.

The History of Analytics at the College

Throughout the 1980s and 1990s, Montgomery County Community College's (MCCC) institutional research (IR) and information technology (IT) were in the same department, which was led by the chief information officer (CIO), who reported directly to the college president. During the early 1980s, the IR functions were performed by the CIO with the support of the administrative programming team. In the mid-1980s the first dedi-cated IR position was created, with primary responsibility for completing Integrated Postsecondary Education Data System (IPEDS) reporting, devel-oping surveys, providing data for academic program reviews, and reporting grant information. Most often, business unit staff (e.g., admissions, enroll-ment, financial aid) data requests were provided by IT in the form of reports. IT also supported IR data requests. The most significant difference in skill set between IR and IT during this period was that IR often used a statistical software package to analyze information, while IT pulled data and formatted that data into row and column reports.

In early 2000 IR was moved from IT to student affairs—where it would spend the next 10 years. With that move came an increase in the number of IR staff, an increase in IR responsibilities and expectations, and a title change. The office became known as the Office of Institutional Effectiveness and Institutional Research and the IR director's title was changed to the executive director of institutional effectiveness and institutional research. In addition, the institution hired a full-time and part-time IR researcher to support the executive director of IR, allowing for a substantial expansion of the responsibilities of IR. New duties for IR included developing an institutional effectiveness model for the institution and developing, monitoring, and measuring key performance indicators (KPIs). In addition, data analysis expanded in the academic area and also moved into student affairs. IR was recognized institution-wide as an important strategic partner to all departments throughout the institution.

Also during this period, business unit staff from finance, human resources, academic, and student affairs began to request more reporting. Due to IR staff limitations, IT continued to fulfill the information requests from these units unless analysis was involved. In the mid-2000s analytics began to take hold, with the publication of *Competing on Analytics: The New Science of Winning* by Davenport and Harris (2007)—a frequent read for those interested in and/or responsible for reporting and analytics. In addition, in 2006 MCCC joined Achieving the Dream (ATD), an organization that focuses on helping community colleges with their student success initiatives. As ATD's student success model is rooted in data-informed decision-making, becoming an ATD member necessitated that MCCC engage in additional reporting and analysis to aid in the identification and evaluation of initiatives that would support improved student success (Glover, 2009).

With the necessity for more in-depth analysis, there was a critical need to build out our data, reporting, and analytics capacity. To accomplish this institutional strategic goal, the institution needed to explore, design, and implement new processes, tools, and job duties—with some components of reporting and analytics moving to a more distributed model (Figure 12.1).

The analytics timeline shows the formation of a cross-functional data team, comprising representatives from IR, IT, academic administrators, faculty, and student affairs administrators, who supported our student success initiatives. While the IT/IR relationship had always been strong and collaborative, the formation of the data team in 2006 set in motion campus-wide cultural change focused on the importance of reporting and analytics and the use of data to inform decision-making. Both IT and IR staff were members of the data team, with faculty and administrators further strengthening the institution's collaborative approach to reporting and analytics.

Shortly after the formation of the data team, the college's IT department implemented an off-the-shelf data warehouse containing student, finance, and human resource system data. With the implementation of the data warehouse,

Figure 12.1. MCCC's analytics journey.

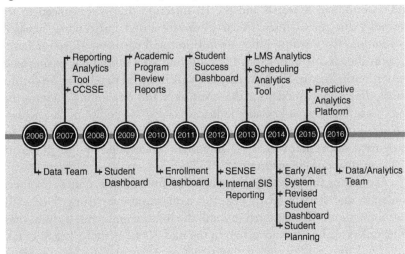

IT supported IR in the design and delivery of a student enrollment dashboard and also provided user departments with the ability to access the data warehouse and create their own ad hoc queries and reports. The institution continued to evolve with their use of data to inform decisions. IT continued to support more complex data pulls from disparate systems, and IR evolved from an organization that completed state and federal reports, created an annual fact book, and provided detailed enrollment reporting to a function that assisted in analyzing academic programs, measuring institutional effectiveness, and benchmarking the institution against peer and aspirant institutions.

During this time, the institution was evolving into an organization that valued self-assessment and review as a way to enhance and improve institutional programs and services to its students and community. There was a growing expectation that data would be provided and used to make informed decisions, with the days of "I think" (with no evidence) becoming a thing of the past. The use of data to inform decisions could be found in all areas of the institution (e.g., budget development, annual and strategic plan development, goal setting and progress monitoring, and new programs and services analysis). This was made possible because of a strong IR and IT team, whose working relationship was supportive and collaborative. Together, these two functions had earned the trust of the entire college community by creating products, reports, and insight that were considered highly credible. Furthermore, there was a core group of end users who were supportive in taking on basic query building and reporting for their specific area—providing bandwidth for IT and IR to provide more technical reporting and in-depth analysis.

In addition to building out the organizational structure in reporting, there were systems enhancements, as noted previously, in building a data warehouse, setting data standards, and integrating improved data cleaning processes to ensure data integrity. These initiatives, developed over several years, provided the pathway enabling the institution to move to the architecture that could support actionable analytics, the setting and monitoring of key performance indicators, and the ability to create institutional and departmental dashboards. Building this culture of evidence required new skill sets in data warehousing, data stewardship, and data architecture, in addition to the training of end users in query building, report development (using drag and drop tools), and the understanding of data elements. The building of this culture of evidence was essential to our ability to measure the effectiveness of student success interventions and invest in those that were shown to be effective, and to the institution's ability to move from an organization that, at times, made decisions based on anecdote to an organization that made informed decisions based on data.

In 2014, the college extended its reporting and analytics capabilities beyond data stored in the student information system (SIS) through vendor provided analytics from an early alert system (EAS), learning management system (LMS), and space management system. During this same time frame the college enhanced its accountability and benchmarking measures through annual participation in the voluntary framework of accountability (VFA) and, every other year, participation in the survey of entering student engagement (SENSE) and the community college survey of student engagement (CCSSE). Finally, in 2015 the college began implementation of a predictive analytics tool using the college's SIS, LMS, and EAS data.

Entering the Predictive Analytics Space

Predictive analytics was a natural next step as the college moved from a data-informed decision-making institution using descriptive analytics to a data-informed decision-making institution using both descriptive and predictive analytics.

Early Forays: Institutional Context

MCCC's movement into predictive analytics was driven by the knowledge that predictive data models can help improve institutional decision-making

(Daniel, 2015), create competitive advantages, and positively impact student success (Norris & Baer, 2013). This movement coincided with a series of significant changes at MCCC. Concurrent to the college's decision to pursue predictive analytics and their selection of a vendor with whom to partner, MCCC experienced a change of leadership, with the president of the college leaving. Additionally, key personnel changed in IR and IT, a new office of business analytics was created, and several of the college's power users left.

Although these changes impacted the continuity of existing teams and processes around analytics at the college, in retrospect, they also offered opportunities for bringing in personnel with new skill sets and the establishment of new institutional organizations and processes—opportunities that other institutions have reported successfully leveraging to positively impact analytics capacity and culture (Civitas Learning, n.d.).

MCCC ultimately identified a vendor to provide the college's predictive analytics technology and worked with them to stand up their platform—which allows users to identify the various predictors highly related to student persistence at one's institution. The predictive analytics tool became the technological centerpiece of the new cross-functional working group at MCCC, which was populated with leaders from across the divisions of the college.

Determining the people and roles that comprised the MCCC working group was an important decision that leadership at the college considered carefully. In the forefront was the key role that personnel play in determining an institution's analytics capacity (Norris & Baer, 2013) and the importance of identifying the right people to marry to the right processes and technologies. The college determined that the working group would include personnel who had both knowledge of key processes and policies at the college and the authority to make decisions. The staff selected had the contextual knowledge of college-specific data points, policies, processes, and capacities and the empowerment to take action at the college.

Interestingly, the college's decision to appropriate such key institutional team members to the working group was facilitated by an institution-wide presentation by our technology partner, who highlighted the potential of the predictive analytics tools to provide actionable insights by analyzing some key pieces of the college's data. This presentation, which occurred around the time membership in the working group was being formalized, increased institutional buy-in and ensured that leadership was willing to appropriate key personnel to the group (which ultimately included directors from enrollment, financial aid, advising, marketing, business intelligence [BI], IT, and IR).

In fact, the presentation by the college's technology partner proved to be an important catalyst for the work around predictive analytics, not only

Figure 12.2. Impact of institution-wide presentation on predictive analytics.

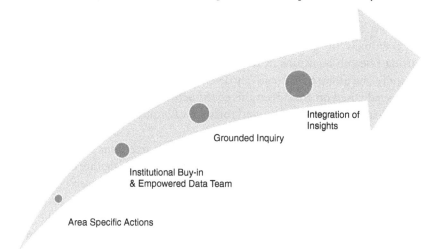

Integration of
Insights

Grounded Inquiry

Institutional Buy-in
& Empowered Data Team

Area Specific Actions

impacting the department that had its data analyzed (tutoring) but also facilitating buy-in (as mentioned), empowering the working group, and helping to move forward the institutional discussion around actionable data and lines of inquiry and the necessity of integrating insights in an iterative loop (Figure 12.2). Indeed, it is likely that without the aforementioned presentation, which engaged a significant portion of the college faculty and staff, the working group would have faced greater difficulty in building momentum around their charge.

Early Forays: Processes and Structures

Early forays by the group into the predictive analytics work were tentative and gradual, as there were several structural, procedural, and knowledge factors that needed to be addressed at the onset. One of the first issues the group worked to tackle revolved around developing a shared understanding of the predictive analytics tool: how it worked, what it was capable of, and how it could be leveraged. Despite having several trainings prior to the first convening of the group, led by our technology partner, it was found early on that comfort with and understanding of the tool varied significantly among group members. This necessitated that time be spent so that all members could reach a base level of proficiency.

Structures and procedures guiding the operation of the working group also needed to be established. Over the first several biweekly meetings, the group tried a variety of approaches: working in the analytics tool collectively to unearth meaningful patterns/insights, working in the tool in small groups around key topics, and generating research questions in the group and engaging in related data exploration in the tool outside of the group, to name a few. Eventually, the group settled on a process whereby all actions began with crafting research questions in response to the ongoing needs of the college. Critically, the group collaboratively determines which research questions will be pursued based on considerations of the actionability of the resulting data, the capacity of the institution, and the lines of inquiry likely to have the biggest potential impact on student success.

In the current working group structure, once questions are selected the group identifies the relevant actions that need to be taken, whether that involves data gathering/exploration/analysis or development and/or implementation of an intervention. Indeed, it is a key feature of the working group that every working session ends with a plan for actions to be taken prior to the next meeting and individuals being assigned to, and accountable for, those actions.

It was also determined in the period of group "norming" that beyond the aforementioned processes, the group would adopt a flexible approach to structure/process, which would be dictated by where the group was in regard to the particular line of inquiry that it was pursuing. Thus, the group might spend time reviewing data during one working session, while discussing a relevant college policy the next. This flexibility has proved critical to maintaining the group's momentum and cohesion.

An important decision was also made around the role that the college's predictive analytics tools would play. Specifically, the group shifted its focus from considering the predictive analytics tools in isolation (an initial model) to a model whereby the predictive analytics tools were integrated as one element, albeit a powerful one, in the group's analytics repertoire.

Early Forays: Initial Efforts

While the evolution of the working group required an initial investment of group time, it did not preclude the group from simultaneously working on lines of inquiry. Two of the early efforts of the group focused on targeted outreach to students who were likely to be able to increase their course load and analysis of the college's first-term online students.

The first of these lines of inquiry was taken up in response to the college's ongoing focus on decreasing students' time to completion. The goal of increasing course load was decided upon as the avenue to attempt to impact students' time to completion after considering student course success rates, the rate of major changes among students, and the high percentage of students at the college who take less than a full-time course load (currently approximately 70%), among other factors. The group then decided that the predictive analytics tool would be used to identify students who would be able to increase course load without any likely negative impact to their likelihood to persist. It was also decided within the working group that students in the identified group would be contacted by student services and offered the chance to take an additional course in the current semester (the college has multiple start dates for courses within the semester) at a reduced rate (so as to incentivize participation).

To be sure, this description is not meant to be an exhaustive review of all the decision points and processes around this line of inquiry. Rather, it is meant to illustrate that contextual information is considered in the working group and that the actions of the group are grounded in a spirit of informed and iterative experimentation.

With respect to the outcomes of the pilot around increasing course load, they ultimately proved informative in several respects. First, it was found that student participation in the initiative was very limited. To be sure, some students who were contacted reported not wanting to increase their course load. Others reported that they did not have the time. Notably, students also commonly reported that the courses they might be interested in taking during a late start session were either not offered or not offered at a time that fit their schedule. This piece of feedback was used by group members in future conversations regarding course scheduling.

Another outcome of the pilot was that the group realized the need to more closely consider the people, processes, messaging, and data documentation involved in the implementation process of working group initiatives. Understandably, for the first working group action there was a considerable sense of accomplishment around actually being able to roll out an initiative informed by the data/insights. Fortunately, the working group was able to move quickly past this early mode of implementation and into a more mature model. It is illuminating, however, to consider that new working groups will be unlikely to begin their work as optimally functioning units, but will take time (often many years), effort, and adaptation to reach higher degrees of functionality (Baer & Norris, 2015).

The other initial piece of work undertaken by the working group focused on identifying and supporting an analysis of the college's first-term online students. This student group was identified as a focus following exploration in the predictive analytics tool by a subgroup of working group members focused on online student success. In the course of their work this group identified a ~15%-point decrease in persistence likelihood for first-semester students taking all online courses. Notably, this marked decline was not evidenced for second-semester (or beyond) online students. This information prompted an internal review of the online course readiness self-assessment tool the college provides to students, the conversations advisers have with first-semester students, the potential for early alerts to be prompted based on course scheduling behavior, and the ability for first-term students to take all online courses.

Thus, this example of early work by the group illustrates that actions taken from insights and/or to gain insights need not fit one mold. Indeed, considering potential avenues of action as broadly as possible opens the door for creativity within the group and helps prevent the working group from becoming stuck.

Early Forays: A Later Example

As the working group matured, by continually integrating feedback from prior actions taken by the group and building a more advanced shared knowledge base, the process of taking data-informed action became easier and more refined. For example, a later set of actions focused on using the college's predictive analytics tool to help build a stratified random sample of students for A/B testing around a two-way text campaign. The goal of the work was to help identify target audiences that would most benefit from receiving text-based outreach early in the semester. As the college did not want to overwhelm students with text messages and thereby dilute their effect, the working group took up the task of piloting a text message outreach to students who were at various levels of risk of not persisting to the next semester. By being able to identify students within different risk bands, sending them a carefully crafted message (via a platform that enabled the working group to capture all text exchanges between students receiving the texts and the team organized by the working group to respond to them), and analyzing the resulting data relative to persistence and other academic outcomes, the group was able to gain insight that will inform the college's texting strategy and protocols going forward.

Thus, through considering strategic college goals, context, capacity, scalability, the implementation and data-gathering process, outcome measures, and the set of future actions that could result from the initiative in concert, the working group was able to move toward a more holistic and mature model of functioning that closed the loop of inquiry, insight, evaluation, and action.

Analytics: Obstacles and Adaptation

Like many other colleges, MCCC's data team is faced with several challenges: limited resources, competing initiatives, and end user data literacy.

Some of the challenges are beyond the college's control to a large extent (e.g., limited resources), while others are more modifiable through process improvement, prioritization, and professional development.

As noted, one of the critical challenges facing the college is the lack of resources around data and reporting. For the recent past the college has had 2.5 full-time employees (FTEs) devoted to IR and, in the past year, an additional person in BI. While the size of the IR office is not uncommon for a community college, the challenge around resources exists for the following central reasons: (a) the demand for data and reporting, both internally and externally, has grown exponentially in the last several years, a trend widely acknowledged (Association for Institutional Research, 2015), while the FTEs devoted to providing data and reporting have not kept pace; (b) nearly all discussions at the college require insights regarding data and analytics, and having an IR person participate in those discussions takes capacity away from IR's ability to produce data, reports, and analysis; and (c) many colleges have experienced declines in enrollment and or funding recently, thus precluding the adding of more positions to the data teams.

To deal with these challenges, MCCC has reorganized the IT and IR departments. The reorganization was aided by the help of an external consultant, who was brought in to review IT and IR structures and processes and to identify key needs and opportunities for increased efficiencies. The reorganization, based on the consultant's findings, recast 1.5 FTEs into the BI team, increasing capacity without any additional staff being added to the division.

The college has sought to stem the ever-increasing flow of data requests by requiring that all individuals requesting data complete an electronic form identifying the purpose of the data requested and requiring all data requests to be approved by division heads before being submitted to IR. This data request form was implemented with the goal that the approval process will help ensure that requests align with the strategic goals of the college and that this will limit the impact of competing initiatives on the capacity of the data teams. The process should also help develop a culture where data requestors will be more forward-thinking about their data requests, which should decrease the number of last-minute data requests that flood IR/BI/IT and constrain their ability to complete larger and more complex tasks.

The college has also sought to deal with issues of data literacy on campus (i.e., end user issues with understanding/interpreting data) by having IR/BI be more involved throughout the life cycle of data-dependent programs, initiatives, and assessments on campus. Moreover, in addition to the creation of the cross-functional working group around predicative analytics, the college has recently bolstered and diversified membership in its data steward-ship committee. This has helped to facilitate a shared understanding of the college's data structures across a wider array of departments and functional units.

Finally, IR/BI have prioritized getting accurate, clear, visually appealing, actionable data in the hands of end users. By improving the user experience around data delivered by the IR/BI teams, IR/BI is attempting to limit mis-interpretation and increase the use of data to inform decision-making at the college.

Takeaways

Over the course of MCCC's evolution with analytics, several insights were achieved, which may be useful for institutions looking to advance their ana-lytics work.

Assembling the Team

Analytics is more about people and processes than about tools. Too often the focus is on the tools—with users hoping for amazing results without considering the importance of including the right people and making pro-cess changes necessary for data-informed action. The right data models and tools can facilitate insights, but in order to take action, a contextual understanding of the institution and an empowered and data-savvy team are necessary.

Critical to the success of analytics work is building a cross-functional team. Institutions should consider representation from IR/IT, enrollment management, student affairs, academic affairs, and marketing and commu-nications. This cross-functional composition allows the team to consider the initiatives and processes that are occurring across the institution while they are distilling their insights and developing their targeted interventions.

Indeed, it is critical to ensure that this group is operating and making decisions in the context of existing outreach and initiatives. For example, if outreach and intervention ideas are generated but are not evaluated in the larger context of existing touchpoints, the student experience might be over-whelming and disjointed and the impact of the initiatives might be difficult to evaluate.

Additionally, to keep the data team's work from being seen as just another meeting, each person around the table needs to be empowered to make decisions within their respective area. Team members should also have an understanding of the data definitions and a familiarity with the tools.

Data as the Starting Point

In a metrics-driven culture, data are often viewed as the output at the end of a line. Data requests are submitted, with the intention of reporting on numbers like enrollment or assessing outcomes. However, when venturing into the world of analytics, the data need to be viewed as the starting point for the conversation. When this transition is made successfully, data and analytics become an organic part of any decision-making process at the institution and perpetuate an iterative cycle of inquiry, insight, action, and assessment.

Action–Research Mind-Set

A mind-set shift is often required in how teams approach data. End users often expect the data and "the analytics" to "tell them something"—as if the data are magically going to dictate the next steps one should take to improve outcomes. Unfortunately, that is not how it works. End users need to enter the conversation not only with a research question but also with a potential action that they could take, depending on what they find. Institutional team members working with data and analytics constantly need to be asking themselves, "So what? What's my next step? How do I integrate what I have uncovered and how does that impact how I move forward?" This shift to an iterative action–research mind-set is key for analytics working groups. It's incredibly easy to get pulled into a rabbit hole of data on a seemingly endless quest to better understand the data.

Changing Results Versus Changing Behaviors

Most institutions have metrics and benchmarks against which they are consistently being measured at the highest level: enrollment, retention rate, completion rate, and so on. However, when an analytics working group sits down to try to "move the needle," they are often left feeling discouraged because they are focusing on shifting the highest-level metrics.

One way to make this work more digestible for the group is to break down those metrics and focus on one submetric. For example, overall retention rate might be broken down to first-semester retention rate. Then it becomes important to identify behaviors that may impact that submetric and to develop an aligned research question and a clear potential action. For example, "Are students more likely to persist if they use the tutoring center during their first semester?" If the data indicate that tutoring increases a student's likelihood to persist, the "So what" will focus on trying to change the behavior of students who do not use the tutoring center during their first semester.

The group can then identify a benchmark for the percentage of first-semester students who use the tutoring center and strategically attempt to increase that percentage through, for example, awareness campaigns and outreach. If the outreach is successful and more first-semester students use the tutoring center, then you would expect to see first-semester retention rates improve.

Focus on the Student Experience

It's important that data group members are aware that initiatives developed and executed as a result of the analytics work are not occurring in a vacuum. There are often a multitude of initiatives that are occurring in the midst of the standard streams of interaction at institutions. In order to execute an effective intervention, the group must consider the point of view of the intended recipient, who will experience numerous touchpoints with the institution.

For example, too often for student-directed initiatives, departments across campus forget that they are not the only ones communicating to a student. From the student's point of view, every communication, regardless of department, is coming from the institution. Understanding and coordinating such efforts is key to ensuring that outreach that is part of analytics-informed initiatives has the intended effect.

Close the Loop

Despite the prevalence of data and analytics in the everyday happenings and conversations at institutions across the country, many higher education professionals may not be aware of the true impact that analytics has, or can have. It's important for analytics working groups to evaluate their efforts and tell the resulting stories to their campus communities. Whether successful or not, such stories increase the data-informed knowledge base of an institution. Mini case studies presented to the college community, which demonstrate how a data team is using data and the impact that it has on the institution, may be especially useful in helping institutions contextualize the importance of this work and find ways to integrate it.

Conclusion

This case study from MCCC highlights several key factors for community colleges as they begin to explore the espoused promises of analytics. In order to improve student success through the use of data analytics, community colleges will need to attend to these critical factors.

The first key factor is time. In the case of MCCC, the transition was a gradual transformation of both practice and infrastructure over more than a decade. Community colleges cannot expect to move to an effective use of analytics overnight, and despite frequent promises of immediate impact, effective implementation of data analytics requires a thoughtful and persistent approach that results not only in better data but also better use of the analysis.

The second factor is leadership commitment. While not explicitly indicated in this case study, the college demonstrated a strong leadership commitment to improving the use of data and analytics. The transformational change demonstrated at MCCC did not occur in a vacuum. It took a commitment from leadership to provide human and financial resources, as well as an environment that leads to a culture of inquiry and evidence where data can be acted upon. Many of these qualities are delineated in a report on effective community college leaders produced by the Aspen Institute and Achieving the Dream (2014).

The third factor is an environment of institution-wide inclusion in the process. MCCC engaged individuals across many parts of the college. This provides several benefits. It improves the value and utility of the analytics across the college. Engagement in the process also helps individuals understand the value of data input into the system and drives better data inputs. Engagement also helps the development team better focus efforts on areas of need, not just desired data.

The fourth factor is flexibility. MCCC demonstrated the need to constantly review and evaluate their approach to developing and effectively using their analytics solution. This flexibility included organizational structures and staffing, continuous evaluation of their data infrastructure, and policies and practices to drive equitable use of analytics across the college. This flexibility, however, needs to be rooted in a broader strategy to improve institutional effectiveness. The college needs to have a vision of where it is going and how the analytics will help meet the college's strategic goals.

Analytics holds the potential to help colleges improve student success. But it is not an endeavor that colleges should undertake lightly. In the current resource-constrained environment facing many community colleges, it is important that there is a clear commitment to the process of designing, developing, and using a data analytics solution, for if the ability to use the data is not concomitantly developed with the data tools and faculty and staff are not involved in the process, the college will have data, but an inability to use that data to improve student outcomes.

References

Aspen Institute & Achieving the Dream, Inc. (2014). *Crisis and opportunity: Aligning the community college presidency with student success* [Project report]. Retrieved from http://kresge.org/sites/default/files/Edu-CC%20Leadership%20Final%20 Report.pdf

Association for Institutional Research. (2015). *Impact of business intelligence on institutional research* [White paper]. Retrieved from https://www.airweb.org/eAIR/ Surveys/Documents/ImpactofBusinessIntelligenceonInstitutionalResearch.pdf

Baer, L. L., & Norris, D. M. (2015). *What every leader needs to know about student success* [White paper]. Retrieved from https://cdn2.hubspot.net/hubfs/488776/ Summit/Partner_Summit_2016/White_Paper_What_Leaders_Need_to_ Know_About_Analytics.pdf

Boggs, G. R. (2010). *Democracy's colleges: The evolution of the community college in America.* Washington DC: American Association of Community Colleges. Retrieved from http://www.aacc.nche.edu/AboutCC/whsummit/Documents/ boggs_whsummitbrief.pdf

Civitas Learning. (n.d.). *Learning brief: Using predictive analytics to increase retention to 90 percent by 2020.* Austin, TX: Civitas Learning.

Daniel, B. (2015). Big data and analytics in higher education: Opportunities and challenges. *British Journal of Educational Technology, 46,* 904–920. doi:10.1111/ bjet.12230

Davenport, T. H., & Harris, J. G. (2007). *Competing on analytics: The new science of winning.* Boston, MA: Harvard Business School Press.

Desrochers, D. M., & Kirshstein, R. J. (2012). *College spending in a turbulent decade: Findings from the Delta Cost Project; A Delta Data Update, 2000–2010.* Washington DC: American Institutes for Research.

Glover, R. (2009). *Strengthening institutional research and information technology capacity through Achieving the Dream: Principles and practices of student success.* Chapel Hill, NC: Achieving the Dream.

Norris, D. M., & Baer, L. L. (2013). Building organizational capacity for analytics. *EDUCAUSE.* Retrieved from https://library.educause.edu/~/media/files/ library/2013/2/pub9012-pdf.pdf

13

UNPACKING THE MESSINESS OF HARNESSING THE ANALYTICS REVOLUTION

Jonathan S. Gagliardi

Powerful forces have converged to wield a great deal of pressure on American higher education, which faces an imperative to improve student outcomes, lower costs, and maintain quality. This has been made more difficult due to resource contraction, the changing nature of the student body, and growing demands for transparency and accountability. While a culture of assessment has taken root across many campuses, some are still struggling with the transition into an environment that focuses on outcomes as much as access (Yeado, Haycock, Johnstone, & Chaplot, 2014). College and university leaders need to meet the challenges of student success and sustainability head-on. Many are taking an approach centered around data analytics to strategically invest scarce resources into student services, academic programs, and institutional priorities (Gagliardi & Wellman, 2015; Wellman & Ewell, 2010). Those who do not will risk the competitiveness and survival of their institutions (Lubin & Esty, 2010). Simply put, the need for a systemic, data-informed approach to higher education innovation has never been more apparent (Bhattacharya, 2013; Gagliardi, 2015; Guenther & Guenther, 2013; Rogers, 2003; Swing, 2016).

In recent years, technological advances have given rise to an analytics revolution, which makes it possible for colleges and universities to satisfy these demands. The emergence and growing accessibility of big data and spread of analytics tools have led institutions to explore how they can improve their capacity to learn (Foss, 2014; Gagliardi & Wellman, 2015; Lane, 2014). Some institutions have focused on the use of data and evidence to improve student learning, increase retention and completion, and close equity gaps (Gagliardi, Espinosa, Turk, & Taylor, 2017). A growing number have begun to focus on optimizing resource allocation (Anguiano et al., 2017; Wellman & Ewell, 2010). All campuses will have to do both to provide a superior and sustainable education given the level of environmental volatility they face (Anguiano et al., 2017).

The analytics revolution represents an opportunity for colleges and universities to undertake needed structural shifts, but only if decision makers can use it to extract valuable insight that promotes student success and quality outcomes and supports the institutional mission (Foss, 2014; Gagliardi & Wellman, 2015). Institutional research (IR) professionals will play a crucial role in leading colleges and universities as they embark on their analytics journeys. They are uniquely situated to do so because of their familiarity with campus data, deep institutional knowledge, blend of skills and competencies, and understanding of the needs of senior leadership (Cheslock, Hughes, & Umbricht, 2014).

Still, differences in institutional traits and arrangements make it difficult to get the most out of analytics assets, including functions like IR (Bichsel, 2012; Foss, 2013; Swing, 2016). In many instances data are not commonly understood or centrally linked, making it hard to develop minimum data collection standards and analysis use cases. These barriers to using data analytics are magnified by a lack of capacity (Gagliardi & Wellman, 2015; Swing, 2016). Many institutions have only enough resources to fulfill mandatory reporting requirements and information requests that originate from high priority stakeholders including lawmakers, board members, and accrediting agencies. As a result, many IR teams spend most of their time supporting the completion of information requests from internal and external stakeholders that are of limited value (Bichsel, 2012; Gagliardi & Wellman, 2015; Swing, 2016).

Demands for insight have outstripped the capacity of IR as currently composed to supply it (Gagliardi & Wellman, 2015; Swing, 2016). These capacity issues will persist barring a change in how colleges and universities prioritize resource investment. The likelihood of such a change in mind-set occurring is low given how tight the budgets of many institutions are. To overcome these challenges some campuses have begun to reassess the composition of their analytics functions. They are strategically and creatively scaling data analytics across the entirety of the institution. The emergence of more profuse data analytics models, bolstered by strong leadership, adoption, and implementation, make it possible for institutions to consistently and cohesively develop the kinds of insight that are needed to improve performance, create efficiencies, and foster innovation. This chapter seeks to highlight some of the key takeaways for institutional leaders seeking to maximize the value of their IR function and analytics assets.

Building Analytics Functions for Modern Needs

As evidenced by this volume, many colleges and universities are overcoming the challenges they face in harnessing the analytics revolution by positioning IR at the hub of a more widespread analytics function. A more collaborative function that encompasses the use of accurate, timely, relevant, integrated, and secure data to create predictive and prescriptive insight and strategic action is as much of an art as it is a science. It requires IR to blend its traditional functions with new ones, leading to the use of data analytics in goal setting, performance evaluation, and strategic planning in more nuanced and sophisticated ways.

Many institutions are eager to use their analytics functions in ways that move beyond the traditional reflective and descriptive reporting that they do, with an eye toward adopting more prescriptive models of data analytics. But moving toward assessment and application and away from counting represents a major shift for most campuses. For example, many institutions want to increase their use of predictive and prescriptive analytics for the purposes of improving student outcomes. However, they remain sparsely used in higher education due to a lack of vision, strategy, planning, and capacity. Institutions are either missing or have an underdeveloped data analytics vision and plan, and they often lack comprehensive strategies for implementation, adoption, and use of predictive and prescriptive analytics. The human and technical capacities to conduct such analyses are absent or disorganized at many colleges and universities, which complicates efforts to improve student outcomes through the effective use of predictive and prescriptive analytics (Arroway, Morgan, O'Keefe, & Yanosky, 2016). Still, that has not stopped institutions from reconsidering and restructuring their analytics functions in order to reap the benefits of the analytics revolution, and some of the key steps are described in the paragraphs that follow.

Key Themes

Realizing the full potential of the analytics revolution requires leadership from IR in many areas. The following are clear steps that can be taken by institutional leaders seeking to support the maturation of their analytics assets.

Frame Data as an Accessible Asset of Value

Data need to be viewed as an institutional asset, rather than something that falls squarely in the dominion of one or a handful of groups. Too often the data housed in IR, IT, budget and finance, or assessment have remained disconnected and inaccessible to the stakeholders who could use them the most. These units have only recently begun developing collaborative models to integrate and distribute data. One major element of this is ascribing the appropriate value to data so that people feel empowered to use them properly. This is easier said than done. For example, deans and department chairs could make better use of metrics in the evaluation of programs and courses, but they would be mistaken if they used metrics as the sole tool for the assessment of individual faculty for the purposes of promotion or tenure review. The same applies to student programs and services. People need to know where and how data analytics are useful. This can be a difficult needle to thread. If the data are perceived as too fragile, then they can get walled off. If data are not seen as being of quality, then they may become delegitimized. In either case, the data are not used. This works against the development of a cohesive campus plan about how data are used to improve institutional performance and student success. Data need to be seen as both valuable and durable.

Double Down on Data Governance

A data governance plan is a framework for data use, collection, definition, and analysis. It should be structured enough to create a minimum set of standards and a common language around formulating data definitions, ensuring accuracy and security, and developing processes and standards for information and analytics requests. It should also be flexible enough to accommodate different user needs and the evolutionary nature of data and analytics tools. Many campuses have elements of a sound data governance plan, but few have one that is cohesive and dynamic. The absence of a strong and flexible data governance plan can stall the maturation of campus-wide analytics functions. Developing one is a resource-intensive process, but if done right, it can set institutions up to benefit greatly from the analytics revolution.

Get Champions and Resources

The early stages of creating a culture of data analytics requires buy-in from senior administrative and academic leaders at the cabinet level. This involves advocacy for and investment into data analytics use. It also requires that they use data analytics themselves. Buy-in and use at the senior-most levels can help ensure that analytics cultures have time to grow and take root across the institution. Without this level of commitment, campuses are likely to revert to old patterns of operating, and this will make future efforts at resuscitating analytics efforts harder and more complicated. Incentives are also needed, and they can take many forms. Money is always helpful, particularly in early phases of analytics adoption. Dedicated talent and staff can help ensure that someone is always focused on data analytics. Requiring the use of data in program assessment and evaluation by senior administrators, deans, and department chairs provide additional anchors that eventually find their way to all of the corners of the campus. Regardless, people and incentives need to be pointed toward the same goals. If they run counter to one another, they will be a source of future conflict and potentially lead to entrenchment against or the counterproductive use of data analytics.

Start Small and Scale Later

Due to the resource-intensive and time-consuming nature of harnessing the analytics revolution, it is advisable to start small. Creating a pilot for the more comprehensive use of data analytics can help create champions at all levels of the institution. Pilots should be carefully designed, acknowledged as imperfect, and refined based on feedback. The movement from pilot to proof of concept should help people to see the value of data analytics, particularly if this has been done collaboratively, as this creates a sense of ownership and sustains momentum. Once the pilot becomes a proof of concept, then it's ready to be scaled and implemented across an institution in a phased manner.

Ask the Right Questions

Institutions should define a core set of data questions and views which drive continuous improvement in mission-centered ways. These questions and views will vary to a certain extent across campuses or departments because context matters. Asking the right questions allows for the creation of analytics platforms that focus on a set of key performance metrics that matter most to the success of the institution and its students. These questions and metrics should be used to develop core products (e.g., analyses, visualizations, dashboards) that are used to drive continuous improvement. These measures should be periodically reviewed and changed to reflect the evolving nature of institutional goals and priorities and the growing sophistication of data collection, preparation, storage, and analysis tools and techniques. This approach is far more productive than throwing every last byte of data into a warehouse or a model, which can be wasteful and difficult to navigate. It also allows campuses to work through challenges related to the ethical and secure use of data before something slips through the cracks.

Be Ethical and Transparent About Data Use

Institutions are entering a space where data are used more globally and in a more targeted and prescriptive fashion. Issues related to the privacy, security, and ethical use of data analytics will surface in expected and unexpected ways. Institutions will need to proactively develop plans to communicate transparently with students, faculty, and staff about the nature of data collection and will need to seek consent to use it. Additionally, institutions will have to develop the policies, procedures, and infrastructure necessary to ensure data security, which remain areas of high risk. Once the data are secure and their use clearly and transparently communicated, institutions will also have to be diligent about using data in ethical ways that support students instead of reinforcing bias. The use of analytics should not impede student success or limit student choice or enrollment. It should not be used as the sole determinant of decisions about staff and program investment. It is the responsibility of the institution to ensure that data are used ethically and responsibly regardless of whether an analytics solution is homegrown or vendor developed. Outsourcing does not absolve an institution from deeply understanding the potential benefits and drawbacks of the development and deployment of analytics solutions.

Facilitate Institution-Wide Change

The use of analytics typically focuses on intervening on behalf of students who need support or are at risk, but more power lies in using analytics to identify structural flaws in programs and services that have developed over time. As such, the focus should be on how analytics can be used to facilitate structural changes across the campus. Many student success challenges exist due to misalignments of academic or administrative programs and services with student needs. These misalignments are design flaws that have emerged over time and become more obvious as the student body has diversified and funding streams have shifted. The analytics revolution offers institutions a chance to shape institutional reforms in evidence-based and contextualized ways. Using it effectively can change student engagement and resource use. This requires providing support, facilitation, human capacity development, and educational resources that help students, faculty, and staff interpret data analytics in appropriate and effective ways.

Get Comfortable With Internal Change

Data analytics is becoming an institution-wide affair, and this has implications for the ways in which analytics functions operate and are structured. The capacity to leverage analytics will increase as an analytics culture grows, infrastructure matures, and more people use it for the purpose of decision support. Roles will change and more stakeholders will feel a sense of ownership and empowerment over the use of data. This will lead to more analyses occurring outside of traditional analytics functions like IR. In the future, IR will find itself providing support for others to do analyses rather than doing them internally. This evolution will be a conflictual one, and those conflicts are sometimes internal in nature. Getting comfortable with the idea of consequential validity versus statistical validity and being open to alternative interpretations of data analytics will create tensions. These tensions need to be acknowledged and soothed if they are to be overcome, making it important to create a forum for the evolving use of data analytics.

Communicate Clearly and Own a Unified Message

Effectively and adaptively communicating insight is crucial to realizing the full value of the analytics revolution. This is a complex process that requires faculty, staff, and senior leaders to have a common understanding about the use and interpretation of data analytics. The different perspectives of these internal stakeholders can make that difficult. Still, the entire campus has to be on the same page about how to do that. Collaboratively defining problems, guiding analyses, embedding data into routines, and creating the space to tackle issues that arise from data analytics are important to implement. Doing so allows institutions to fulfill the information needs and address in a unified fashion the questions that external stakeholders, such as boards, legislators, and other policy-focused organizations are bound to have. Efforts to do this are strengthened by creating a data-informed institutional value proposition that is clear and impactful. In short, institutions need to own the message shaped by data analytics or get comfortable with others doing so.

Be Dynamic; Don't Fall Into Old Habits

It is natural to get complacent after all the legwork that goes into creating a data-informed campus, but that cannot happen. Creating plans, implementing new structures, and building out culture and infrastructure are starting points for a process of evidence-based continuous improvement and adaptation that has no end. These building blocks should be used in a fluid and routine fashion. If they are not, they will eventually become rigid and functionally obsolete, and campuses will find themselves back at square one. Dynamic policies, structures, assets, analyses, and teams are needed to prevent that.

Build a Bridge Between Senior Leadership and Analytics

For many institutions, a gap exists between the IR function and senior leaders who need insight from data analytics. This gap can be a major barrier to fully optimizing valuable analytics assets, and it needs to be bridged. The best way to do so is by creating a new analytics leadership role at the cabinet level of the institution (if it does not already exist). This requires someone who can lead the coordination of analytics assets in ways that support a shared vision for the future. The role involves strategy, relationship building, implementation, vision, and communication and is key to embedding a campus-wide analytics culture. Creating such a role and placing it at an appropriately high level within campus administration also helps to legitimize data analytics use.

Create Diverse and Complementary Analytics Teams

Data analytics teams with diverse skill sets are required to successfully fulfill the modern information needs of colleges and universities. These teams should be led by IR, include a broader array of roles, and use cross-campus collaboration to overcome capacity constraints. The composition of analytics teams should fluctuate throughout the course of any data project involving the creation of insight-driven products. While in the process of data collection and preparation, a project might require database developers and administrators, applications developers, data scientists and IR analysts, and end users. When data are collected and ready for analysis, IR analysts should conduct the analysis and test the quality of the product and findings with select stakeholder groups. Once the analysis is conducted, data visualization experts and IR analysts should work together to create compelling stories. At each stage, end users should be engaged for testing. This will require IR and IT to interface more effectively than ever before. In short, IT is the tool to scale out sound IR and evidence-based innovations.

Discussion and Conclusion

The value of the analytics revolution to colleges and universities is clear given the increasing pace of changes that are occurring to enrollments, funding streams, and expectations around performance and accountability. Institutions now have available to them the data and analytics tools to break free from traditional structures and create new forms of program and service delivery. These new data-informed business models promise to offer innovative approaches to improving student outcomes and resource utilization. Simply put, the analytics revolution, if harnessed effectively, represents a rare opportunity for higher education to fundamentally reconfigure itself for the better.

It is worth noting that realizing the value of the analytics revolution will not happen overnight, nor will it turn higher education into a giant algorithm. It will instead build on the high-quality education already provided by American colleges and universities. The process of transformation will be a lengthy and difficult one because institutions often mirror the era in which they were created, and it takes a lot for cultures, infrastructures, and business models to evolve. This will be particularly true for institutions, as they have become inflexible after decades of relative stability. Even so, new campus infrastructures that are centered on organizational learning and adaptation fueled by the analytics revolution offer a lot of hope for the future vitality of colleges.

Stakeholders hold lofty expectations regarding the possible impact of the analytics revolution on higher education. In some cases, the magnitude of those expectations can be daunting, and in some cases paralyzing. Still, it is worth remembering that they are a positive force in American higher education. This is especially important for leaders of IR and other analytics functions to remember, given the pressures they face in promoting institutional reforms that benefit students. Everyone needs to be reminded that higher education has proven innovative in the past, but that such changes have typically taken time, patience, hard work, persistence, collaboration, and productive discomfort.

Still, by embracing the analytics revolution and recognizing the value of data analytics, higher education as a whole has signaled its seriousness about reconsidering itself. Institutions of all types—ranging from community colleges to research universities to higher education systems—see data and analytics as fundamental to satisfying growing demands in spite of the challenges presented by social, political, economic, and technological changes. Some institutions are more mature than others in their capacity to extract value out of the analytics revolution, but all are intentionally exploring how to best do so while staying true to their mission and values. That should be celebrated.

This volume includes a host of examples of efforts undertaken by institutions and systems to harness the analytics revolution. The unique circumstances of each institution fundamentally shape how they use timely, transparent, accessible, relevant, and insightful data to make better decisions. Some, like the University of Minnesota, have focused on developing data governance frameworks that can be shaped by the user. Others, like the California State University System, have created the infrastructure and platforms for sharing the insight created by data analytics in actionable ways. To do that, new and collaborative analytics teams, like that developed at the University of Georgia at Athens, have been created. At Montgomery County Community College, a culture of analytics has permeated the entire institution. Certain cases require a fundamental restructuring of analytics functions that are better suited to improving student outcomes, like what has occurred at the University of Arizona. This has led certain institutions, like the University of Texas System, to seek out ways to connect education and workforce outcomes data in unprecedented ways. All of the examples of institutions embracing the analytics revolution have been shaped by context and setting.

Amid a growing sea of demands and thirst for data, different institutions have traveled similar but different paths to becoming smarter universities. Each path is uneven, often rugged, and fraught with tensions as boundaries related to the use of data get redrawn. Doing so successfully has often required that IR bring new stakeholders into the fold on matters that typically fall squarely in its domain. These include data collection, governance, use, analysis, and application. This necessitates some change within IR functions, which are now refocusing on guiding institutions through a process of embracing data analytics rather than being a one-step shop for all of it.

These changes can be uncomfortable, as IR has long enjoyed its status as the gatekeeper of data and analysis. It is now at a point where its scope and impact are broadening as a result of the analytics revolution. More and more, campus leaders expect IR to meet increasingly diverse and growing needs for analysis, insight, and translatable knowledge that promote accountability and transparency, drive student outcomes, and lead to improved organizational performance. That starts with effective data governance and stewardship, but it ends in the hands of key decision makers and leaders who are littered across the higher education landscape. It is in that process of refining data into something with utility where there are messy spaces related to the roles and capacities, cultures, and structures of IR relative to other analytically inclined functions. There can be a lot of apprehension in that for IR professionals, because these pressures will shift the way IR functions and its staff perform their duties. This has led IR and analytics professionals to be of two minds when it comes to welcoming ongoing changes with open arms.

The image of a lean and mean institution fueled by reams of data conjures up the boldest of aspirations among all vested stakeholders. Some seek real-time student success and workforce data that drive advising and academic program review in ways that get students degrees and jobs. Others are seeking out cross-functional data that identify cost savings without sacrificing quality. Many hope to use more comprehensive and accurate data to improve presidential and chancellor evaluations. Aspirations around data use are wide-ranging, and they have merit, even if they are currently unattainable. As a function, IR has to help colleges and universities figure out how to use data from internal and external, structured and unstructured sources optimally to turn analytics dreams into a reality.

To do that, data must be viewed as a valuable institutional asset. Data governance needs to become a campus-wide affair. Consensus needs to be reached around data definitions, collection and storage methods, quality control, performance measures, and analyses. Data will need to become less siloed, and student success and resource optimization need integration. Conflicts around the ethical and responsible use of data will need to be resolved. IR needs to ensure that data analytics are not seen as a panacea. The function will need to blend art and science in order to derive the greatest value from the analytics revolution. It will have to work diligently to ensure that the human elements of the academy—teaching, learning, and advising—are enhanced and that students are not put at risk as a result of flawed or biased analyses.

IR professionals need to be ready and willing to confront these concepts, manage those expectations, and offer solutions based on the assets that are available today, not promised tomorrow. IR professionals alone are ideally positioned to blend data science and decision-making. It will likely require that the position of IR or analytics be elevated to a more senior level within institutions and systems. For that to occur, IR professionals need to illustrate value actively in leading those conversations, rather than waiting for others to have an epiphany. History, culture, and perceptions are all opposing forces that can prevent that from happening.

Through this murky ongoing process of change one thing is clear: The role of IR is vital to the success of higher education now, more than ever. IR professionals should feel empowered by this reality, even if the future holds some degree of uncertainty. Embracing the analytics revolution will empower IR to own the future of the function and ensure data are used contextually and effectively, taking into consideration the distinctiveness of colleges and universities and student needs, and wielded in ways that complement to the wisdom of leadership. Together, institutional leaders and IR have a unique opportunity to use the analytics revolution as a tool to effect transformational change that has equal benefits for students and institutions. Seizing it will help to ensure that the future of American higher education is a bright one.

References

Anguiano, M., D'Anieri, P., Hull, M., Kasturiraman, A., & Rodriguez, J. (2017). *Optimizing resource allocation for teaching: An experiment in activity-based costing in higher education* [White paper]. Retrieved from https://www.ucr.edu/about/admin/docs/ucr_abc_whitepaper.pdf

Arroway, P., Morgan, G., O'Keefe, M., & Yanosky, R. (2016). *Learning analytics in higher education*. EDUCAUSE Center for Analysis and Research. Retrieved from https://library.educause.edu/~/media/files/library/2016/2/ers1504la.pdf

Bhattacharya, C. B. (2013). The importance of marketing for social innovation. In T. Osburg & R. Schmidpeter (Eds.), *Social innovation: Solutions for a sustainable future* (pp. 147–154). New York, NY: Springer.

Bichsel, J. (2012). *Analytics in higher education: Benefits, barriers, progress, and recommendations*. EUCAUSE Center for Applied Research. Retrieved from http://net.educause.edu/ir/library/pdf/ers1207/ers1207.pdf

Cheslock, J., Hughes, R. P., & Umbricht, M. (2014). The opportunities, challenges, and strategies associated with the use of operations-oriented (big) data to support decision making within universities. In J. E. Lane (Ed.), *Building a smarter university: Big data, innovation, and analytics* (pp. 211–238). Albany, NY: SUNY Press.

Foss, L. H. (2014). Integrating data analytics in higher education organizations: Improving organizational and student success. In J. E. Lane (Ed.), *Building a smarter university: Big data, innovation, and analytics* (pp. 187–210). Albany, NY: SUNY Press.

Gagliardi, J. S. (2015). From perpetuation to innovation: Breaking through barriers to change in higher education. In J. E. Lane (Ed.), *Higher education reconsidered: Executing change to drive collective impact* (pp. 61–96). Albany, NY: SUNY Press.

Gagliardi, J. S., Espinosa, L. L., Turk, J., & Taylor, M. (2017). *American college president study 2017*. Washington DC: American Council on Education.

Gagliardi, J. S., & Wellman, J. (2015). *Meeting demand for improvements in public system institutional research: Progress report on the NASH project in IR*. Washington DC: National Association of System Heads.

Guenther, E., & Guenther, T. (2013). Accounting for social innovations: Measuring the impact of an emerging intangible category. In T. Osburg & R. Schmidpeter (Eds.), *Social innovation: Solutions for a sustainable future* (pp. 155–170). New York, NY: Springer.

Lane, J. E. (Ed.). (2014). *Building a smarter university: Big data, innovation, and analytics*. Albany, NY: SUNY Press.

Lubin, D., & Esty, D. C. (2010, May). The sustainability imperative. *Harvard Business Review*. Retrieved from https://hbr.org/2010/05/the-sustainability-imperative

Rogers, E. M. (2003). *Diffusion of innovations* (5th ed.). New York, NY: Free Press.

Swing, R. L. (2016). *Institutional research capacity: Foundations of federal data quality*. Association for Institutional Research. Retrieved from https://www.airweb.org/Resources/IRStudies/Documents/institutional_research_capacity.pdf

Wellman, J. V., & Ewell, P. T. (2010). *Connecting the dots between learning and resources*. National Institute for Learning Outcomes Assessment. Retrieved from http://www.learningoutcomeassessment.org/documents/Wellman-Occasional%20Paper%203%2010-20.pdf

Yeado, J., Haycock, K., Johnstone, R., & Chaplot, P. (2014). *Learning from high-performing and fast-gaining institutions*. The Education Trust. Retrieved from https://edtrust.org/resource/education-trust-higher-education-practice-guide-learning-from-high-performing-and-fast-gaining-institutions/

EDITORS AND CONTRIBUTORS

Editors

Julia Carpenter-Hubin serves as assistant vice president for institutional research and planning at The Ohio State University, where she and her team of data analysts focus on turning data into strategic information to support faculty and student success. A past president of the Association for Institutional Research, Carpenter-Hubin has also served as chair of the Association of American Universities Data Exchange and as a panelist for both the National Postsecondary Education Cooperative on the Integrated Postsecondary Education Data System and on Sample Surveys. Additionally, Carpenter-Hubin is a peer reviewer and a member of the Team Chair Corps for the Higher Learning Commission. Her service in these positions has given her a view of how data are currently used beyond her own institution and informed her understanding of the need for more effective use of data in decision-making nationally. A member of the Advising Board for Academic Analytics, LLC, Carpenter-Hubin engages regularly with a forward-thinking private company to discuss new directions and uses for faculty scholarly productivity data.

Carpenter-Hubin's research interests include performance measurement in higher education and using performance measurement to develop improvement strategies. Among her previous publications relevant to this topic are "Data Exchange Consortia: Characteristics, Current Examples, and Developing a New Exchange," with Rebecca Carr and Rosemary Hayes (*Handbook for Institutional Research*, edited by Howard, McLaughlin, and Knight, Jossey-Bass, 2012, pp. 420–433), and "Making Measurement Meaningful," with Eunice Hornsby (*Association for Institutional Research Professional File*, No. 97, Fall 2005).

Jonathan S. Gagliardi currently serves as the associate director for the American Council on Education Center for Policy Research and Strategy and as a visiting fellow for the Rockefeller Institute of Government. Previously, Gagliardi was a chancellor's fellow of the State University of New York System and the deputy director of the National Association of System Heads. In these roles he helped create and implement national completion initiatives aimed at scaling out evidence-based practices that promote student success. Gagliardi was a coprincipal investigator for the multiyear research project *Meeting Demands for Improvements in Public System Institutional Research,* which focused on examining and transforming the IR function.

Gagliardi previously served the Kentucky Council on Postsecondary Education on matters related to research, economic and community development, efficiency and innovation, and data governance and stewardship. He is recognized for his expertise in innovation and entrepreneurship, serving as an advisory board member for the Association of Public and Land-grant Universities Commission on Innovation, Competitiveness and Economic Prosperity, and for the Center for Leadership and Service at the University at Albany. He holds a PhD and an MS in higher education policy and leadership and a BA (history and sociology) from the University at Albany. Gagliardi's research has focused on innovation, organizational transformation, the intersection of higher education and the workforce, and student success.

Amelia Parnell is vice president for research and policy at NASPA—Student Affairs Administrators in Higher Education, where she directs the Research and Policy Institute (RPI), which links research, policy, and effective student affairs practice in support of student success. Parnell is leading NASPA's examination of several critical higher education issues, including colleges' use of emergency aid programs to address student needs. Prior to her arrival at NASPA, Parnell was director of research initiatives at the Association for Institutional Research, where she conducted two national studies related to future directions of the institutional research function. Her current research portfolio also includes studies on leadership attributes of college presidents and vice presidents, documenting and assessing cocurricular learning, and assessment and evaluation in student affairs.

Parnell is an advisory board member for the DC Public Schools' Urban Education Leaders Internship Program Alumni Board and an advisory committee member for Lumina Foundation's Beyond Financial Aid toolkit. Parnell holds a PhD in higher education from Florida State University and MA and BA degrees in business administration from Florida A&M University.

Contributors

Angela Y. Baldasare serves as the assistant provost for institutional research at the University of Arizona (UA), providing data to support strategic planning, decision-making, and reporting. In collaboration with her colleagues in University Analytics and Institutional Research (UAIR) and stakeholders across campus, Baldasare focuses on better telling of the university's story at all levels and improving and expanding the delivery of actionable information through data visualizations, interactive dashboards, modeling tools, and predictive analytics.

Baldasare earned her PhD in sociology from UA and was an assistant professor at the University of Dayton from 2000 through 2003. Baldasare then spent 10 years as a consultant on international public health projects, as well as statewide and tribal initiatives for multiple branches of the Arizona Governor's Office, U.S. Health and Human Services, and U.S. Department of Justice. From 2010–2014, Baldasare served as the director of Assessment and Research for Student Affairs and Enrollment Management at UA.

Angela Bell is the associate vice chancellor of research and policy analysis for the University System of Georgia (USG). Her division is responsible for meeting the information needs of the USG ranging from overseeing collection of campus data, responding to internal and external data requests, and conducting research and analysis to guide planning, policy, and decision-making. A key responsibility is harnessing the system's vast data holdings into actionable information for campus and system leadership. In this role, she led the agency's collaboration with the Carl Vinson Institute of Government on the Student Success Analytics Project, which has garnered awards from both the Georgia Technology Authority and the Technology Association of Georgia. Before coming to the USG, Bell worked at the West Virginia Higher Education Policy Commission as the vice chancellor of Policy and Planning and received her doctorate in higher education administration at the University of Georgia.

Desdemona Cardoza served as the director of institutional research at Cal State Los Angeles for 2 years. Subsequently, as assistant vice president for information resources management and vice president for information resources management, she oversaw that department for 12 years. She also served as dean of the College of Natural and Social Sciences and Provost. For the past 6 years she has served as a faculty member in the Department of Psychology and works as a special consultant at the Office of the Chancellor for the California State University System. She has been involved in the development and implementation for the Student Success Dashboard that supported the 2009 CSU Graduation Initiative as well as the Graduation Initiative 2025. Her primary role has been to develop the predictive analytic models in the dashboard that are designed to assist campuses in gauging progress toward achieving their graduation and achievement gap closing goals.

Timothy M. Chester is vice president for information technology (IT) at the University of Georgia, where he operates a unit that combines IT operations with administrative and academic information systems together with institutional research (IR), thereby ensuring tighter integration between the systems that store information, the offices that produce and consume information, and the offices that analyze it for strategic needs and reporting. The economies of scale that come from this combination allow the organization to be more responsive when it comes to IT–IR overlapping activities such as data standards, governance, business transactions, and data analysis. A social scientist by training, Chester was previously the vice provost at Pepperdine University, where he held similar responsibilities for both IT and IR.

Daniel R. Cohen-Vogel, PhD, is the vice president for data and analytics at the University of North Carolina System Office, the system office for the 17-campus University of North Carolina. His unit's primary responsibility is to meet the information needs of the system office leadership and the Board of Governors that oversees the university, as well as the needs of other key stakeholders. His unit maintains the university's central data system and draws on those campus data as well as community college, K–12, and numerous other data sources to conduct federal and state reporting on behalf of its constituent institutions, to respond to internal and external information requests, and to engage in various decision support activities. Recently, Cohen-Vogel's unit has led the development and implementation of the UNC Student Data Mart, the university's student data warehouse, and has engaged in private sector collaborations—such as those with SAS, HelioCampus, and Hobson's—to build a strong, system-wide analytical environment supported by the Data Mart foundation.

Daniel previously served in a similar role in the Board of Governors Office of the State University System of Florida, and prior to that he was a legislative analyst in Florida and Tennessee. He received an undergraduate degree from the University of Pennsylvania and master's and doctoral degrees in agricultural and resource economics from the University of California, Berkeley.

Jeff Gold has been the assistant vice chancellor for student success strategic initiatives at the Office of the Chancellor for the California State University (CSU) System for over 15 years. During his tenure he developed and implemented the strategic vision for the system-wide Graduation Initiative to raise freshman graduation rates by eight percentage points, and cut in half the degree attainment gap by CSU's underrepresented students. He led and managed the creation of a system-wide Student Success Dashboard, which used predictive analytics to guide campus leadership to improve graduation rates and close achievement gaps. He currently serves as the assistant vice president chancellor for student success initiatives and research and has primary responsibility for overseeing the 2025 Graduation Initiative for the CSU. He oversees the development of the Student Success Dashboard for this new initiative and has developed accountability measures based on predictive analytics for both faculty and administrators.

Steve A. Gillard is the University of Minnesota's data custodian and has been a central figure responsible for establishing and operationalizing the Enterprise Data Management and Reporting (EDMR) strategy and governance structure at the University of Minnesota. He is responsible for providing leadership and coordination of the EDMR strategy through advancing system-wide governance and analytic initiatives. This includes interfacing with the EDMR governance structure, data custodians, data stewards, administrative officers, and technical and analytic staff across the university. In executing these responsibilities, he leads the Data Governance Program, coordinates the Analytics Collaborative, and serves as the representative of the Office of Institutional Analysis in fulfilling its role as business owner of the University of Minnesota reporting and analytics program.

Ronald L. Huesman Jr. is the director of institutional assessment at the University of Minnesota; in this role, he has broad responsibilities for the analytic capacity of the Office of Institutional Research. Huesman leads a team of analysts and graduate students that works collaboratively with many diverse units (e.g., equity and diversity, student and academic affairs) to design research studies, collect data, provide analysis, and report results to inform campus assessment efforts, policy development, and decision-making that supports the university's strategic mission of providing an exceptional student experience. He has been involved with and led national data exchange consortiums among research universities for the purpose of developing comparable data needed for benchmarking and assessing institutional improvement. Huesman earned a PhD in educational measurement and statistics from the University of Iowa.

Stephanie A. Bond Huie is the vice chancellor for the Office of Strategic Initiatives for the University of Texas (UT) System. Huie leads several functional teams including institutional research and analysis, business intelligence and data warehousing, strategic project management, and information technology, among others. She oversees the UT System Dashboard, a business intelligence system that provides publicly accessible web-based applications for extracting and analyzing institutional data. Promoting data sharing and collaboration, she also directs seekUT, a free online tool and website that provides postgraduation outcomes of UT System graduates by major. A recent first-of-its-kind agreement with the U.S. Census Bureau will provide a national picture for postgraduation success. Huie received her undergraduate degree as well as her master's and doctoral degrees in sociology, from the University of Texas at Austin. She completed the educational leadership program at Harvard University's Institute for Education Management.

David Kowalski is the executive director of institutional research at Montgomery County Community College, where he leads the college's predictive analytics team and conducts research and analysis to support institutional decision-making. Kowalski has worked in educational research in both the K–12 and higher education environment and has also worked as a consultant for educational technology companies. In addition to his work in research, Kowalski has served as a faculty member in the college's psychology department for the past 10 years and also works as a licensed clinician in private practice. He holds a PhD in educational psychology from Temple University and an MA in clinical psychology from La Salle University. He frequently presents at national conferences on the topics of student identity, motivation, engagement, analytics, and student success.

Jason E. Lane is the founding executive director of the SUNY Academic & Innovative Leadership (SAIL) Institute as well as chair of the Department of Educational Policy and Leadership at the State University of New York at Albany. He has extensive experience leading multicampus transformational change initiatives in higher education and is a recognized expert in data analytics, system thinking, and leadership development. Currently, he is the colead of the predictive analytics stream of the Taking Student Success to Scale (TS3) initiative of the National Association of System Heads (NASH), which is focused on using data to drive student success. Previously, he served as vice provost for academic planning and strategic leadership and senior associate vice chancellor for the State University of New York, the largest comprehensive system of higher education in the United States. In this role, he led efforts focused on student transfer and mobility, creating a student longitudinal data, and involving New York in the Multi-State Longitudinal Data Exchange. An award-winning author and invited speaker, Lane has published 12 books, including *Academic Leadership and Governance of Higher Education* (Stylus Press, 2012), *Higher Education Systems 3.0* (SUNY Press, 2013), and *Building a Smarter University: Big Data, Innovation, and Data Analytics* (SUNY Press, 2014).

Kent Phillippe serves as the associate vice president of research and student success at the American Association of Community Colleges (AACC), where he has been responsible for research for over 20 years. In his time at the association, he has been instrumental in developing a strong, reliable research capacity at the association. He has integrated diverse national data sets including census, Department of Education, and association data files to better understand and describe community colleges, and the communities in which they reside. Phillippe also leads the association's work for the Voluntary Framework of Accountability (VFA), a major national initiative to provide community colleges with better data for institutional improvement and accountability. He serves on a wide variety of advisory panels for national research projects, including the U.S. Department of Education's National Postsecondary Student Aid Study, Beginning Postsecondary Student Longitudinal Study, and Integrated Postsecondary Education Data System, as well as Department of Labor, Lumina, and FIPSE funded projects. He obtained a BA in psychology from Hamline University in St. Paul, Minnesota; an MA in clinical and counseling psychology from Southern Methodist University; and attended a Michigan State University doctoral program where he studied child/family clinical psychology.

Angela Polec is the executive director of marketing and communications at Montgomery County Community College in Pennsylvania. In this role, she oversees branding, enrollment marketing, digital strategy, and strategic communications. Polec collaborates with colleagues across the college to leverage data and analytics to improve the student experience and support student success. She is a member of the project team managing the college's Integrated Planning and Advising for Student Success (iPASS) grant from the Bill & Melinda Gates Foundation, is a core member of the institution's enrollment management leadership team, and serves on the college-wide curriculum committee. She holds an MS and a BBA in marketing from Temple University's Fox School of Business and is pursuing her PhD in higher education management from The University of Pennsylvania.

Celeste M. Schwartz is the vice president for information technology and chief digital officer at Montgomery County Community College. In this role, Schwartz is responsible for academic and administrative technology and technology-supported process improvements. In addition to her technology focus, she provides leadership support for the college's Student Success initiatives, iPASS (Integrated Planning and Advising for Student Success) and College Sustainability initiatives and oversees institutional research. Schwartz is an active member of and contributor to EDUCAUSE and a variety of organizations, including The Pathway School Board of Directors, KINBER Board of Directors, and The Rotary Club of Blue Bell. She holds an AAS from Montgomery County Community College, a BS from St. Joseph's University, an MS in information technology from Villanova University, and a PhD in education, with specialization in community college leadership, from Walden University.

Jason Sullivan holds an MA in psychology from the University of Illinois at Urbana-Champaign and a BS in Psychology from the University of Michigan–Ann Arbor. His original research background is in psycholinguistics and cognitive neuroscience. In the Office of Institutional Research and Planning, Sullivan helps design research strategies, provides statistical consultation, and analyzes complex data sets. Prior to his work in institutional research and planning, Sullivan was a research staff member of The Ohio State University Center for Family Research, where he designed and coordinated data collection strategies for county-level agencies that oversaw programs for youths in the mental health or juvenile justice systems, along with analyzing data and creating reports for a diverse array or projects run by the Center.

Randy L. Swing focuses on postsecondary student success, data-informed decision-making, and workforce readiness. He is an independent consultant, with prior career appointments including executive director of the Association for Institutional Research, a professional association serving over 1,500 postsecondary institutions (2007–2016); codirector and senior scholar at the Policy Center on the First Year of College (1999–2007), and leadership of academic advising, first-year seminars, and outcomes assessment at Appalachian State University (1980–1999). Randy is a frequent speaker at national and international conferences and author of books and articles on assessment, institutional research, and student success, especially the first-year experience and a new vision for institutional research (*Change Magazine*, March 2016). He holds a PhD from the University of Georgia and is a fellow of the Institute of Higher Education at UGA and a fellow of the National Resource Center on the First-Year Experience and Students in Transition.

Degrees that Matter
Moving Higher Education to a Learning Systems Paradigm

Natasha A. Jankowski and David W. Marshall

"By rethinking tired conventions, by questioning long held assumptions, and by pointing to the most useful and applicable resources, Jankowski and Marshall offer practical steps for making education more effective and students more successful. Every college or university could stand to benefit from the practical and principled advice this book advances."—*Paul L. Gaston*, *Trustees Professor, Kent State University*

Concerned by ongoing debates about higher education that talk past one another, the authors of this book show how to move beyond these and other obstacles to improve the student learning experience and further successful college outcomes. Offering an alternative to the culture of compliance in assessment and accreditation, they propose a different approach which they call the Learning System Paradigm. Building on the shift in focus from teaching to learning, the new paradigm encourages faculty and staff to systematically seek out information on how well students are learning and how well various areas of the institution are supporting the student experience and to use that information to create more coherent and explicit learning experiences for students.

Real-Time Student Assessment
Meeting the Imperative for Improved Time to Degree, Closing the Opportunity Gap, and Assuring Student Competencies for 21st-Century Needs

Peggy L. Maki

Foreword by George D. Kuh

"Real-Time Student Assessment is the absolute best book on the market today for anyone engaged in student learning outcomes assessment. It is current, based on exhaustive research and actual practice, exemplified through multiple case studies and extensive references for follow-up. . . . I will be buying copies for many of my colleagues myself!"—*Ralph Wolff*, *President, The Quality Assurance Commons for Higher and Postsecondary Education; former President, WASC Senior Accrediting Commission*

Peggy Maki advocates for real-time assessment processes to identify patterns of under-performance and obstacles that require timely interventions for enrolled students to succeed. In tandem with the sets of educational practices and policies that many institutions have now undertaken to close achievement and graduation rates across our diverse student demographics, such as developing clear degree pathways, she calls on all higher education providers—if they are to remain relevant and meet their social purpose in our complex world—to urgently recalibrate their assessment processes to focus on currently enrolled students' progress towards achieving a high-quality degree, regardless of when they matriculate or re-enter higher education.

Sty/us

22883 Quicksilver Drive
Sterling, VA 20166-2019   Subscribe to our e-mail alerts: www.Styluspub.com

Celebrating its centennial in 2018, the American Council on Education (ACE) is the major coordinating body for all the nation's higher education institutions, representing nearly 1,800 college and university presidents and related associations. It provides leadership on key higher education issues and influences public policy through advocacy. For more information, please visit *www.acwenet.edu* or follow ACE on Twitter *@ACEducation*.

ASSOCIATION FOR INSTITUTIONAL RESEARCH
Data and Decisions for Higher Education

The Association for Institutional Research

The Association for Institutional Research (AIR) is the world's largest association of higher education professionals working in institutional research, assessment, planning, and related postsecondary education fields. The organization provides educational resources, best practices and professional development opportunities for more than 4,000 members. Its primary purpose is to support members in the process of collecting, analyzing, and converting data into information that supports decision-making in higher education.

The field of institutional research (IR) is over 50 years old and is embedded in nearly every college and university in the United States and many others around the world. Often working behind the scenes, IR professionals support campus leaders and policy makers in wise planning, programming, and fiscal decision-making covering a broad range of institutional responsibilities. These areas can include research support to senior academic leaders, admissions, financial aid, curriculum, enrollment management, staffing, student life, finance, facilities, athletics, alumni relations, and many others. In addition to providing the data-informed foundation for good decision-making, institutional researchers use the data they collect for governmental reporting and to benchmark their results against similar institutions.

In short, most of the important decisions made on campuses regarding an institution's most vital programs and responsibilities are based on analytics produced by IR professionals. AIR makes sure these professionals are fully equipped to perform their jobs at the highest levels.

For further information, see the following:

Website: www.airweb.org

Telephone: 850-385-4155

E-mail: air@airweb.org